NAZI POLICY, JEWISH WORKERS, GERMAN KILLERS

Nazi Policy, Jewish Workers, German Killers focuses on controversial issues in current Holocaust scholarship. How did Nazi Jewish policy evolve during the first years of the war? When did the Nazi regime cross the historic watershed from population expulsion and decimation ("ethnic cleansing") to total and systematic extermination? How did Nazi authorities attempt to reconcile policies of expulsion and extermination with the wartime urge to exploit Jewish labor? How were Jewish workers impacted? What role did local authorities play in shaping Nazi policy? What more can we learn about the mind-set and behavior of the local perpetrators? Using new evidence, this book attempts to shed light on these important questions.

Christopher Browning is Frank Porter Graham Professor of History at the University of North Carolina, Chapel Hill. He is the author of four previous books: *The Final Solution and the German Foreign Office* (1978); *Fateful Months: Essays on the Emergence of the Final Solution* (1985); *Ordinary Men: Reserve Police Battalion 101 and the Final Solution in Poland* (1992); and *The Path to Genocide* (Cambridge University Press, 1992).

NAZI POLICY, JEWISH WORKERS, GERMAN KILLERS

CHRISTOPHER R. BROWNING

CAMBRIDGE
UNIVERSITY PRESS

PUBLISHED BY THE PRESS SYNDICATED OF THE UNIVERSITY OF CAMBRIDGE
The Pitt Building, Trumpington Street, Cambridge, United Kingdom

CAMBRIDGE UNIVERSITY PRESS
The Edinburgh Building, Cambridge CB2 2RU, UK
http://www.cup.cam.ac.uk
40 West 20th Street, New York, NY 10011-4211, USA
http://www.cup.org
10 Stamford Road, Oakleigh, Melbourne 3166, Australia
Ruiz de Alarcón 13, 28014 Madrid, Spain

First published 2000

Printed in the United States of America

Typeface Sabon 10.25/13.5 pt. *System* QuarkXPress™ [HT]

A catalog record for this book is available from the British Library

Library of Congress Cataloging-in-Publication Data

Browning, Christopher R.
Nazi policy, Jewish workers, German killers/Christopher R. Browning.
p. cm
Includes bibliographical references.
ISBN 0-521-77299-0 hb
1. Holocaust, Jewish (1939–1945) 2. World War, 1939–1945 – Conscript labor – Poland.
3. Germany – Population policy. I. Title.

D804.3 .B769 2000
940.53′18 – dc21 99-040042

ISBN 0 521 77299 0 hardback
ISBN 0 521 77490 x paperback

In memory of
George L. Mosse
1918–1999

CONTENTS

INTRODUCTION

In November 1995 I received the singular honor of being invited to deliver the George Macaulay Trevelyan Lectures at Cambridge University in the Lent Term of 1999. I deeply appreciated the opportunity given me by the Electors to present the twentieth set of biennial lectures in this very distinguished series that began in 1959. But I must admit to some initial trepidation, for the letter of invitation indicated that the lectures were intended to commemorate Trevelyan by attending to aspects of history that interested him. Trevelyan was at home in the seventeenth, eighteenth, and nineteenth centuries. He wrote broad synthetic national histories that focused on the emergence of a distinct English political culture marked by liberty, civility, decency, and moderation on the one hand and heroic biographies of figures he deemed exemplary and inspirational on the other. In contrast, he wrote of the twentieth century: "I don't understand the age we live in and what I do understand I don't like."[1] That was in 1926, and the following decades were even more disagreeable. Moreover, my own subject was to be the most tragic and terrifying event of those terrible decades. But Trevelyan also believed that history had a public function – to instruct about the frailty of the human condition and the necessity for civic virtue. In this regard, at least, I hope that he would not consider lectures addressing the topic of the Holocaust an inappropriate commemoration of his legacy.

I am also acutely aware that this was the first occasion on which a relatively new field of historical study, the Holocaust – the Nazi attempt to destroy the Jews of Europe – was the topic of these lectures. As an academic field characterized by university courses, scholarly conferences and journals, and a growing body of literature based on archival research, the field of Holocaust studies began to

[1] David Cannadine, *G. M. Trevelyan: A Life in History* (London, 1992), p. 153.

emerge only some twenty-five years ago. It is useful in this regard to remind ourselves, for example, that in the 1950s and 1960s, the pioneering scholar in the field, Raul Hilberg, could find no university press to publish and no academic journal to review his now classic work, *The Destruction of the European Jews*.[2] Such academic marginalization of the Holocaust is no more, and it is increasingly recognized as an event central to our understanding of western civilization, the nation-state, and modern bureaucratic society, as well as human nature.

However, it was not my intention in these lectures to deal with this wider issue of the general importance of the Holocaust as a topic of historical study. That is, I believe, a battle that has already been fought and won. Rather, in three pairs of lectures I examine three issues at the forefront of current Holocaust scholarship: (1) decision and policy making at the heart of the Nazi regime, out of which emerged the so-called Final Solution – the systematic attempt to murder every last Jew, man, woman, and child, within the German grasp; (2) the pragmatic and temporary use of Jewish labor, which was potentially in conflict with but also clearly subordinate to the regime's ideological commitment to total destruction, and the resulting impact on the victims whose lives were thus briefly spared; and (3) the attitudes, motivations, and adaptations of the "ordinary" Germans who implemented Nazi policy at the local level.

In addition to this thematic division of lecture topics, there is a methodological division as well. The first three lectures deal with what is often termed "history from above." The focus is on the decisions and policies of the Nazi leadership, though not to the exclusion of the initiatives and actions of local and regional authorities that affected and interacted with the central authorities. The last three lectures deal with "history from below." Here the focus shifts to the activities, experiences, and memories of both victims and perpetrators on the local level. The source materials include both postwar testimonies and rare contemporary letters and document files that speak less to the issue of decision and policy making and more to those elusive issues of individual attitudes and behavior.

[2] For his own reflections on this matter, see: Raul Hilberg, *The Politics of Memory: The Journey of a Holocaust Historian* (Chicago, 1996).

As with any other work of history, these lectures could not have been written without the indispensable aid and support from the staffs of numerous archives and libraries. The United States Holocaust Memorial Museum (where I had the opportunity to serve as the J. B. and Maurice Shapiro Senior Visiting Scholar), Yad Vashem, the Zentrale Stelle der Landesjustizverwaltungen in Ludwigsburg, the National Archives, the Bundesarchiv, the Fortunoff Archive in Sterling Library at Yale University, and the interlibrary loan services at Pacific Lutheran University Library deserve particular mention. I owe a special debt of gratitude to Ella Waşowska–Benson and Sylvia Noll, who translated key survivor testimonies given in Polish, Yiddish, and Hebrew.

President Loren Anderson, Provost Paul Menzel, and the board of regents of Pacific Lutheran University – my academic home for the past 25 years – provided unstinting support and release time from my teaching obligations, without which the lectures could not have been written. Jonathan Steinberg of Cambridge University and Trinity Hall College was an exemplary host and, along with many of his colleagues, helped make my stay in Cambridge a truly joyous occasion.

Just weeks before I departed for Cambridge, historians were deeply saddened by the death of George L. Mosse, a man who had been for me a very special scholar, mentor, and friend. This book is dedicated to his memory.

N
W
E
S
ESTONIA
SWEDEN
BALTIC SEA
Riga
LATVIA
SOVIET UNION
LITHUANIA
Tilsit
Kovno
Vilna
Danzig
EAST PRUSSIA
Marcinkance
Minsk
Mir
WEISSRUTHENIAN
BIALYSTOK
Bialystok
GERMANY
WEST PRUSSIA
ZICHENAU
Treblinka
WARTHEGAU
Brest-Litovsk
Warsaw
Chelmno
WARSAW DISTRICT
Lodz
Sobibor
Kovel
Radom
RADOM DISTRICT
Lublin
VOLHYNIA-PODOLIA
LUBLIN DISTRICT
Starachowice
Nisko
EAST UPPER SILESIA
Belzec
Czeladz
Sosnowiec
CRACOW DISTRICT
Cracow
Lwow (Lemberg)
Mährisch Ostrau (Ostrava)
Auschwitz-Birkenau
GALICIA DISTRICT
CZECHOSLOVAKIA
AUSTRIA
Danube R.
HUNGARY
ROMANIA
YUGO.
0 50 100 mi
0 50 100 km
POLAND
Death Camp
Poland boundary before Sept. 1, 1939
Russian-German line, 1939
Annexed Land
General government
Generalkommissariats

I

FROM "ETHNIC CLEANSING" TO GENOCIDE TO THE "FINAL SOLUTION"

The Evolution of Nazi Jewish Policy, 1939–1941

Why the emphasis on decision and policy making, it might be asked. Is this not an exhausted topic whose time has come and gone with the intentionalist/functionalist controversy of the late 1970s and early 1980s, characterized by unduly polarized alternative interpretations? The intentionalists emphasized the centrality of Adolf Hitler's ideology, predetermined plans, and opportunistic decision making, whereas the functionalists emphasized the dysfunction and unplanned destructive implosion of an unguided bureaucratic structure and tension-filled political movement that had driven themselves into a dead end. One approach perceived the Final Solution as being more like the Manhattan Project, a massive and well-planned program that produced the destruction intended, whereas the other perceived it as a kind of Chernobyl, the unintended but all too predictable by-product of a dysfunctional system.

If the intentionalist/functionalist controversy in this highly polarized form is no longer at the center of Holocaust research, nonetheless a much more nuanced debate over Hitler and the origins of the Final Solution, based on a much vaster documentary collection, has found new life in the 1990s. In this debate, virtually all the participants agree on the centrality of the year 1941 and an incremental decision-making process in which Hitler played a key role. What is being debated are the relative weighting of the different decisions taken in 1941 and the different historical contexts invoked to explain the importance and timing of those decisions. What is at stake is our differing understandings of how Hitler and the Nazi system functioned and how historically the fateful line was crossed between population decimation and genocide on the one hand and the Final Solution and Holocaust on the other.

The most recent controversy in this ongoing debate over the decisions for the Final Solution is the topic of my second lecture. But part of my argument is that the pattern of decision making that was practiced and the frustrations and failures that the Nazis experienced in racial empire building in Poland in the years 1939–41 are important for understanding the "fateful months" in which the Final Solution emerged. One crucial historical context for understanding the origins of the Final Solution, until recently overshadowed by the history of European and German anti-Semitism, the development of the eugenics movement, and the functioning of the Nazi system of government, is the visions of demographic engineering and plans for population resettlement that both inspired and frustrated Nazi racial imperialism in Poland between 1939 and 1941. I will argue that the theory and practice of what we now call ethnic cleansing was an important prelude to the decisions for the Final Solution that followed.

More specifically, I will argue that between September 1939 and July 1941, Nazi Jewish policy, as one component of a broader racial imperialism in the east, evolved through three distinct plans for ethnic cleansing to a transitional phase of implicit genocide in connection with preparations for the war of destruction against the Soviet Union. Hitler was both the key ideological legitimizer and decision maker in this evolutionary process, which also depended crucially upon the initiatives and responses elicited from below. For Hitler the historical contexts for his key decisions were the euphoria of victory in Poland and France and the galvanizing anticipation of a territorial conquest of *Lebensraum* and an ideological and racial crusade against "Judeo-Bolshevism" in the Soviet Union. Additionally, for the middle and lower echelon, regional and local authorities, key factors were not only their identification with Hitler's goals and personal ambition to make a career but also frustration over the impasse created by the ideological imperatives of the regime and their failure to implement the previous policies of ethnic cleansing.

In the months before the invasion of Poland, Hitler made clear on several occasions that the outbreak of war would set a new level of expectation on his part. For instance, in his Reichstag speech of January 1939, he prophesied that a world war would mean the destruction of the Jews in Europe. And to his generals on August 22, he called for a "brutal attitude," "the destruction of Poland," and the "elimination of living forces."[1] When Quartermaster General Eduard Wagner asked Reinhard Heydrich about the tasks of the Einsatzgruppen, he was bluntly informed: "Fundamental cleansing: Jews, intelligentsia, clergy, nobles" *(Flurbereinigung: Judentum, Intelligenz, Geistlichkeit, Adel).*[2] But what did *Flurbereinigung* mean? How were Hitler's prophesies and exhortations transformed by his eager subordinates, especially Heinrich Himmler and Heydrich, into specific and concrete policies?

The arrest and decimation of Poland's leadership classes seem to have been decided even before the invasion.[3] But plans for a more sweeping demographic reorganization of Poland, including a solution to the Jewish question, emerged only during the month of September. On September 7 Heydrich told his division heads that Poland would be partitioned and Germany's boundary would be moved eastward. Poles and Jews in the border region annexed to the Third Reich would be deported to whatever remained of Poland.[4] A week later Heydrich discussed the Jewish question before the same audience and noted: "Proposals are being submitted to the Führer by the Reichsführer, that only the Führer can decide, because they will be of considerable significance for foreign policy as well."[5] The nature of these proposals was

[1] *Nazi Conspiracy and Aggression* (hereafter cited as NCA), III, p. 665 (1014-PS); Franz Halder, *Kriegstagebuch* (Stuttgart, 1962), I, p. 25; Winfried Baumgart, "Zur Ansprache Hitlers vor den Führern der Wehrmacht am 22. August 1939," *Vierteljahresheft für Zeitgeschichte* (hereafter cited as VfZ), 1968, pp. 120–149.

[2] Halder, *Kriegstagebuch,* I, p. 79.

[3] Heydrich and Quartermaster General Eduard Wagner reached agreement in August that the Einsatzgruppen would arrest all potential enemies – that is, all "who oppose the measures of the German authorities, or obviously want and are able to stir up unrest due to their position and stature" (*die sich dem Massnahmen der deutschen Amtsstellen widersetzen oder offensichtlich gewillt und auf Grund ihrer Stellung und ihres Ansehens in der Lage sind, Unruhe zu stiften*). According to Wagner, the Einsatzgruppen had lists of 30,000 people to be sent to concentration camps. Edward Wagner, *Der Generalquartiermeister: Briefe und Tagebuch Eduard Wagners,* ed. by Elisabeth Wagner (Munich, 1963), pp. 103–4. In early September, Wilhelm Canaris pointed out to Wilhelm Keitel that he "knew that extensive executions were planned in Poland and that particularly the nobility and the clergy were to be exterminated." Keitel confirmed that "the Führer had already decided on this matter." NCA, V, p. 769 (3047-PS).

[4] National Archives (hereafter cited as NA), T175/239/2728499-502 (conference of Heydrich's division heads, 7.9.39).

[5] NA, T175/239/2728513-5 (conference of Heydrich's division heads, 14.9.39).

revealed the following week, when Heydrich met not only with his division heads but also the Einsatzgruppen leaders and his expert on Jewish emigration, Adolf Eichmann. Concerning Poles, the top leaders were to be sent to concentration camps, the middle echelon were to be arrested and deported to rump Poland, and "primitive" Poles were to be used temporarily as migrant labor and then gradually resettled, as the border territories became pure German provinces. According to Heydrich, "The deportation of Jews into the non-German region, expulsion over the demarcation line is approved by the Führer." This "long-term goal," or *Endziel,* would be achieved over the next year. However, "in order to have a better possibility of control and later of deportation," the immediate concentration of Jews into ghettos in the cities was an urgent "short-term goal," or *Nahziel.* The area east of Cracow and north of the Slovak border was explicitly exempted from these concentration measures, for it was to this region that the Jews as well as "all Gypsies and other undesirables" were eventually to be deported.[6]

This plan was slightly altered the following week when Germany surrendered Lithuania to the Soviet sphere and received in return Polish territory around the city of Lublin between the Vistula and Bug Rivers. On September 29, Hitler told Alfred Rosenberg that all Jews, including those from the Reich, would be settled in this newly acquired territory between the Vistula and the Bug. Central Poland west of the Vistula would be an area of Polish settlement. Hitler then broached yet a third resettlement scheme. Ethnic Germans repatriated from the Soviet sphere would be settled in western Polish territories incorporated into the Third Reich. Whether "after decades" the German settlement belt would be moved eastward, only time would tell.[7]

[6] NA, T175/239/2728524-8 (conference of Heydrich's division heads, 21.9.39); NCA, VI, pp. 97–101 (3363-PS); Helmuth Groscurth, *Tagebücher eines Abwehroffiziers 1938–40,* ed. by Helmuth Krausnick and Harold Deutsch (Stuttgart, 1970), p. 362 (document nr. 14, Groscurth memorandum over verbal orientation by Major Radke, 22.9.39).

[7] *Das politische Tagebuch Alfred Rosenbergs,* ed. by Hans-Günther Seraphim (Göttingen, 1956), p. 81. NA, T175/239/2728531-2 (conference of Heydrich's division heads, 29.9.39). According to Götz Aly, *"Endlösung": Völkerverschiebung und der Mord an den europäischen Juden* (Frankfurt/M., 1995), p. 39, the decision to repatriate all Baltic Germans from the Soviet sphere was reached between Hitler and Himmler only on September 27.

In short, by the end of September 1939 Himmler had proposed and Hitler had approved a grandiose program of demographic engineering based on racial principles that would involve the uprooting of millions of people. These policies were fully consonant with Hitler's underlying ideological assumptions: a need for *Lebensraum* in the east justified by a Social-Darwinist racism, a contempt for the Slavic populations of eastern Europe, and a determination to rid the expanding German Reich of Jews. These policies were also very much in tune with widely held views and hopes in much of German society concerning the construction of a German empire in eastern Europe. There was no shortage of those who now eagerly sought to contribute to this historic opportunity for a triumph of German racial imperialism. And the degree to which the widely held hopes and visions of these eager helpers would subsequently founder on stubborn reality, the greater their willingness to resort to ever more violent solutions. The broad support for German racial imperialism in the east was one foundation upon which the future consensus for the mass murder of the Jews would be built.[8]

Heydrich's plans for the immediate concentration of Jews in urban ghettos had to be postponed owing to army concerns over undue disruption.[9] But that did not deter one young and ambitious Schutzstaffel (SS) officer from taking the initiative to jump from the short-term to the long-term goal and implement the immediate expulsion of the Jews. On October 6, 1939, Eichmann met with the head of the Gestapo, Heinrich Müller, who ordered him to contact Gauleiter Wagner in Kattowitz concerning the deportation of 70,000 to 80,000 Jews from East Upper Silesia. Eichmann noted the wider goal of this expulsion: "This activity shall serve first of all to collect

[8] Aly, *"Endlösung,"* esp. pp. 13–17; Aly and Susanne Heim, *Vordenker der Vernichtung. Auschwitz und die Pläne für eine neue europäische Ordnung* (Hamburg, 1991); Michael Burleigh, *Germany Turns Eastward. A Study of Ostforschung in the Third Reich* (Cambridge, 1988); Hans Mommsen, "Umvolkungspläne des Nationalsozialismus und der Holocaust," *Die Normalität des Verbrechens: Bilanz und Perspektiven der Forschung zu nationalsozialistischen Gewaltverbrechen* (Berlin, 1994), pp. 68–84. Deborah Dwork and Robert Jan van Pelt, *Auschwitz: 1270 to the Present* (New York, 1996), pp. 66–159.

[9] Klaus-Jürgen Müller, *Das Heer und Hitler. Armee und nationalsozialistische Regime 1933–40* (Stuttgart, 1969), pp. 671–2 (document nr. 47: Heydrich to Einsatzgruppen leaders, 30.9.39).

experiences, in order . . . to be able to carry out evacuations in much greater numbers."[10]

Within days Eichmann had expanded this program to include deportations from both Mährisch Ostrau in the Protectorate and Vienna. He had also located a transit camp at Nisko on the San River on the western border of the Lublin district, from which the deportees were to be expelled eastward. By October 11, German officials in Vienna were informed that Hitler had ordered the resettlement of 300,000 Reich Jews, and Vienna would be completely cleared of Jews in 9 months.[11] And on October 16, Eichmann confidently informed Artur Nebe, head of the Criminal Police, that Jewish transports from the Old Reich would begin in 3 to 4 weeks, to which train cars of "Gypsies" could also be attached.[12]

In short, between mid-September and mid-October 1939, Nazi plans for the ethnic cleansing of the Third Reich of Jews and "Gypsies" from both its old and new territories had taken shape in the form of a vast deportation and expulsion program to the farthest extremity of Germany's new eastern empire – the Lublin district on the German–Soviet demarcation line.

Barely was implementation of the Nisko Plan underway, however, when it was abruptly aborted. On October 19, as the second and third transports were being prepared for departure, Gestapo Müller from Berlin ordered "that the resettlement and deportation of Poles and Jews in the territory of the future Polish state requires central coordination. Therefore permission from the offices here must on principle be in hand." This was quickly followed by the clarification that "every evacuation of Jews had to be stopped."[13]

[10] Yad Vashem Archives (hereafter cited as YVA), 0-53/93/283, Eichmann Vermerk, 6.10.39. For general studies of the Nisko Plan, see: Seev Goshen, "Eichmann und die Nisko-Aktion im Oktober 1939," VfZ 19/1 (January 1981), pp. 74–96; Jonny Moser, "Nisko: The First Experiment in Deportation," *The Simon Wiesenthal Center Annual,* II (1985), pp. 1–30; H. G. Adler, *Der Verwaltete Mensch* (Tübingen, 1974), pp. 126–140.

[11] Gerhard Botz, *Wohnungspolitik und Judendeportation in Wien 1938 bis 1945: Zur Funktion des Antisemitismus als Ersatz nationalsozialistischer Sozialpolitik* (Vienna, 1975), pp. 164–86 (document VII: Becker memorandum, 11.10.39).

[12] YVA, 0-53/93/299-300 (Eichmann to Nebe, 16.10.39) and 227–9 (Günther-Braune FS-Fernspräch, 18.10.39.

[13] YVA, O-53/93/235-8 (R. Günther Tagesbericht, 19.10.39), 220 (undated R. Günther telegram), and 244 (R. Günther Vermerk, 21.10.39).

The stop order in fact came personally from Himmler, which he justified to the irate Gauleiter of Vienna on the basis of so-called technical difficulties.[14] But what difficulties had caused Himmler to abort the Nisko Plan just days after it had been set in motion? Expelling Jews and "Gypsies," it turned out, was not the most urgent item on Himmler's agenda for the demographic reorganization of eastern Europe. Himmler had just gained jurisdiction over the repatriation and resettlement of ethnic Germans, and the first Baltic Germans had arrived in Danzig on October 15.[15] The problem of finding space for the incoming ethnic Germans now took priority over deporting Jews from East Upper Silesia, the Protectorate, and Vienna. The geographic center of Nazi resettlement actions suddenly shifted northward to West Prussia and the Warthegau as policy priorities shifted from expelling Jews to finding lodging and livelihood for ethnic Germans.

But despite the sudden demise of the Nisko Plan, the goal of ethnic cleansing remained, though it was now to be implemented in more gradual stages. On October 18 Hitler reiterated that "Jews, Polacks and riff-raff" ("*Juden, Polacken u. Gesindel*") were to be expelled from Reich territory – both old and new – into what remained of Poland, where "devils' work" ("*Teufelswerk*") remained to be done.[16] On October 30, Himmler issued overall guidelines for the *Flurbereinigung* of the incorporated territories that Hitler had once again sanctioned. Within 4 months, *all* Jews (estimated at 550,000) were to be expelled from the incorporated territories to a Lublin reservation between the Vistula and Bug Rivers. Also to be expelled were post-1919 Polish immigrants (so-called Congress Poles) and a sufficient number of anti-German Poles to bring the total to 1 million.[17] Jews in the recently

[14] Botz, *Wohungspolitik und Judendeportationen*, p. 196 (document X, Himmler to Bürckel, 9.11.39).

[15] Hans Umbreit, *Deutsche Militärverwaltungen 1938/39* (Stuttgart, 1977), p. 218.

[16] *Trials of the War Criminals before the International Military Tribunal* (hereafter cited as IMT), vol. 26, pp. 378–9, 381–3 (864-PS).

[17] *Faschismus, Getto, Massenmord* (hereafter cited as FGM) [Berlin (East), 1960], pp. 42–3 (NO-4059); YVA, JM 21/1, Frank Tagebuch: Streckenbach report of 31.10.39; *Biuletyn Glownej Komisji Badania Zbrodni Hitlerowskich W Polsce* (hereafter cited as *Biuletyn*), XI, pp. 11F–14F, and Hans Frank, *Diensttagebuch des deutschen Generalgouverneurs in Polen 1939–1945*, ed. by Werner Präg and Wolfgang Jacobmeyer (Stuttgart, 1975), pp. 60–1 (conference of 8.11.39).

established General Government were to be moved from west to east of the Vistula the following year.[18]

No one misunderstood the implications of this plan for a Jewish reservation in Lublin. Arthur Seyss-Inquart reported that the "extreme marshy nature" of the Lublin region "could induce a severe decimation of the Jews."[19] And the newly appointed general governor, Hans Frank, exulted: "What a pleasure, finally to be able to tackle the Jewish race physically. The more that die, the better."[20]

Clearly there were many Germans who were intoxicated by Hitler and Himmler's vision of vast and brutal population transfers within 4 months and who welcomed the loss of life, particularly Jewish life, that this would entail. But turning this vision into reality would prove difficult for the Germans actually entrusted with the task of implementation. The first flood of ethnic Germans arrived in Danzig–West Prussia, where space was found by both brutally clearing half the population of Gdynia (Gotenhafen)[21] and murdering the patients of mental hospitals.[22] But Gauleiter Albert Forster proved increasingly uncooperative about resettling further ethnic Germans.[23] By late November the higher SS and police leader for Danzig and West Prussia, Richard Hildebrandt, announced that "in the Danzig district itself the Baltic Germans will no longer remain but rather be sent on."[24]

On November 28, Heydrich intervened from Berlin, drastically scaling down the immediate task facing the Germans to a "short-range plan" (*Nahplan*) that differed from Himmler's guidelines of October 30 in significant ways. First, immediate expulsions were to take place only from the Warthegau rather than throughout the incorporated territories. Second, the quota was sharply cut from 1 million to 80,000 "Poles and Jews," whose removal would make room for 40,000 "incoming Baltic Germans." And finally, the racial and political crite-

[18] United States Holocaust Memorial Museum (hereafter cited as USHMM), RG 15.005m, 2/104/15 (Müller, RSHA, to EG VI in Posen, 8.11.39).

[19] IMT, vol. 30, p. 95 (2278-PS).

[20] FGM, p. 46 (Frank speech in Radom, 25.11.39).

[21] Umbreit, *Militärverwaltung,* pp. 216–21.

[22] Aly, "*Endlösung,*" pp. 114–26.

[23] Herbert Levine, "Local Authority and the SS State: The Conflict over Population Policy in Danzig–West Prussia," *Central European History,* II/4 (1969), pp. 331–55.

[24] YVA: O-53/69/639–41 (Polizeisitzung in Danzig, 15.11.39) and 642–3 (conference of 20.11.39); JM 3582 (Hildebrandt speech, 26.11.39).

ria emphasized by Himmler gave way to more practical concerns. Housing and livelihoods had to be procured for incoming ethnic Germans, and "urgently needed" manual laborers were to be exempted.[25]

As a consequence, the emphasis on deporting Jews was diminished. Although by far the largest concentration of Jews in the Warthegau, those in the city of Lodz were not to be included, because it was not yet clear whether that city would ultimately be part of the General Government or end up within the boundaries of the Third Reich. Other Warthegau Jews were to constitute a deportation reservoir and be expelled only when needed to fill gaps and prevent delays, if the other priority-target groups were not available in sufficient numbers to fill the deportation quotas.[26]

The Germans in the Warthegau exceeded the quota and reported triumphantly that they had succeeded in deporting over 87,000 "Poles and Jews" by December 17, 1941. The primary thrust of the "first short-range plan" (*1. Nahplan*) was not to solve the Jewish question but rather to remove Poles who posed "an immediate danger" and find space for the Baltic Germans.[27] The reason why the precise number or percentage of Jews among the expellees was not reported becomes clear from local documents. In Lodz local authorities had been too incompetent or inefficient to identify "politically suspicious and intellectual Poles" in sufficient numbers to fill their quotas. Thus they had "had to fall back on Jews."[28] The indiscriminate seizure of Jews was obviously administratively easier than the selective seizure of Poles. In the end, about 10,000 Jews were deported, mostly from Lodz after all, owing to the insufficient number of deportable Poles identified and listed by the local authorities. This figure of 10,000 Jewish deportees from Lodz was not included in the self-congratulatory final reports on the "first short-range plan," because it was evidence not of a success in

[25] *Biuletyn,* XII, pp. 15F–18F (Heydrich to HSSPF Cracow, Breslau, Posen, Danzig, 28.11.39; and Heydrich to Krüger, Streckenbach, Koppe, and Damzog, 28.11.39).

[26] USHMM, RG 15.015m, 1/5/4-7 (Rapp draft, 10.11.39) and 2/99/1-5 (Koppe circular, 12.11.39).

[27] *Biuletyn,* XII, pp. 22F–31F, and USHMM, RG 11.001m, 1/88/185–202 (Rapp report, 18.12.39); YVA, JM 3582, and USHMM, RG 15.015m, 3/208/1–12 (Rapp report, 26.1.40).

[28] USHMM, RG 15.015m, 3/218/13–14 (undated Richter report) and 27–35 (Richter report, 16.12.39).

deporting Jews but rather of a failure to identify and seize Polish political activists and intelligentsia.

Immediately following the conclusion of the "first short-range plan," Heydrich's Jewish experts in Berlin once again posed the question "whether a Jewish reservation shall be created in Poland. . . ."[29] Heydrich's response was threefold: he appointed Eichmann as his "special adviser" (*Sonderreferent*),[30] for the moment postponed any Jewish deportations from the Old Reich,[31] and ordered a "second short-range plan" for "the complete seizure of all Jews without regard to age or gender" in the incorporated territories and "their deportation into the General Government."[32] On January 4, 1940, Eichmann reaffirmed that "On the order of the Reichsführer-SS the evacuation of all Jews from the former Polish occupied territories is to be carried out as a priority."[33]

However, despite the German recommitment to the immediate expulsion of all Jews from the incorporated territories, the problems that stood in the way of realization of expelling both Jews and Poles only multiplied in the new year. The arrival of 40,000 Baltic Germans was to be quickly followed by a further deluge of 120,000 Volhynian Germans. Hans Frank, so enthusiastic the previous fall, was now considerably sobered. He complained bitterly about the impact of the chaotic deportations of the "first short-range plan" and emphasized the limited absorptive capacity of the General Government.[34] The latter had been a matter of no concern in the fall of 1939 but increasingly became so as Hermann Göring insisted upon harnessing the productive capacities of the conquered territories to the war effort.[35] There were other problems as well. No trains were available until mid-February.[36] And Himmler, worried about a sufficient stock of German

[29] YVA, JM 3581 (RSHA II/112 an den Leiter II im Hause, 19.12.39).

[30] YVA, JM 3581 (Heydrich to Sipo-SD in Cracow, Breslau, Posen, Danzig, and Königsberg, 21.12.39).

[31] YVA, JM 3581 (Müller to all Staatspolizeistellen, 21.12.39).

[32] USHMM, RG 15.015m, 2.97/1–7 (2. Nahplan, 21.12.39).

[33] *Biuletyn*, XII, pp. 37F–39F (Abromeit Vermerk of 8.1.40 on conference of 4.1.40).

[34] *Biuletyn*, XII, pp. 37F–39F (Abromeit Vermerk of 8.1.40 on conference of 4.1.40; FGM, pp. 48 and 53 (reports of Gschliesser and Wächter); *Documenta Occupationis* (hereafter cited as DO), vol. 8, pp. 37–8 (report of Mattern); IMT, vol. 26, pp. 210–12. (661-PS); Frank, *Diensttagebuch*, pp. 93–7 (Abteilungsleitersitzung, 19.1.40).

[35] Aly, "*Endlösung*," pp. 113–14.

[36] USHMM, RG 15.015m, 1/96/12–13 (Krumey report, 30.1.40, on Leipzig Fahrplanbesprechung of 26–27.1.40).

blood to repopulate the incorporated territories, insisted that cases of contested ethnic German status and Poles capable of Germanization not be deported without screening; hence only Jews and recent Polish emigrants but not longtime Polish residents were to be deported.[37] But that often meant exempting the political and economic leadership classes whose property was needed for accommodating incoming ethnic Germans while deporting the propertyless Polish workers most needed for economic production. The labor issue was intensified further when the Warthegau was targeted to provide 800,000 agricultural workers for the Reich. German occupation authorities immediately demanded that further deportations to the General Government had to be stopped if local labor needs were to be covered.[38]

Thus within the overall scheme for a demographic reorganization of eastern Europe that Himmler had proposed and Hitler approved in the fall of 1939, the Nazis had set for themselves three tasks: the ethnic cleansing of Jews from the Third Reich, of Poles from the Third Reich, and the repatriation of ethnic Germans from abroad. The plan for expelling the Jews had not been generated by the need to make space for the ethnic Germans but rather preceded it. But then the immediate urgency of resettling the Baltic Germans led to the temporary curtailment of Jewish expulsion, for the latter did not provide the necessary housing and jobs for the former. This conflict within German racial and resettlement policy was soon complicated by additional economic factors: the concern for labor and production, the shortage of trains, and the limited absorptive capacity of the General Government. The Nazi empire builders and demographic engineers had tied themselves in knots.

The Nazi leadership attempted to solve this welter of self-imposed contradictions with very limited success. On January 30, 1940, Heydrich chaired a meeting of leading officials from the occupied east, his own Reich Security Main Office, and Göring's representative, at which the hoped-for expulsion of all Jews was postponed once again. The deportation of 40,000 Jews and Poles for the purpose of "making room" (*Platzschaffung*) for the remaining Baltic Germans –

[37] Nuremberg Document NO-5411 (Creutz to Koppe, 18.1.40); *Biuletyn,* XII, pp. 44F–45F (Vermerk of Eichmann Seidl conversation, 22–23.1.40).

[38] USHMM, RG 15.015m, 2/146/9–15 (meeting of 11.1.40).

the so-called intermediate plan (*Zwischenplan*) – was now to be followed by an "another improvised clearing" of 120,000 Poles to provide space for the Volhynian Germans – a "second short-range plan." Unlike the urban Baltic Germans, the Volhynian Germans were a rural population, for whom the removal of Jews was even less relevant. Thus the evacuation of all Jews from the incorporated territories would take place only "as the last mass movement."[39]

The discussion was continued at a higher level yet, when Göring hosted Himmler, Frank, and the eastern Gauleiter at his Karinhall estate on February 12, 1940. Göring insisted that the first priority was to strengthen the war potential of the Reich, and in this regard the incorporated territories were to be the granary of Germany. Thus, "all evacuation measures are to be directed in such a way that useful manpower does not disappear." Jewish transports were to be sent only in an orderly manner, with prior notification and approval. Frank immediately adhered to Göring's position.

Himmler took for granted that the Baltic and Volhynian resettlements would continue in what were now designated the "intermediate" and "second short-range" plans. But Himmler agreed to postpone the resettlement of a further 40,000 Lithuanian Germans, 80,000 to 100,000 Bukovinian Germans, and 100,000 to 130,000 Bessarabian Germans, as well as the ethnic Germans west of the Vistula. However, the 30,000 ethnic Germans in the Lublin district east of the Vistula would have to be resettled, he insisted, because their present homeland was destined to become the *Judenreservat.* Finally, Himmler assured Frank that they "would reach agreement upon the procedures of future evacuations."[40]

Back in the General Government in early March, Frank explained what he thought had been agreed upon. The General Government would receive 400,000 to 600,000 Jews, who would be placed along the eastern border. "It is indescribable, what views have formed in the Reich, that the region of the General Government east of the Vistula is increasingly considered as some kind of Jewish reservation," he noted. The final goal was to make the German Reich free of Jews, but "that

[39] *Biuletyn,* XII, pp. 66F–75F (NO-5322: conference of 30.1.40); USHMM, RG 15.015m, 12/109/1–3 (Rapp Vermerk, 1.2.40).

[40] IMT, vol. 36, pp. 300–306 (EC-305).

that shall not occur in a year and especially not under the circumstances of war, Berlin also recognizes." Moreover, no resettlement actions would take place without prior approval from the General Government. And most important, "the great resettlement ideas have indeed been given up. The idea that one could gradually transport 7.5 million Poles to the General Government has been fully abandoned."[41]

When Himmler attempted to exceed the Karinhall agreement and add Jewish deportations from Stettin to the "intermediate" and "second short-range plans," Göring and Frank exercised their power to block unauthorized transports. Himmler had to concede once again that the expulsion of Jews would commence only in August after the completion of the Volhynian Aktion or "second short-range plan."[42]

Himmler had seen his grandiose design for the sweeping racial reorganization of eastern Europe steadily whittled away. In the fall of 1939, he had envisaged the deportation of 1 million people (including *all* Jews) from the incorporated territories by March 1940, and eventually the removal of all Poles as well. By the spring of 1940, however, the deportation of Jews had been postponed to August, and Frank was boasting that the expulsion of 7.5 million Poles from the incorporated territories had been "fully abandoned." Moreover, Hitler himself seemed to have lost interest in the Lublin reservation as a solution to the Jewish question as well, indicating even to foreign visitors in mid-March 1940 that he had no space available for Jews there.[43]

Then suddenly Germany's stunning victory in France emboldened Himmler once again to try to override the pragmatic considerations of Göring and Frank. Himmler seized the propitious opportunity to revitalize his plans for the total expulsion of Poles from the incorporated territories and to suggest an even more radical expulsion plan for the Jews.

Sometime in May 1940 Himmler drafted a memorandum entitled "Some Thoughts on the Treatment of Alien Populations in the East."

[41] Frank, *Diensttagebuch,* pp. 131 and 146–7 (Sitzung des Reichsverteidigungsausschuss, Warsaw, 2.3.40, and Dienstversammalung der Kreis und Stadthauptmänner des Distrikts Lublin, 4.3.40).

[42] Frank, *Diensttagebuch,* pp. 158 (entry of 5.4.40) and 204 (entry of 19.5.40); *Dokumently i Materialy Do Dziejow Okupacji Niemieckiej W Polsce,* III, *Getto Lodzkie* (Warsaw, 1946), pp. 168–9 (Riegierungspräsident to officials of Bezirk Lodz and Kalish, 8.5.40).

[43] *Documents on German Foreign Policy,* D, VIII, p. 912–13.

The 15 million people of the General Government and 8 million of the incorporated territories – "ethnic mush" (*Völkerbrei*) in Himmler's view – were to be splintered into as many ethnic groups as possible for "screening and sifting" (*Sichtung und Siebung*). Himmler wanted "to fish out of this mush the racially valuable" to be assimilated in Germany, with the rest to be dumped into the General Government, where they would serve as a reservoir of migrant labor and eventually lose their national identity.

Along with the denationalization, in effect cultural genocide, of the various ethnic groups of eastern Europe, the Jews were to disappear in a different way. "I hope completely to erase the concept of Jews through the possibility of a great emigration of all Jews to a colony in Africa or elsewhere," he proposed. Concerning this systematic eradication of the ethnic composition of eastern Europe, Himmler concluded: "However cruel and tragic each individual case may be, this method is still the mildest and best, if one rejects the Bolshevik method of physical extermination of a people out of inner conviction as un-German and impossible" ("*So grausam und tragisch jeder einzelne Fall sein mag, so ist diese Methode, wenn man die bolschewistische Methode der physischen Ausrottung eines Volkes aus innerer Überzeugung als ungermansich und unmöglich ablehnt, doch die mildeste und beste*").

With impeccable timing, Himmler submitted his memorandum to Hitler on May 25, a week after the German army had reached the English Channel. "The Führer read the six pages through and found them very good and correct" (*sehr gut und richtig*), Himmler noted. Moreover, "The Führer desires that I invite Governor Frank back to Berlin, in order to show him the memorandum and to say to him that the Führer considers it correct." Not content with this triumph, Himmler obtained Hitler's authorization also to distribute the memorandum to the eastern Gauleiter and Göring as well, with the message that the Führer had "recognized and confirmed" (*anerkannt und bestätigt*) the guidelines.[44]

This episode is of singular importance in that it is the only firsthand account by a high-ranking participant – Himmler – of just how a Hitler decision was reached and a "Führer order" disseminated in the shap-

44 Helmut Krausnick, ed., "Einige Gedanke über die Behandlung der fremdvölkischen im Osten," VfZ, V/2 (1957), pp. 194–98.

ing of Nazi racial policy during this period. Hitler indicated a change in expectations, in this case his abandonment of the Lublin reservation. At the opportune moment, Himmler responded with a new initiative in the form of a general statement of intent and policy objectives known to be in line with Hitler's general ideological outlook. Hitler indicated not only his enthusiastic agreement but also with whom this information could be shared. He gave no specific orders to the likes of Göring, Frank, and the eastern Gauleiter but simply allowed it to be known what he wanted or approved. The stage was then set for a new round of planning in the search for a solution to the Jewish question through expulsion or ethnic cleansing.

Heydrich rather than Himmler in fact met with Hans Frank on June 12. However, "in view of the dire situation" in the General Government it was agreed for the moment not to go beyond the Karinhall accord – that is, the Volhynian action then in progress followed by the general expulsion of Jews scheduled for August.[45] For Frank, even these expulsions loomed as catastrophic, given the food shortages in the General Government.[46] For the beleaguered Frank, a surprising order from Himmler suddenly stopping the impending expulsion of the Jews into the General Government came as a veritable deliverance.[47] Himmler had found his colony in Africa for the Jews!

For decades the island of Madagascar had exercised a fantastical attraction for European anti-Semites as a place for Europe's expelled Jews.[48] It had been frequently mentioned by leading Nazis since 1938, most recently by Frank in January 1940.[49] With the lightning defeat of France, it was a freakish idea whose time had suddenly come. In another example of timely initiative from below that dovetailed with changes in circumstance and policy at the top, the newly appointed Jewish expert of the German Foreign Office, Franz Rademacher, pro-

[45] *Biuletyn,* XII, pp. 94F–95F (R. Günther to Höppner, 1.7.40).

[46] Frank, *Diensttagebuch,* pp. 210, 216 (Polizeisitzung, 30.5.40); Nuremberg Document NG-1627 (Frank to Lammers, 25.6.40).

[47] *Biuletyn,* XII, pp. 96F–97F (Vermerk on Höppner-IV D 4 discussion, 9.7.40).

[48] For the most recent scholarship on the European anti-Semitic tradition and the Madagascar Plan, see: Magnus Brechtken, *"Madagaskar für die Juden": Antisemitische Idee und politische Praxis 1995–1945* (Munich, 1997), and Hans Jansen, *Der Madagaskar-Plan: Die beabsichtigte Deportation der europäischen Juden nach Madagaskar* (Munich, 1997).

[49] IMT, vol. 26, pp. 210–22 (661-PS).

posed that in planning for the peace treaty with France, Germany consider removing the newly acquired west European Jews to the French colony of Madagascar.[50] The proposal not only moved up the hierarchy with incredible speed but also was quickly expanded to include all European Jews. On June 18, both Hitler and Joachim von Ribbentrop mentioned the plan to use Madagascar for a Jewish reservation to Benito Mussolini and Galeazzo Ciano respectively in their talks in Munich over the fate of the French empire.[51] By June 24, 1940, Heydrich had gotten wind of the project and asserted his long-standing jurisdiction over Jewish emigration. He insisted that he be included in any discussions Ribbentrop was planning on a "territorial solution" to the Jewish question.[52] Ribbentrop immediately conceded, and henceforth planning on the Madagascar Plan was a mixture of cooperation and competition between the Foreign Office and SS.[53]

The demise of the Lublin reservation and the emergence of the new Madagascar Plan was, in Frank's words, a "colossal relief" ("*kolossale Entlastung*") for German officials in the General Government.[54] Two fundamental changes in policy immediately resulted. First, "an order from Cracow [Frank's capital] was issued to stop all work on ghetto construction in view of the fact that, according to the plan of the Führer, the Jews of Europe were to be sent to Madagascar at the end of the war and thus ghetto building was for all practical purposes illusory."[55] Second, when Frank met with Gauleiter Arthur Greiser of the Warthegau in late July, the latter conceded that according to Himmler the Jews were now to be sent overseas. Nevertheless, as an interim measure he was still des-

50 Politisches Archiv des Auswärtigen Amtes (hereafter PA), Inland II A/B 347/3, Rademacher memorandum "Gedanken über die Arbeit und Aufgaben des Ref. D III, 3.6.40." A synopsis of this memorandum is Nuremberg Document NG-5764.

51 Paul Schmidt, *Hitler's Interpreter* (New York, 1951), p. 178; Galeazzo Ciano, *The Ciano Diaries 1939–43* (Garden City, NY, 1947), pp. 265–6. Two days later, on June 20, Hitler repeated his intention to resettle the European Jews on Madagascar to Admiral Raeder. Klaus Hildebrand, *Vom Reich zum Weltreich: Hitler, NSDAP, und koloniale Frage 1919–1945* (Munich, 1969), pp. 651–2.

52 PA, Inland IIg 177, Heydrich to Ribbentrop, 24.6.40.

53 For the details of this planning, see: Christopher R. Browning, *The Final Solution and the German Foreign Office* (New York, 1978), pp. 35–43.

54 Frank, *Diensttagebuch*, p. 248 (entry of 10.7.40) for HSSPF Friedrich Wilhelm Krüger's announcement of the news), and pp. 252 and 258 (Abteilungsleitersitzung, 12.7.40, and entry of 25.7.40) for Frank's boisterous reception.

55 FGM, p. 110 (Schön report, 20.1.40).

perate to resettle Jews from the starving Lodz ghetto into the General Government in August as previously planned. Frank flatly refused and advised Greiser instead to see that the Lodz Jews were considered first in line for Madagascar if their situation were so impossible.[56]

Planning for Madagascar continued fervently until the end of August and then stopped abruptly. The defeat of France and seemingly imminent victory over Great Britain had promised both the colonial territory and the merchant fleet necessary for the plan's realization. But failure to defeat Great Britain was fully apparent in September, and the frenetic urgency behind its preparation in the summer months suddenly dissipated. Like Eichmann's Nisko Plan, Rademacher's Magadascar Plan was a timely low-level initiative that offered a way to implement policy decisions just made at the top. And like Nisko, real work on Madagascar was abruptly halted when circumstances changed. Just as the idea of the Lublin reservation continued as the official goal, even though it was consistently postponed in favor of more limited but temporarily more urgent Polish expulsions tied to ethnic German repatriation, Madagascar lingered as the official policy until an alternative was proclaimed. Not a "phantom solution" at first, it became one. Like Nisko/Lublin, Madagascar implied a murderous decimation of the Jewish population. If actually implemented, Hitler's Reichstag prophecy would have been proclaimed as completely fulfilled. And like the failure of Nisko/Lublin, the failure of Madagascar left the frustrated German demographic planners receptive to ever more radical solutions.

In the summer and fall of 1940, German ethnic cleansing continued to encounter difficulties. The Germans expelled over 70,000 people from Alsace–Lorraine and blocked the return of an additional 70,000 refugees who had fled.[57] Gauleiter Robert Wagner took the opportunity to propose expelling the Jews of Baden and Pfalz at the same time, and Hitler "impulsively" agreed.[58] Some 6,500 German Jews were expelled

[56] Frank, *Diensttagebuch*, pp. 261–3 (entry of 31.7.40).

[57] IMT, vol. 31, pp. 283–94 (2916-PS); Akten der Partei-Kanzlei der NSDAP, 101 23821 (Chef der Zivilverwaltung in Elsass, 22.4.41, to Martin Bormann).

[58] Bundesarchiv Koblenz, All. Proz. 6/Eichmann Interrogation, I, pp. 141–5; Jacob Toury, "Die Entstehungsgeschichte des Austreibungsbefehle gegen die Juden der Saarpfalz und Baden (22/23. Oktober 1940) – Camp de Gurs," *Jahrbuch des Instituts für Deutsche Geschichte*, Beihefte X (1986), pp. 435–64.

over the demarcation line into southern France, but the ensuing diplomatic complications with the Vichy government ensured that this measure was not repeatable.

In the east, the "second short-range plan" was somewhat expanded and considerably delayed. As part of the expanded plan, the so-called Cholmer Aktion for the repatriation of ethnic Germans from the eastern border of the Lublin district was particularly significant because it also involved the reciprocal exchange of Poles and ethnic Germans between the Lublin district and the incorporated territories.[59] These ethnic Germans came from within the German sphere and were thus in no imminent danger. In short, repatriating ethnic Germans to the incorporated territories was not just a reactive measure to rescue ethnic Germans from the Soviet sphere but a program carried out for its own sake. The vision of Germanizing the new borderlands fired Himmler's imagination as a historic mission of great consequence. This was the construction of German *Lebensraum* as understood at the time. Two years later, the Germans would try to reverse the Cholmer Aktion with the Zamosc Aktion, resettling Germans in areas from which they had in fact been recently removed. With ethnic German resettlement as with the Lublin and Madagascar plans, the hindsight perspectives of Generalplan Ost and Auschwitz are not the proper yardstick by which to measure Himmler's ideological horizon in the summer of 1940.

By the time the "second short-range plan" was concluded six months behind schedule in December 1941, the Germans had expelled some 460,000 people, of whom at least 36,000 or approximately 8 percent were Jews.[60] (Vastly greater numbers of Jews, of course, had fled on their own as refugees from the incorporated territories to the General Government and from the General Government over the demarcation line into the Soviet sphere). The Nazis, therefore, had achieved only a pathetic fraction of the overall goals and expectations of ethnic cleansing that they had set in the fall of 1939. Progress toward solving their self-imposed Jewish problem in particular was

[59] USHMM, RG 15.015m: 2/115/38 (conference of Ansiedlugnstab, Posen, 12.7.40), 40–41 (Höppner to Eichmann and Ehlich, 12.7.40), and 50 (Krumey Aktenvermerk, 21.8.40); 3/228/3 (Aufstellung der Cholmer Aktion).

[60] The sources for these statistics are too lengthy to include here but are based on my manuscript, "The Origins of the Final Solution: The Evolution of Nazi Jewish Policy, September 1939–March 1942," to be published as part of Yad Vashem's multivolume history of the Holocaust.

even more scant. In the repatriation of ethnic Germans, at least from the Soviet zone, they had come closer to meeting expectations, but the difficulties and delays in moving them from transit camps to permanent resettlement was yet another source of frustration.

Not surprisingly, therefore, the Nazis attempted to reinvigorate their lagging schemes for ethnic cleansing at the end of 1940. On three occasions – in the successive months of October, November, and December 1940 – Hitler made clear to Frank his "urgent wish" that more Poles be taken into the General Government, along with the Jews of Vienna.[61] With Hitler's support to override Frank, who now had no choice but to accept the expulsions as "one of the great tasks that the Führer has set for the General Government," Heydrich produced his "third short-range plan" (*3. Nahplan*) for 1941. Ethnic Germans were to be repatriated from the Balkans (Bessarabia, Bukovina, and Dobrudja) as well as a remnant from Lithuania. To make room in the incorporated territories, over 1 million Poles (200,000 of them at the behest of the army to clear land for a vast military training ground) were to be expelled into the General Government in one year, dwarfing the expulsions of 1939–40.[62]

As the pioneering research of Götz Aly has now shown, the "third short-range plan" for the intensified expulsion of Poles was paralleled by yet another plan for the expulsion of the Jews beyond those of Lublin and Madagascar. On December 4, Eichmann submitted to Himmler a brief summary on the status of the Jewish question, noting that 5.8 million European Jews had to be taken into consideration for resettlement to a destination mysteriously characterized as "a territory yet to be determined" ("*ein noch zu bestimmendes Territorium*"). Clearly the General Government was not this mysterious destination, for its Jews formed the bulk of the 5.8 million to be expelled, and as Himmler wrote concerning the General Government, in notes for a speech delivered 1 week later: "Jewish emigration and thus yet more space for Poles"

61 At the October 2, 1940, meeting of Hitler and the eastern Gauleiter: IMT, vol. 39, pp. 426–9 (USSR-172). At the November 2, 1940, meeting of Hitler with Frank and Greiser: Frank, *Diensttagebuch,* p. 302 (entry of 6.11.40). For December: Ibid., p. 327 (entry of 15.1.41). For the Vienna Jews: NCA, IV, p. 592 (1950-PS).

62 Frank, *Diensttagebuch,* p. 327 (conference of 15.1.41); USHMM, RG 15.105m, 3/199/4-6 (Vermerk on conference of 8.1.41) and 8-9 (Höppner Aktenvermerk on Fahrplankonferenz in Posen on 16.1.41); *Biuletyn,* XII, p. 127F (Krumey to Eichmann, 6.1.41); YVA, JM 3582 (Abschlussbericht 1941).

("*Judenauswanderung und damit noch mehr Platz für Polen*").[63] Himmler's speech was given on the eve of the finalization of two important policies in December 1941, namely the "third short-range plan" for sending more than 1 million Poles from the incorporated territories into the General Government and the decision to invade the Soviet Union. The latter, because it obviously could not be talked about openly, had to be referred to in code language as a "territory yet to be determined" and was to provide the destination for Jewish expulsion. This in turn would break the demographic impasse in the General Government and create space for the realization of the ambitious "third short-range plan."

Planning for Operation Barbarossa remained secretive, and hence use of code language about "a territory yet to be determined" continued. The most detailed reference to this planning is contained in a memorandum written by Eichmann's close associate, Theodore Dannecker, on January 21, 1941:

> In conformity with the will of the Führer, at the end of the war there should be brought about a final solution of the Jewish question within the European territories ruled or controlled by Germany.
>
> The Chief of the Security Police and the Security Service [Heydrich] has already received orders from the Führer, through the Reichsführer-SS, to submit a project for a final solution. . . . The project in all its essentials has been completed. It is now with the Führer and the Reichsmarschall [Göring].
>
> It is certain that its execution will involve a tremendous amount of work whose success can only be guaranteed through the most painstaking preparations. This will extend to the work preceding the wholesale deportation of Jews as well as to the planning to the last detail of a settlement action *in the territory yet to be determined* [italics mine].[64]

[63] Susanne Heim and Götz Aly, eds., *Beiträge zur nationalsozialistischen Gesundheits und Sozialpolitik,* vol. 9: *Bevölkerungsstrukture und Massenmord: Neue Dokumente zur deutschen Politik der Jahre 1938–1945* (Berlin, 1991), pp. 24–7 (Eichmann summary "submitted to the RFSS," 4.12.40; Aly, *"Endlösung,"* pp. 195–200.

[64] Cited in: Serge Klarsfeld, *Vichy-Auschwitz: Die Zusammenarbeit der deutschen und französischen Behörden bei der "Endlösung der Judenfrage: in Frankreich* (Nördlingen, 1989), pp. 361–3. In February 1941 Heydrich also dropped reference to the Madagascar Plan and wrote Undersecretary Martin Luther in the Foreign Office about a "later total solution to the Jewish question" ("*späteren Gesamtlösung des Judenproblmes*") to be achieved through "sending them off to the country that will be chosen later" ("*nach dem zukünftigen Bestimmungslande abzutransportieren*") PA, Inland II A/B 809-41 Sdh. III, Bd. 1, Heydrich to Luther, 5.2.41.

That Heydrich had indeed prepared and submitted a plan to Göring is confirmed in a meeting of the two on March 26, 1941. Heydrich's memorandum of the meeting, another archival find by Götz Aly, noted as point 10:

Concerning the solution to the Jewish question, I reported briefly to the Reichsmarschall and submitted my draft to him, which he approved with one amendment concerning the jurisdiction of Rosenberg and ordered to be resubmitted.

As Aly has pointed out, the reference to Rosenberg's jurisdiction – he was soon to be designated the future minister of the occupied Soviet territories – indicates once again that the proverbial territory yet to be determined was the Soviet Union.[65]

If Heydrich was busy drafting and submitting plans in the early months of 1941, what did Himmler think about it? There is an indication that at least in one regard he was somewhat troubled. In early 1941 he approached Viktor Brack of the Führer Chancellery and expressed concern that "through the mixing of blood in the Polish Jews with that of the Jews of Western Europe a much greater danger for Germany was arising than even before the war. . . ." It is important to emphasize that such a concern made sense in the bizarre mental world of Heinrich Himmler only if a massive concentration of east and west European Jews were actually being envisaged in some area of resettlement, where this mix of Jews would produce offspring reaching adulthood in some 20 years! Clearly in Himmler's mind, this expulsion plan was not merely a cover for an already decided upon policy of systematic and total extermination. Himmler asked Brack, who worked with the "many scientists and doctors" assembled for the euthanasia program, to investigate the possibility of mass sterilization through X-rays. Brack submitted a preliminary report on March 28, 1941, which Himmler acknowledged positively on May 12.[66] Thereafter, however, Himmler showed no further interest.

65 Cited in: Aly, *"Endlösung,"* p. 270, with Aly's analysis, pp. 271–2. The document is from the Moscow Special Archives, 500/3/795.

66 *Trials of the War Criminals before the American Military Tribunal,* I, p. 732 (testimony of Viktor Brack, May 1947); Nuremberg Documents NO-203 (Brack to Himmler, 28.3.41) and NO-204 (Tiefenbacher to Brack, 12.5.41).

The documentation for this last plan for expelling Jews into the Soviet Union is quite fragmentary and elusive in comparison to the Lublin and Madagascar Plans. This was due in part to the need to preserve secrecy concerning the identity of "the territory yet to be determined." And perhaps it was also because the Nazi leadership was caught up in the immediate preparations for Operation Barbarossa. But perhaps it was also because their hearts were no longer in it – that in the minds of Hitler, Himmler, and Heydrich the notion was beginning to take shape of another possibility *in the future,* if all went well with the imminent military campaign. Indeed, it was precisely in March 1941 that Hitler's exhortations for a war of destruction against the Soviet Union – like his earlier exhortations in 1939 preceding the invasion of Poland – were setting radically new parameters and expectations for Nazi racial policies.

Hitler's declarations that the war against the Soviet Union would not be a conventional war but rather a conflict of ideologies and races and that one avowed war aim was the "removal" of "Judeo-Bolshevik intelligentsia"[67] evoked responses from both the SS and the Wehrmacht. Himmler and Heydrich created the Einsatzgruppen and procured military agreement for their operation up to the front lines. The German military itself stripped the civilian population of protection of law by restricting military court martial jurisdiction and mandating collective reprisal. And it prepared to make its own contribution to the elimination of Judeo-Bolshevism through dissemination of the infamous "commissar order" and the equally infamous guidelines for troop behavior that equated Jews with Bolshevik agitators, guerrillas, and saboteurs.[68]

[67] *Kriegstagebuch des Oberkommandos der Wehrmacht 1940–1941,* I, pp. 341–2 (entry for 3.3.41).

[68] For the growing body of literature on Germany's preparation for a war of destruction in the Soviet Union, see: Hans-Adolf Jacobsen, "Kommissarbefehl und Massenexekutionen sowjetischer Kreigsgefangener," *Anatomie des SS-Staates* (Freiburg, 1965), II, pp. 161–278; Andreas Hillgruber, "Die 'Endlösung' und das deutsche Ostimperium als Kernstück des rassenideologischen Programmes des nationalsozialismus," VfZ, 20 (1972), pp. 133–53; Christian Streit, *Keine Kameraden: Die Wehrmacht und die sowjetischen Kreigsgefangenen, 1941–1945* (Stuttgart, 1978); Helmut Krausnick and Hans-Heinrich Wilhelm, *Die Truppe des Weltanschauungskrieges: Die Einsatzgruppen des Sicherheitspolizei und des SD, 1938–1942* (Stuttgart, 1981); Helmut Krausnick, "Kommissarbefehl und 'Gerichtsbarkeiterlass Barbarossa' in neuer Sicht," VfZ, 25 (1977), pp. 682–738; and especially the contributions of Jürgen Förster in *Das Deutsche Reich und der Zweite Weltkrieg,* IV, *Der Angriff auf die Sowjetunion* (Stuttgart, 1983), pp. 3–37, 413–47, 1030–88.

German preparations for the economic exploitation and demographic transformation of Soviet territory implied even greater destruction of life. The Economic Staff East (Wirschaftsstab Ost) of General Georg Thomas made plans for both feeding the entire German occupation army from local food supplies and exporting vast amounts of food to Germany.[69] The staff had no doubt that the "inevitable" result would be "a great famine," and that "tens of millions" of "superfluous" people would either "die or have to emigrate to Siberia."[70] The state secretaries fully concurred: "Umpteen million people will doubtless starve to death when we extract what is necessary for us. . . ."[71]

Himmler was not to be outdone by the military and ministerial plans for the starvation death of "umpteen million" Soviet citizens and the forced migration to Siberia of millions more. Meeting on June 12–15, 1941, in his renovated Saxon castle at Wewelsburg with his top SS associates and the designated higher SS and police leaders (HSSPF) for Soviet territory, Himmler sketched out his own vision of the coming conflict. "It is a question of existence, thus it will be a racial struggle of pitiless severity, in the course of which 20 to 30 million Slavs and Jews will perish through military actions and crises of food supply."[72] And on June 24, 1941, Himmler entrusted one of his demographic planners, Professor Konrad Meyer, with drawing up Generalplan Ost, which in one version would call for the expulsion of 31 million Slavs into Siberia.[73] In short, within the SS, ministerial

[69] For military plans for economic exploitation: Rolf-Dieter Müller, "Von Wirtchaftsallianz zum kolonial Ausbeutungskrieg," *Das Deutsche Reich und der Zweite Weltkrieg*, IV, *Der Angriff auf dem Sowjetunion*, esp. pp. 125–29 and 146–52.

[70] IMT, vol. 36, pp. 141–45 (126-EC: report of Wirtschaftsstab Ost, 23.5.41).

[71] IMT, vol. 31, p. 84 (2718-PS: state secretaries' meeting, 2.5.41).

[72] The Wewelsburg meeting has now been dated to June 12–15, 1941, according to Himmler's Terminkalendar found in the Moscow Secret Archives (Osobyi 1372-5-23. The accession number for the copy in the US Holocaust Memorial Museum is: 1997.A.0328). I am grateful to Dr. Jürgen Matthäus for providing me with a copy of this document. Testifying at the trial of Karl Wolff in Munich, Bach-Zelewski erroneously dated the meeting to March 1941. JNSV, XX (Nr. 580, LG München II 1 Ks 1/64), p. 413. At his even earlier Nürnberg testimony, Bach-Zelewski said that it had taken place early in 1941. IMT, vol. 4, pp. 482–88.

[73] Dietrich Eichholz, "Der 'Generalplan Ost.' Über eine Ausgeburt imperialistischer Denkart und Politik," *Jahrbuch für Geschichte*, 26 (1982), p. 256 (Doc. Nr. 2: Meyer to Himmler, 15.7.41). Richard Breitman, *The Architect of Genocide: Himmler and the Final Solution* (New York, 1991), p. 168. Helmut Heiber, "Der Generalplan Ost," *Vierteljarhshefte für Zeitgeschichte*, 3 (1958), 300–313 (Doc.Nr. 2: Stellungnahme und Gedanken zum Generalplan Ost des Reichsführer SS, by Wetzel, 27.4.42).

bureaucracy, and military, there was a broad consensus on what the German scholar Christian Gerlach has aptly dubbed the "hunger plan" as well as ever vaster schemes of "ethnic cleansing."[74]

None of the Barbarossa planning documents or criminal orders of this period contain explicit plans concerning the fate of the Jews on Soviet territory. Certainly verbal orders were given to the Einsatzgruppen just prior to the invasion, the "most important" of which Heydrich relayed to the HSSPF "in compressed form" on July 2, 1941. Along with the general exhortation to carry out pacification measures "with ruthless severity," Heydrich's explicit orders for those to be executed included Communist functionaries, anyone engaged in any form of resistance, and "Jews in state and party positions."[75] Some historians, such as Helmut Krausnick, have interpreted this Heydrich execution order "in compressed form" as code language for the explicit and comprehensive verbal order given to the Einsatzgruppen prior to the invasion to murder all Soviet Jewry.[76] In contrast, I now share the view first advanced by Alfred Streim[77] and Christian Streit[78] and gradually endorsed by many other scholars[79] that the ultimate decision was made and orders were given for the Final Solution on Soviet territory beginning some 4 weeks after the invasion.

In my opinion, the last months before and the first weeks after the invasion of the Soviet Union can best be seen as an important transi-

[74] Christian Gerlach, *Krieg, Ernährung, Völkermord: Forschungen zur deutschen Vernichtungspolitik im Zweiten Weltkrieg* (Berlin, 1998) pp. 13–30.

[75] Heydrich to HSSPFs Jeckeln, v.d. Bach, Prützmann, and Korsemann, 2.7.41, printed in: Peter Klein, ed., *Die Einsatzgruppen in der besetzten Sowjetunion 1941/42: Die Tätigskeits und Lageberichte des Chefs der Sicherheitspolizei und des SD* (Berlin, 1997), pp. 324–5.

[76] Helmut Krausnick and Hans-Heinrich Wilhelm, *Die Truppe des Weltanschauungskrieges: Die Einsatzgruppen der Sicherheitspolizei und des SD 1938–1942* (Stuttgart, 1981), pp. 150–65; *Der Mord an den Juden im Zweiten Welktrieg*, ed. by Eberhard Jäckel and Jürgen Rohwer (Stuttgart, 1985), pp. 88–106.

[77] Alfred Streim, *Die Behandlung sowjetsicher Kriegsgefangenen im "Fall Barbarossa"* (Heidelberg and Karlsruhe, 1981), pp. 74–93.

[78] Christian Streit, *Keine Kameraden: Die Wehrmacht und die sowjetischen Kriegsgefangenen 1941–1945* (Stuttgart, 1978), pp. 127 and 356.

[79] In particular, see: Peter Longerich, "Vom Massenmord zur 'Endlösung.' Die Erschiessungen von jüdischen Zivilisten in den ersten Monaten des Ostfeldzuges im Kontext des nationalsozialistischen Judenmords," *Zwei Wege Nach Moskau: Vom Hitler-Stalin-Pakt zum 'Unternehmen Barbarossa,'* ed. by Bernd Wegner (Munich, 1991), pp. 251–74; and Ralf Ogorreck, *Die Einsatzgruppen und die "Genesis der Endlösung"* (Berlin, 1996).

tion period in the evolution of Nazi Jewish policy. The first two resettlement plans had failed and the third languished as the feverish and murderous preparations for Operation Barbarossa rendered it increasingly obsolete. Clearly, plans for the war of destruction entailed the death of millions of people in the Soviet Union, and in such an environment of mass death, Soviet Jewry was in grave peril. Indeed, Nazi plans for the war of destruction, when seen in the light of the past Nazi record in Poland, *implied* nothing less than the *genocide* of Soviet Jewry. In Poland, when large numbers of people had been shot, Jews had been shot in disproportionate numbers. When massive expulsions had taken place, it was never intended that any Jews would be left behind. And when food had been scarce, Jews had always been the first to starve. Now mass executions, mass expulsions, and mass starvation were being planned for the Soviet Union on a scale that would dwarf what had happened in Poland. No one fully aware of the scope of these intended policies could doubt the massive decimation and eventual disappearance of all Jews in German-occupied Soviet territories. Within the framework of a war of destruction, through some unspecified combination of execution, starvation, and expulsion to an inhospitable Siberia, Soviet Jewry, along with millions of other Slavs, would eventually be destroyed.

But the *implied genocide* in the future of Jews on Soviet territory was not yet the Final Solution for all Soviet Jewry, much less the other Jews of Europe. The old resettlement plans were dead, replaced by a vague genocidal vision that was unspecific about timetable and means and still comingled the fates of Jewish and non-Jewish victims. However, this vagueness and lack of specificity would soon come to an end. In the "fateful months" following Operation Barbarossa, a series of decisions would be made. Out of these decisions would emerge what the Nazis called "the Final Solution to the Jewish Question," a program of systematic and total mass murder, to begin and be completed as soon as feasibly possible, and for the first time with clear priority for the implementation of Jewish policy over the various other Nazi demographic schemes affecting ethnic Germans and Slavs.

2

NAZI POLICY

Decisions for the Final Solution

Historians have offered a broad spectrum of conflicting interpretations concerning the nature and timing of the decisions for the Final Solution. To outsiders the debate on the decision-making process in general, and both Hitler's role and the timing of decisions in particular, may often seem the arcane equivalent of a medieval scholastic dispute over the number of angels that can stand on the head of a pin. But to participating scholars this debate has remained of central importance because understanding the decision-making process has proved inseparable from understanding both the wider historical context for these decisions and the structure and functioning of the Nazi system. The debate over decision making has quite simply refused to go away precisely because it is indispensable for shedding light on other questions.

This debate over the decision-making process for the Final Solution has now entered a third stage. In the first stage – the intentionalist/functionalist controversy of the late 1970s and early 1980s – the debate encompassed an extraordinarily wide spectrum of interpretation, ranging from those who argued for a basic Hitler decision in the 1920s to those who argued that he made no decision at all.[1] In a second stage, the debate in the late 1980s and early 1990s was conducted on the much narrower front of the single year of 1941. American historian Richard Breitman argued that there was a fundamental decision early in the year as part of the preparation for Operation Barbarossa. Swiss historian Philippe Burrin argued that there was a decision in early October, made within the context of the

[1] For my summary of this first stage, see: Christopher R. Browning, *Fateful Months: Essays on the Emergence of the Final Solution* (New York, 1985), pp. 8–38.

collapse of Hitler's plans for quick victory against the Soviet Union and the looming entry of the United States into the war on the one hand and Hitler's preexisting "conditional intention" to murder the Jews of Europe if he found himself caught in a war on all fronts on the other. I argued that there was a two-stage decision-making process, one for Soviet and another for European Jewry, with each stage reaching closure at the successive peaks of Nazi victory euphoria in mid-July and early October 1941, respectively.[2]

Though Burrin and I disagreed over the military context of frustration or euphoria, we agreed on dating Hitler's decision sealing the fate of European Jewry to early October. And Breitman's chronology placed what he considered Hitler's implementation decisions (as opposed to a basic decision) in late August and early September, only a month ahead of the date agreed upon by Burrin and me. The subsequent interpretations of Dieter Pohl,[3] Götz Aly,[4] and Peter Witte[5] likewise emphasized October as a turning point.

Now, however, the debate has entered a third stage, in which December 1941 has been suggested as a key chronological turning point and the entry of the United States into the war as a key factor in the explanatory historical context. Hans Safrian,[6] L. J. Hartog,[7]

[2] For my summary of this second stage, see: Christopher R. Browning, *The Path to Genocide* (New York, 1992), pp. 86–121.

[3] Dieter Pohl, *Von der "Judenpolitik" zum Judenmord: Der Distrikt Lublin des Generalgouvernements 1939–1944* (Frankfurt/M., 1993), pp. 97–101, 105–6.

[4] Götz Aly, *"Endlösung": Völkerverschiebung und der Mord an den europäischen Juden* (Frankfurt/M., 1995), especially pp. 333 and 358–9, accepted mid-August as the point by which Himmler had ordered the mass murder of Jewish women and children on Soviet territory and the first two weeks of October as the "political caesura" (*politische Zäsur*) when confusion and uncertainty gave way to goal-directed decisions for systematic mass murder of European Jewry. Though Aly emphasizes the "dashed expectation of victory" (*enttäuschte Siegeserwartung*) as vital to the overall radicalization of Nazi racial policy, he admits that it is "conceivable" (*vorstellbar*) that Hitler had "illusions" about the possibility of victory in early October. (p. 358, fn 73). Aly's interpretation differs from mine most sharply in the relatively diminished role he attributes to Hitler in the decision-making process.

[5] Peter Witte, "Two Decisions Concerning the 'Final Solution to the Jewish Question': Deportations to Lodz and the Mass Murder in Chelmno," *Holocaust and Genocide Studies*, 9/3 (winter 1995), pp. 318–45.

[6] Hans Safrian, *Die Eichmann-Männer* (Vienna, 1993), especially pp. 149, 154, and 169–73.

[7] L. J. Hartog, *Der Befehl zum Judenmord: Hitler, Amerika und die Juden* (Bodenheim, 1997), initially published in Dutch in 1994. Hartog's study is based on printed documents interpreted almost entirely within a framework of ideology and foreign policy, and with the United States rather than the USSR at the center of Hitler's concerns.

and Christian Gerlach[8] have all placed the key decision in December 1941, and the latter two have offered extraordinarily precise dates – December 8 and 12, respectively. Safrian has argued that expulsion of Jews into the Soviet Union was foreclosed by the failure of Operation Barbarossa and the Soviet counteroffensive in early December, and the Wannsee Conference was rescheduled from December 9 to January 20 to allow the Nazis time to consider a different option. Hartog argues that the Japanese attack on Pearl Harbor, bringing the United States into the war, ended the usefulness of European Jews as hostages for U.S. neutrality, fulfilled the conditions of Hitler's January 1939 Reichstag prophecy, and freed him to carry out the mass murder he had long desired but pragmatically postponed. As Christian Gerlach's highly stimulating, deeply researched, and powerfully articulated recent article, published in Germany in December 1997 and in English translation in the United States in December 1998,[9] includes both these and additional arguments, as well as much fuller – and in some cases new – documentation, I will return to it in greater detail later.

Before focusing on the contested issues of this latest stage in the debate over the decision-making process, however, it is useful first to review the many areas in which disagreement has diminished and something approaching a general consensus – however temporary we do not yet know – has been achieved. First, most historians agree that there is no "big bang" theory for the origins of the Final Solution, predicated on a single decision made at a single moment in time. It is generally accepted that the decision-making process was prolonged and incremental. The debate is really about the nuances of weighting and emphasis. Which in a series of decisions should be considered more important, more pivotal, than others? For instance, both Gerlach and I accept that important decisions were made in both October and December 1941, but we disagree on the meaning, location, and relative significance of those decisions.

[8] Christian Gerlach, "Die Wannsee-Konferenz, das Schicksal der deutschen Juden und Hitlers Grundsatzentscheidung, alle Juden Europas zu ermordern," *Werkstattgeschichte* 18 (1997), pp. 7–44.

[9] Christian Gerlach, "The Wannsee Conference, the Fate of German Jews, and Hitler's Decision in Principle to Exterminate All European Jews," *Journal of Modern History*. 12 (1998), pp. 759–812.

Second, there has been a shift toward emphasizing continuity over discontinuity in the decision-making process. In the early 1980s, for instance, I referred to the decision for the systematic mass murder of Soviet Jewry as a "quantum leap" in Nazi Jewish policy. I still think this step was one of the two most important turning points in the decision-making process, but today I would not use language that implied such a dramatic rupture. In recent years historians have increased their focus on the hitherto relatively ignored period of 1939–40 and taken the Nazis' expulsion plans and visions of demographic engineering more seriously than before.[10] But in doing so they have also seen the Nazi policies of this period not as sharply juxtaposed to the Final Solution but rather as destructive and murderous steps in their own right in a process of "radicalization" and "escalation" leading toward the Final Solution.

Peter Longerich, perhaps the most emphatic advocate of an explicit continuity thesis, has argued that the decisive transition from *Judenpolitik* to *Vernichtungspolitik* should be dated to the fall of 1939 and that all policies thereafter implied murderous destruction.[11] Magnus Brechtken concluded, in his recent book, that the Madagascar Plan amounted to a "death sentence" for European Jewry that differed from Auschwitz only in the place and method of murder.[12] And Christian Gerlach has articulated the notion of a German "hunger plan" on the eve of Operation Barbarossa that had vast genocidal implications.[13] As I argued in my previous lecture, I still think that there is

[10] The pathbreaking work in this regard is: Götz Aly, *"Endlösung": Völkerschiebung und der Mord and den europäischen Juden* (Frankfurt/M., 1995), which has the added merit of also integrating aspects of the so-called euthanasia program into the evolution of Nazi policy. For the earliest pioneering work on Nazi population policy, see Robert L. Kochl, *RKFDV: German Resettlement and Population Policy 1939–1945* (Cambridge, MA, 1957).

[11] Peter Longerich, "Die Eskalation der NS-Judenverfolgung zur 'Endlösung': Herbst 1939 bis Sommer 1942," presented at the University of Florida/German Historical Institute Symposium on the Origins of Nazi Policy, Gainesville, Florida, April 1998. Not available at the time this lecture was originally written is Peter Longerich's massive and important *Politik der Vernichtung: Eine Gesamtdarstellung der Nationalsozialistische Judenverfolgung* (Munich, 1998).

[12] Magnus Brechtken, *"Madagaskar für die Juden: Antisemitische Idee und politische Praxis 1885–1945* (Munich, 1997), esp. p. 295.

[13] Christian Gerlach, *Krieg, Ernährung, Völkermord: Forschungen zur deutschen Vernichtungspolitik im Zweiten Weltkrieg* (Hamburg, 1998), pp. 13–30.

merit in identifying and preserving the distinctions between policies of population decimation, genocide, and Final Solution, but I am fully in accord with this recent tendency to recognize and emphasize the elements of continuity in German racial policies between 1939 and 1941.

Third, most – though certainly not all – scholars in the field have gravitated toward the position first articulated by Christian Streit and Alfred Streim some 20 years ago that the decision and dissemination of orders for the murder of all Soviet Jewry down to the last man, woman, and child, with only a temporary exemption for indispensable skilled workers, did not occur until after the initial invasion.[14] On the empirical side, it is generally accepted that in the first weeks of Operation Barbarossa the Jewish victims were primarily adult male Jews, and that beginning in late July – at different times in different places at different rates – the killing was gradually expanded to encompass all Jews except indispensable workers – a process that was nearly complete in the Baltic by the end of the year but not yet elsewhere on occupied Soviet territory until 1942.

There is still considerable difference of interpretation on at least two issues concerning this transition to the systematic and total mass murder of Soviet Jewry: first, the relative roles of regional and local authorities on the one hand and Hitler and the central authorities on the other, and second, the historical context of euphoria of victory or growing frustration and desperation. A number of very important regional studies incorpo-

[14] For example, Peter Longerich, "Vom Massenmord zur 'Endlösung.' Die Erschiessungen von jüdischen Zivilisten in den ersten Monaten des Ostfeldzuges im Kontext des nationalsozialistischen Judenmords," *Zwei Wege, Nach Moskau: Vom Hitler-Stalin-Pakt zum 'Unternehmen Barbarossa',* ed. by Bernd Wegner (Munich, 1991), pp. 251–74; Ralf Ogorreck, *Die Einsatzgruppen und die "Genesis der Endlösung"* (Berlin, 1996); Christian Gerlach, *Krieg, Ernährung, Völkermord,* pp. 56–81. For recent scholarship on Lithuania, where the transition to the Final Solution was first implemented, see: Jürgen Matthäus, "Jenseits der Grenze: Die ersten Massenerschiessungen von Juden in Litauen," *Zeitschrift für Geschichtswissenschaft* 2 (1996), pp. 101–17; Christoph Dieckmann, "Der Krieg und die Ermordung der litauischen Juden," *Nationalsozialistische Vernichtungspolitik 1939–1945: Neue Forschungen und Kontroversen,* ed. by Ulrich Herbert (Frankfurt/M., 1998), pp. 292–329; Konrad Kwiet, "Rehearsing for Murder: The Beginning of the Final Solution in Lithuania in June 1941," *Holocaust and Genocide Studies* 12 (spring 1998), pp. 3–26; and Michael MacQueen, "The Context of Mass Destruction: Agents and Prerequisites of the Holocaust in Lithuania," *Holocaust and Genocide Studies* 12 (spring 1998), pp. 27–48. For a dissenting opinion to the general trend toward accepting the Streim/Streit thesis: Daniel Jonah Goldhagen, *Hitler's Willing Executioners: Ordinary Germans and the Holocaust* (New York, 1996), pp. 148–53.

rating the archival sources newly available in the 1990s have recently appeared,[15] and others are forthcoming.[16] The interpretive trend is now toward placing greater emphasis on local and regional decision making as a frustrated response to local and regional problems as opposed to my interpretation, which has emphasized the impact of a premature victory euphoria on Hitler in mid-July and the important role of Himmler in disseminating the new policy over the following weeks. This current scholarship, incorporating the new archival sources, is producing many new trees; the shape of the forest, however, remains to be seen.

A fourth area of emerging agreement is that the decision-making process did not end in 1941. Peter Longerich has argued that there was a fourth "stage of escalation" ("*Eskalationsstufe*") in May 1942, characterized by the "indiscriminate murder of all Jews at the end of the deportation."[17] I have sketched out the importance of July 1942 as the point of a "final decision" for the Final Solution.[18] And now Christian Gerlach has developed a much more detailed argument concerning an "acceleration" of the mass murder in the summer of 1942, focusing in particular on the murder of Jewish labor in connection with the height of the Reich's crisis in food production.[19] The fate of Jewish labor is a theme to which we will return later.

And finally, there is considerable agreement among historians that the destructive acceleration during these "fateful months" ought not be studied with sole focus on the roles of central authorities in decision making and the SS in implementing policy. Rather, there is a growing

[15] Galicia has been particularly well served by two monographs: Dieter Pohl, *Nationalsozialistische Judenverfolgung in Ostgalizien 1941–1944: Organisation und Durchführung eines staatlichen Massenverbrechens* (Munich, 1996); and Thomas Sandkühler, *"Endlösung" in Galizien: Der Judenmord in Ostpolen und die Rettungsinitiativen von Berthold Beitz 1941–1944* (Bonn, 1996). For Latvia, see: Andrew Ezergailis, *The Holocaust in Latvia 1941–1944* (Washington, D.C. and Riga, 1996).

[16] For Byelorussia, see: Christian Gerlach, *Kalkulierte Morde: Die deutsche Wirtschafts - und Vernichtungspolitik im Weissrussland* (Hamburg, 1999). Christoph Dieckmann's on Lithuania in particular. The Ukraine is until now the least well served.

[17] Longerich, "Die Eskalation der NS-Judenverfolgung zur 'Endlösung': Herbst 1939 bis Sommer 1942."

[18] Christopher R. Browning, "A Final Decision for the 'Final Solution'? The Riegner Telegram Reconsidered," *Holocaust and Genocide Studies* 10 (spring 1966), pp. 3–10.

[19] Christian Gerlach, "Die Bedeutung der deutschen Ernährungspolitik für die Beschleunigung des Mordes an den Juden 1942: Das Generalgovernement und die Westukraine," *Krieg, Ernährung, Völkermord*, pp. 167–299.

awareness among historians that the Final Solution was based on a form of consensus politics among the Germans.[20] Thus the role of regional and local as well as central authorities must be studied, as must the participation of the military, civil administration, Order Police, and economic planners, as well as local collaborators and police auxiliaries, alongside the Einsatzgruppen and Security Police. Here again the issue is one of finding the appropriate balance. What were the respective roles of central, regional, and local authorities? What were the respective roles of various German and non-German participants? How did these respective roles differ from place to place?

If the focus has been widened and a fair degree of agreement has been attained on so many issues concerning the origins of the Final Solution, why – one might ask – have some historians (including me) remained so concerned with pinpointing the nature and timing of an alleged key decision by Hitler – what Christian Gerlach has called the *Grundsatzentscheidung* – for the Final Solution? I cannot speak for others, but I can explain why I have periodically revisited this question throughout my career and why I do not think this has been a trivial exercise.

I believe that the Holocaust was a watershed event in human history – the most extreme case of genocide that has yet occurred. What distinguishes it from other genocides are two factors: first, the totality and scope of intent – that is, the goal of killing every last Jew, man, women, and child, throughout the reach of the Nazi empire; and second, the means employed – namely, the harnessing of the administrative/bureaucratic and technological capacities of a modern nation-state and western scientific culture. It is precisely these elements that both define the singularity of the Holocaust and distinguish the Nazi Final Solution in its ultimate form from the regime's prior policies of population decimation, genocide, and even the systematic and total mass murder of Soviet – as distinguished from all European – Jewry. It is not, therefore, a trivial historical question to ask when Hitler and the Nazi regime passed the point of no return and committed themselves to a vision of

[20] A pioneering study that demonstrated the importance of regional studies and emphasized the consensus politics behind the Final Solution is: Dieter Pohl, *Von der "Judenpolitik" zum Judenmord: Der Distrikt Lublin des Generalgouvernements 1939–1944* (Frankfurt/M., 1993).

murdering all the Jews of Europe through the most modern and efficient methods available to it.

In addition, I would note, there is a need particularly for Holocaust scholars, insofar as possible, to get the facts right, because there are people who do not wish us well. They stand malevolently prepared to exploit our professional mistakes and shortcomings for their own political agenda. I do not wish to make their dishonest tasks easier.

Whatever nightmarish dreams might have lurked in Hitler's mind and for how long, we can only guess. But I think the preponderance of evidence points to the conclusion that in mid-July 1941 Hitler instigated Himmler and Heydrich to undertake what amounted to a "feasibility study" for the mass murder of European Jews, and in early October 1941 he shared with Himmler and Heydrich his approval of their proposal to deport the Jews of Europe to killing centers in the east. These two dates, mid-July and early October 1941, coincided with the two peaks of victory euphoria on the eastern front, which – as in September 1939 and May 1940 for the Lublin and Madagascar Plans, respectively – provided a conducive context for the radicalization of Nazi Jewish policy. Thereafter, notwithstanding regional variations, temporary exceptions and postponements, trial-and-error experimentation, and a remarkably unsystematic and gradual dissemination of the regime's intentions, Nazi Jewish policy was directed toward realizing this vision.

The most recent alternative interpretation is that of Christian Gerlach. According to Gerlach, prior to December 12, 1941, the fate of German and west European Jews – in contrast to that of Soviet and at least some Polish Jews – was still undecided. As of that date, only 6 of 41 Jewish transports to Lodz, Kovno, Minsk, and Riga had been liquidated upon arrival, so no general destruction order could yet have been given. What became known as the Wannsee Conference, originally scheduled for December 9, was at that time intended primarily to clarify issues relating to the ongoing deportation and still undecided fate of German Jews, he has argued.[21] And Belzec, admittedly under construction in the fall of 1941, had too little gas chamber capacity to indicate an intention to murder all Polish, much less all European,

[21] Gerlach, "Grundsatzentscheidung," pp. 8, 14, 16–20.

Jewry.[22] Insofar as planning and preparation for mass murder were underway in the fall of 1941, Gerlach has characterized these efforts as the product of regional authorities trying to solve regional problems while seeking approval and support from above.

In Gerlach's account, this situation was dramatically transformed in early December. The Japanese attack on Pearl Harbor deprived the Jews of their value as hostages for U.S. neutrality and inaugurated the world war that was the condition of Hitler's January 1939 Reichstag prophecy dooming the Jews to destruction. In the grip of a "fortress mentality" that saw the Jews as a "partisan" threat and determined to retaliate against those he blamed for the war, Hitler acted. As a recently published portion of Joseph Goebbels' diary now reveals, on December 12, 1941, the day after declaring war on the United States, Hitler addressed the top party leaders in his private apartment. He explicitly invoked his Reichstag prophecy: "The world war is here, the destruction of the Jews must be the necessary consequence. . . . The instigators of this bloody conflict must pay for it with their own lives." According to Gerlach, this was not only an "announcement" ("*Bekanntgabe*") to party leaders but also the "basic decision" ("*Grundsatzentscheidung*") sealing the fate of German and west European Jewry.[23] Only then could "systematic planning" for the Final Solution (as opposed to transitional, regionally initiated programs of mass murder) begin.

According to Gerlach, previously known but not fully understood documents of Alfred Rosenberg's meeting with Hitler and Himmler's meeting with Rudolf Brandt on December 14 and Hans Frank's speech on December 16 confirm this interpretation of Hitler's speech.[24] But the new "smoking pistol" document is Himmler's *Terminkalendar* from the Moscow Special Archives,[25] with its cryptic entry from a Himmler – Hitler meeting on December 18: "*Judenfrage. Als Partisanen auszurotten.*" For Gerlach, this is to be understood neither literally nor as a sug-

[22] Moreover, he claims, it was visited by Eichmann only in December after Heydrich and the RSHA (Reichssicherheitshauptamt [Reich Security Main Office]) began searching for ways to implement Hitler's basic decision. Gerlach, "Grundsatzentscheidung," pp. 9, 12, 31.

[23] Gerlach, "Grundsatzentscheidung," pp. 25–8.

[24] Gerlach, "Grundsatzentscheidung," pp. 22–5, 29–30.

[25] Moscow Special Archives (hereafter cited as MSA), 1372-5-23.

gestion of *Tarnsprache* or camouflage language but in the "global sense" ("*globalen Sinn*") as an "instruction" ("*Weisung*") concerning the imaginary Jewish threat everywhere.[26] The postponed Wannsee Conference was rescheduled for January 20, 1942, an unusual and previously unexplained 6-week delay, to give Heydrich and his minions in the Reich Security Main Office time to prepare for the new task posed by the "announcement" of Hitler's "basic decision" of December 12, 1941.[27]

To explain why I do not find this interpretation persuasive, I would like to examine several key documents from the months leading up to December 1941 in light of Gerlach's arguments. Gerlach and especially L. J. Hartog emphasize the key relationship between Hitler's Reichstag prophecy concerning world war and the destruction of European Jewry on the one hand, and the U.S. entry into the war on the other. They suggest that Hitler made a sharp distinction between a "European war" with the Soviet Union and a "world war" against the United States, and that he viewed only the latter as activating his prophecy of January 1939. Such a literal and restrictive interpretation is made doubtful by another entry in Goebbels' diary from August 19, 1941:

> The Führer is convinced that his Reichstag prophecy is coming true; that should the Jews once again succeed in provoking a world war, this would end in their annihilation. It is coming true in these weeks and months with a certainty that appears almost sinister. In the east the Jews are paying the price; in Germany they have already paid in part and they will have to pay still more in the future.[28]

Hitler assured Goebbels that Berlin Jews would be deported to the east as soon as the campaign was over and transportation was available. "Then they will be worked over in the harsh climate there."[29] Here Hitler's prophecy and the murder of Jews, already being realized on Soviet territory and anticipated for German Jews following victory, are clearly not tied to a "world war" defined primarily by American involvement.

[26] Gerlach, "Grundsatzentscheidung," pp. 22, 27.
[27] Gerlach, "Grundsatzentscheidung," pp. 32.
[28] *Die Tagebücher von Joseph Goebbels,* Teil II, Bd. 1, p. 269 (entry of 19.8.41).
[29] *Die Tagebücher von Joseph Goebbels,* pp. 266 and 278 (entries of 19 and 20.8.41).

But what exactly was being anticipated in late August concerning what German Jews "would pay still more in the future"? In mid-July, I have argued, Hitler solicited a plan or "feasibility study" for the destruction of European Jewry. The written authorization for preparing this plan (*not yet* a *decision* or *order* for the Final Solution) was drafted by Heydrich and signed by Göring on July 31. This authorization explicitly requested a plan for a "total solution" encompassing all Jews within the German sphere and made no mention whatsoever concerning the distinction between German and west European Jews on the one hand and east European Jews on the other that is so central to Gerlach's argument. Nor, for that matter, do any other documents of this period, although in contrast many refer explicitly and inclusively to all European Jews.

Heydrich's authorization for planning was not an insignificant document containing empty rhetoric. By late August it was no secret to Eichmann that plans were being prepared. To his year-old formulaic answer to the Foreign Office rejecting requests for Jewish emigration from occupied territories "in view of the imminent Final Solution," he now added the ominous phrase "now in preparation" ("*im Hinblick auf die kommende und in Vorbereitung befindliche Endlösung der europäischen Judenfrage*").[30]

The nature and scope of the proposals under consideration and awaiting approval can be seen in a document submitted to the Reich Security Main Office just days later on September 3, 1941, by Rolf-Heinz Höppner, the head of the Emigration Central (*Umwandererzentrale* or UWZ) in Poznan, who had been in charge of expelling "undesired" Poles and Jews from the Warthegau into the General Government. Höppner's proposals had been drafted "on the basis of the recent consultation" ("*auf Grund der letzten Rücksprache*") with Eichmann, and they did not concern just local solutions to his local problems in the Warthegau. Höppner wanted an expanded Emigration Central – headquartered in Berlin – to be in charge of both deportation and "reception territories" ("*Aufnahmegebieten*") for the resettlement ("*Aussiedlung*") of all "undesired" ("*unerwünschten*") ethnic elements in the Greater German Reich. Concerning the Jews in particular, he took it for granted that "the final solution to the Jewish question . . . will include all states

[30] Politisches Archiv des Auswärtigen Amtes (hereafter cited as PA), Inland II A/B 47/1, Eichmann to Rademacher, 28.8.41.

within the German sphere of influence in addition to the Greater German Reich." He made no distinction between east and west European Jews. But Höppner complained that his proposals concerning "reception areas" had to remain "patchwork" ("*Stichwerk*") for the moment, however, because he did not yet "know the intentions" of Hitler, Himmler, and Heydrich:

> I could well imagine that *large areas of the present Soviet Russia* are being prepared to receive the undesired ethnic elements of the greater German settlement area. . . . To go into further details about the organization of the reception area would be fantasy, because first of all the basic decisions must be made. It is essential in this regard, by the way, that total clarity prevails about what finally shall happen to those undesirable ethnic elements deported from the greater German settlement area. Is it the goal to ensure them a certain level of life in the long run, or shall they be totally eradicated.[31]

When were the "basic decisions" made and "total clarity" achieved – at least concerning the European Jews if not yet other "undesired" elements – that Eichmann was openly discussing and Höppner was impatiently awaiting?

As Peter Witte has documented, on September 16 and 17, 1941, Himmler met with Hitler as well as with a number of other middle-ranking Nazi leaders like Joachim von Ribbentrop, Otto Abetz, Ulrich Greifelt (RKFDV or Reichskommissariat für die Festigung deutschen Volkstums), and the author of the Generalplan Ost, Konrad Meyer.[32] The topics of discussion with Greifelt included the "Jewish Question" and "settlement in the east" ("*Siedlung Ost*").[33] Previously Hitler had repeatedly rejected proposals to begin the deportation of German Jews until "after the war." Now, during this busy weekend of meetings, he apparently concluded that the time for deportations had finally come. On September 18, Himmler informed Gauleiter Arthur Greiser in the Warthegau of Hitler's wish to empty the Old Reich and Protectorate of Jews as soon as possible. This meant deporting Jews to Lodz that fall,

[31] United States Holocaust Memorial Museum (hereafter cited as USHMM), RG 15.007m, roll 8/file 103/pp. 45–62 (Höppner to Eichmann and Hans Ehlich, 3.9.41, with proposal of 2.9.41).

[32] Peter Witte, "Zwei Entscheidungen in der 'Endlösung' der Judenfrage," *Holocaust and Genocide Studies* (hereafter cited as HGS), 9/3 (winter 1995), pp. 318–45.

[33] MSA, 1372-5-23: Himmler Terminkalendar, entry of 16.9.41.

"in order to deport them yet further to the east next spring."[34] Hitler then seemed to hesitate, offering a series of reasons why implementation of the decision he had just made might have to be held in temporary abeyance. On September 24 he expressed concern about "clarification of the military situation in the east," and on October 6 he noted "the great shortage of transport."[35]

One consideration that was at least weighed by Hitler in mid-September 1941 but apparently not found to be of sufficient importance to delay further the deportations of Jews from Germany was the American factor. Before officials of the German Foreign Office knew of the reversal of policy, one of them wrote: "The Führer has not yet made a decision about reprisals against German Jews . . . the Führer considers to hold this measure for an eventual entry of America into the war."[36] Hitler's decision nevertheless to begin deporting Jews from Germany would seem to indicate that the American factor was not decisive after all.

Hitler's last hesitations seem to have disappeared in the euphoria of early October, following the capture of Kiev and in the midst of the great double-encirclement victory at Vyazma and Bryansk, when the road to Moscow seemed open. When Hitler arrived in Berlin on October 4, Goebbels noted:

> He looks at his best and is in an exuberantly optimistic frame of mind. He literally exudes optimism. . . . The offensive has been surprisingly successful so far. . . . The Führer is convinced that if the weather remains halfway favorable, the Soviet army will be essentially demolished in fourteen days.

Three days later, Goebbels again noted: "It goes well on the front. The Führer continues to be extraordinarily optimistic."[37] On October 10, at the peak of victory euphoria, Heydrich in Prague announced the deportation of Reich Jews to camps of the Einsatzgruppen comman-

[34] National Archives, T175/54/2568695: Himmler to Greiser, 18.9.41.

[35] *Die Tagebücher von Joseph Goebbels*, Teil II, Bd, 1, pp. 480–83 (entry of 24.9.41); Koeppen's note of 7.10.41, cited in: Martin Broszat, "Hitler und die Genesis der 'Endlösung': Aus Anlass der Thesen von David Irving," *Vierteljahrsheft für Zeitgeschichte* (hereafter cited as VfZ), 25/4 (1977), 751.

[36] Werner Koeppen's note of 20.9.41, cited in: John Lukacs, *The Hitler of History* (New York, 1997), pp. 191–2. A slightly different translation can be found in Witte, "Two Decisions," p. 343.

[37] *Die Tagebücher von Joseph Goebbels*, Teil II, Bd. 2, pp. 49–50 and 73 (entries of 4 and 7.10.41).

ders in Riga and Minsk as well as the Lodz ghetto, and that therefore "all pending questions must be solved immediately."[38]

Indeed, many "pending questions" were solved immediately. On October 15, the deportation of Reich Jews began, and on October 18 Himmler ordered the emigration gates closed. And sometime in October sites for the future death camps at Chelmno and Belzec were also selected. It is this cluster of events, coinciding with Hitler's mistaken victory euphoria, that I have interpreted as signifying closure to the second stage of the decision-making process of the Final Solution and sealing the fate of European Jewry.

This does not mean that some specific plan was approved or that clear-cut and comprehensive orders were given at this point. Rather it is the point, in my opinion, at which Hitler, Himmler, and Heydrich – and a widening circle of initiates thereafter – were aware that the ultimate goal or vision of Nazi Jewish policy was now the systematic destruction and no longer the decimation and expulsion of all European Jews. No clear and uniform plan as to how this would be accomplished was imposed from above, for no such plan yet existed. Much that would happen in the next months would indeed take place on local or regional initiative. But when such initiatives dovetailed with the vision of the Nazi leadership, they were seized upon with alacrity precisely because they met perceived needs. Those initiatives that did not were rejected or ignored. Berlin was not passive but interacted in a goal-directed manner with local authorities in the surge of killing actions and preparation for killing actions that characterized the fall of 1941.

Christian Gerlach has disagreed with my interpretation of the meaning of this cluster of events. "That the decision to deport German Jews was equivalent to the decision to kill them is proven by nothing," he has written. As for Belzec, he concluded: "What conceptions about the future were linked to the construction of Belzec are still shrouded in mystery."[39] Indeed, taken alone, the decision to deport German Jews does not prove a decision for the Final Solution. It is precisely the *conjuncture* of the deportation decision with other events – the closing of emigration and the planning and construction of gassing facilities and death camps – that is key.

[38] Notes on conference of 10.10.41 in Prague, printed in: H. G. Adler, *Theresienstadt 1941–1945* (Tübingen: second edition, 1960), pp. 720–2.

[39] Gerlach, "Grundsatzentscheidung," pp. 42–3.

Let us first turn to the end of Jewish emigration, with focus on one telling incident from mid-October 1941. Before the war German policy had been to create a *judenfrei* Germany through Jewish emigration. After the outbreak of war, Jewish emigration from the occupied territories was banned in order to monopolize the increasingly scarce emigration possibilities for German Jews. For non-German Jews within the German empire, as well as for the bulk of German Jews who would be unable to emigrate, the Nazis planned a succession of three expulsion schemes whose respective destinations were Lublin, Madagascar, and inhospitable regions of the Soviet Union.[40]

This was the state of German policy toward European Jews when the Germans rounded up thousands of Jews in Paris in August 1941 in retaliation for an attack on German soldiers. Included in the roundup were numerous Jews holding Spanish citizenship, and the Spanish government pressed for their release. As an incentive, the Spanish government even offered to evacuate all Spanish Jews – some 2,000 – from France to Morocco, and Undersecretary Martin Luther in the German Foreign Office urged Heydrich to accept the Spanish proposal. It was, after all, very much in line with previous German policy.

However, on October 17, 1941, just one day before Himmler officially closed the gates for Jewish emigration, Heydrich, in a phone conversation with Luther, rejected the Spanish proposal for evacuating Spanish Jews from German-occupied France to Morocco. He gave two reasons for his surprising opposition to this proposal. First, the Spanish government had neither the will nor experience to guard the Jews in Morocco. "In addition these Jews would also be too much out of the direct reach of measures for a basic solution to the Jewish question to be enacted after the war." ("*Darüber hinaus wären diese Juden aber auch bei den nach Kriegsende zu ergreifenden Massnahme zur grundsätzlichen Lösung der Judenfrage dem unmittelbaren Zugriff allzusehr entzogen*".)[41]

What did Heydrich mean by "measures for a basic solution" to be enacted after the war that were incompatible with the evacuation of Spanish Jews to Morocco, if the eventual murder of German and west

[40] For the first two expulsion plans, see: Christopher R. Browning, "Nazi Resettlement Policy and the Search for a Solution to the Jewish Question, 1939–1941," *German Studies Review*, 9/3 (1986), 497–519; and now in much greater detail and with convincing evidence concerning a third expulsion scheme, see: Götz Aly, *"Endlösung": Völkerverschiebung und der Mord an den europäischen Juden* (Frankfurt/M., 1995).

[41] PA, Politische Abteilung III 245, Luther memoranda, 13 and 17.10.41.

European Jews was still undecided? Did Heydrich really prefer to take on the diplomatic and logistical burden of shipping 2,000 Spanish Jews in France over the Urals to Siberia as part of some future expulsion plan rather than simply to allow the Spanish to evacuate them to Morocco immediately? I consider such a scenario most implausible. To my mind Heydrich's actions become quite explicable, however, if the Nazi leadership was now committed to the murder of all Jews in the German grasp. Let us turn then to the issue of German conceptions about and preparations for the construction of death camps in the fall of 1941.

Construction of Belzec was underway by November 1, 1941. Preconstruction preparations – such as site selection, design, and assembly of materials – must therefore have taken place in October. Even if the proposal to construct Belzec was to some degree an initiative of Odilo Globocnik, the SS and police leader in Lublin, to kill the Jews of the General Government as part of his own plans for total Germanization and not solely due to instructions from above, it was an initiative that Himmler apparently approved almost instantaneously in mid-October and incorporated into his own agenda.[42] Whatever the origins of Belzec and the respective roles of central policy and regional initiative, if Eichmann's visit there took place in the early autumn *after* he had learned from Heydrich of Hitler's decision for the Final Solution (as he repeatedly stated after the war), Gerlach's thesis for a December *Grundsatzendscheidung* is untenable.

Gerlach has not questioned that actual construction was underway in Belzec in November, but he has minimized its significance in several ways. First, because of the relatively small capacity of the initial gas chambers in Belzec, the Germans could not yet have constructed them to murder all Jews in the General Government but rather simply to test the possibility for the mass killing of Jews with poison gas.[43] Second, he has claimed that Eichmann could have visited Belzec in December 1941 at the earliest, given his description of the state of construction

[42] Nürnberg Document NO-5875: Helmut Müller, Lublin SSPF, to Gruppenf. Hofmann, 15.10.41, in: *Trials of the War Criminals before the Nürnberg Military Tribunals,* IV, pp. 864–6. Pohl, *Von der "Judenpolitik" zum Judenmord,* 99–102. The early transfer of euthanasia personnel from Berlin to the General Government in connection with Belzec would indicate that Berlin was not merely the passive recipient of Globocnik's initiatives but an active partner in the planning process.

[43] Gerlach, "Grundsatzentscheidung," pp. 9, 43.

there, and that "Eichmann's testimony would fit well with a Hitler decision of early December 1941."[44] I am not persuaded.

Let us examine the Eichmann testimony first.[45] Eichmann testified that 2 or possibly 3 months after the invasion of the Soviet Union, "in any case late summer," Heydrich informed him of the Führer's order for the physical destruction of the Jews. Eichmann was then sent to report on progress in Lublin, where Globocnik had already been informed of the Führer's order and was going to use antitank ditches. Eichmann was driven from Lublin by a member of Globocnik's staff, Hermann Höfle. After a 2-hour ride, they arrived at a wooden house on the righthand side of the road. There, a police captain, one of only two people he saw there, received Eichmann and led him across the road into a forest to two or three wood huts "under construction" ("*noch im Bau*"). The captain said he had to seal one hut to serve as a gas chamber, which was the first time Eichmann allegedly learned that gassing was the intended technological method for the mass murder program "now in preparation." The motor for producing carbon monoxide (allegedly a Russian U-boat engine) was "not yet there" ("*noch nicht einmal da*") and "the installation had not yet been put into operation." ("*die Anlage war noch nicht einmal in Betrieb gewesen*").

Eichmann vividly remembered that the trees were "in full color"[46] ("*im vollen Schmuck*"), the police captain – who spoke a southwest German dialect – was "in shirtsleeves" ("*in Hemdeärmeln*"), and that he stopped in Prague both coming and going, where he shared all he knew

44 Gerlach, "Grundsatzentscheidung," p. 31.

45 Eichmann's testimony is found in a number of sources: "Eichmann tells his own damning story," *Life Magazine* 49/22 (28.11.60); the handwritten "Meine Memoiren" (Bundesarchiv Koblenz [hereafter BAK], All. Proz. 6/119); the pretrial interrogations (BAK, All. Proz. 6/1–6), Eichmann's *Zeitplan* that he prepared for his defense attorney Servatius (BAK, All. Proz. 6/169), the court testimony; and *Ich Adolf Eichmann. Ein historischer Zeugenbericht*, ed. by Dr. Rudolf Aschenauer (Leoni am Starnberger See, 1980). This last source is, in my opinion, the least reliable for reconstructing Eichmann's chronology, due to Aschenauer's own intrusive agenda and strange omission of many events included in all other Eichmann accounts. Yet this is the account Gerlach cites most prominently. Gerlach, "Grundsatzentscheidung," pp. 30–1 and fn 136.

46 In his recent response to the initial version of this paper, Gerlach has suggested that fall colors would not have reached their peak yet in eastern Poland in October. Christian Gerlach, *Krieg, Ernährung, Völkermord* (Hamburg, 1998), p. 270. Yet Goebbels noted on October 9, 1941, for Berlin: "*Der Winter kündigt sich zwar schon langsam an, das Laub an den Bäumen wird braun und fällt herab.*" If the leaves had turned brown and were falling in Berlin on October 9, surely it is not unlikely that the fall colors reached their peak in eastern Poland in the same month. *Die Tagebücher von Joseph Goebbels*, Teil II, Bd. 2, p. 84.

with his associate Hans Günther. It should be noted that Eichmann was present in Prague on October 10, when Heydrich announced the deportations to Lodz, Riga, and Minsk. It should also be noted that in his notes for his defense attorney Robert Servatius, Eichmann associated this trip to Lublin and Belzec with a "double battle" ("*Doppelschlacht*") that he named Minsk and Bialystok. As these two cities fell to the Germans in the first days of the war, I do not think it wild conjecture to suggest that Eichmann meant instead the double encirclement battle of Vyazma and Bryansk that raged October 2–18, 1941.[47]

A team of 20 Polish workers undertook construction of two barracks and the gas chambers at Belzec between November 1 and December 23, under the supervision of a young ethnic German *Baumeister.* By December Josef Oberhauser (who had been transferred to Lublin in November) was on the scene with a band of 20 black-uniformed Ukrainian guards from Trawniki and was joined by Christian Wirth before Christmas. Thereafter 70 Jewish workers were added, and fencing, guard towers, and further barracks were constructed.[48] This busy scene is hardly the virtually empty site and state of construction described by Eichmann. Quite simply, despite a few minor problems (as occur in virtually any witness accounts given years later), there is much in the Eichmann testimony that strongly indicates on October visit to Belzec, which he remembered as taking place *after* Heydrich informed him of Hitler's decision.[49] On the other hand I can find nothing in it to support

[47] In his subsequent response, Gerlach has suggested that this mention of the *Doppelschlacht* Minsk and Bialystok by Eichmann was an attempt by association to remember the travel destination of Minsk. Gerlach, *Krieg, Ernährung, Völkermord,* p. 270. But Eichmann used this association when constructing a chronology or *Zeitplan* for Servatius – that is, when he was attempting a temporal or chronological, not geographical, association to aid his memory.

[48] Zentral Stelle der Landesjustizverwaltungen (hereafter ZStL), 8 AR-Z 252/59: IV, pp. 656–60 and 763–5 (testimony of Josef Oberhauser, 26.2.60 and 20.4.60); VI, pp. 1037–40 (testimony of Josef Oberhauser, 15.9.60), 1112 (testimony of Ludwik Obalek), 1117–20 (Eustachy Urkainski), 1129–40 and 1195 (Stanislaw Kozak), 1138–40 (Edward Luczynski), 1142–3 (Tadeusz Misiewicz), 1150 (Michal Kusmierczak), 1153 (Maria Baniel), 1156 (Jan Glab), 1184 (Alojzy Berezowski), 1222 (Edward Ferens); IX, pp. 1680–87 (Josef Oberhauser, 12.12.62).

[49] In his subsequent response, Gerlach notes that "once" ("*einmal*") during his interrogation, Eichmann referred to the Belzec trip as taking place after the Wannsee Conference. Gerlach, *Krieg, Ernährung, Völkermord,* p. 272. I do not think one such inconsistent statement can outweigh the many other times in which Eichmann dated this trip to the fall of 1941, including when he had time to reflect and was preparing confidential notes for his attorney.

the notion of a December visit "at the earliest" except Eichmann's reference to two or three "wood huts" under construction.

If Gerlach tried to appropriate the Eichmann testimony without success, Hans Safrian tried to discredit the dating of Eichmann's Belzec visit as a defense strategy falsification.[50] Again, I am not persuaded. As Eichmann's chronology and notes for Servatius indicate, he consistently placed the Belzec trip in the fall of 1941, whereas his major obsession was the claim in the memoirs of the Auschwitz commandant Rudolph Höss that Eichmann had visited Auschwitz repeatedly in 1941 and been involved with the search for a suitable gas. As he wrote for Servatius: "Why do I put so much value on all this? Because I must prove Höss the arch-liar, that I had nothing at all to do with him and his gas chambers and his death camp, because I . . . cannot have been with him at all at this time." ("*Warum lege ich auf all dieser einen solch grossen Wert? Weil ich den Erzleugner Höss beweisen musste, dass ich mit ihm und seinen Gaskammern und seinen Tötungslager überhaupt nichts zu tun gehabt habe, weil ich . . . um diese Zeit gar nicht bei ihm gewesen sein kann.*")[51] Insofar as there was a resulting tendency by Eichmann to modify dating, therefore, it was to move events to a later date so that he could only have been in Auschwitz for the first time in the spring of 1942. He certainly had no defense strategy or motive to move events, such as his visit to Belzec, to an earlier date. And although Eichmann might have confused some elements of different visits or telescoped them into one, I find it most implausible that he invented out of thin air an early visit to Belzec that was both described in considerable detail and contrary to the interests of his defense strategy.

Concerning Gerlach's point about the relatively small capacity of the gas chamber being constructed at Belzec, it may be true that viewed according to the later standards of Auschwitz, the first gas chambers at Belzec were indeed very small. However, I would note that for the Germans at that time they represented a significant increase in scale over the "euthanasia" killing centers in Germany. Furthermore, even Himmler's quick approval to construct and "test" such enlarged gassing facilities was far more likely to have occurred after a decision for the Final Solution than before.

[50] Hans Safrian, *Die Eichmann-Männer,* p. 171.

[51] BAK, All. Proz. 6/169, Eichmann chronologies for 1941 and 1942.

More importantly, the construction of Belzec at this time ought not be viewed in isolation but rather in conjuncture with the evidence of other Nazi plans for gassing facilities in the fall of 1941. Polish judge Jan Sehn and subsequently Frenchman Jean-Claude Pressac have accepted December 1941 as the date of the first gassing in the old crematorium in Auschwitz I,[52] but I am inclined to accept the dating provided by Danuta Czech that the experimental gassings on Soviet prisoners of war (POWs) began in Bunker 11 in late August and in the old crematorium in mid-September.[53] Thereafter Jews rather than Soviet POWs were the test subjects. Particularly persuasive to my mind is the testimony of Hans Stark that in October 1941 he personally participated in gassings in the old crematorium of two groups of Silesian Jews brought to the camp in trucks. On one of these occasions he admitted shaking out the Cyclon B pellets. Stark had no reason to invent such self-incriminating testimony. Moreover, as he was on leave from Auschwitz from December 1941 to March 1942, he could not have been confusing events from the fall of 1941 with the gassing of Silesian Jews in the old crematorium that occurred in late February 1942.[54]

On October 25, 1941, the day Reichskommissar Hinrich Lohse arrived in Berlin to protest the planned deportation of Reich Jews to Riga, the Ostministerium Jewish expert Eberhard Wetzel met with Viktor Brack, the euthanasia coordinator in the Führer's chancellery. According to the draft of a letter that Wetzel prepared for his boss, Alfred Rosenberg, Brack declared himself ready to aid in the construction of "gassing apparatuses" ("*Vergassungsapparate*") on the spot in Riga because they were not in sufficient supply in the Reich. They had yet to be built. (At that time, in fact, the gas van prototype

[52] Jean-Claude Pressac, "The Machinery of Mass Murder at Auschwitz," *Anatomy of the Auschwitz Death Camp* (Bloomington, IN, 1994), pp. 209 and 242–3.

[53] Danuta Czech, *Kalendarium der Ereignisse im Konzentrationslager Auschwitz-Birkenau 1939–1945* (Hamburg, 1989), pp. 115–19, 122. See also: Franciszek Piper, "Gas Chambers and Crematoria," *Anatomy of the Auschwitz Death Camp,* p. 157; *Nationalsozialistische Massentötungen durch Giftgas,* ed. by Eugen Kogon, Hermann Langbein, and Adalbert Rückerl (Frankfurt/M., 1983), p. 204; ZStL, IV, p. 402 AR-Z 37/58 (LG Frankfurt 4 Ks 2/63), Sonderband 16, p. 2475 (testimony of Edward Pys).

[54] ZStL, IV p. 402 AR-Z 37/58, Bd. I, pp. 240–2, and Sonderband 6, p. 970 (testimony of Hans Stark).

was just being constructed and tested.[55]) Brack offered to send his chemist Dr. Helmet Kallmeyer to Riga, where he would take care of everything on the spot. According to Wetzel, Eichmann was in agreement with the sending of Kallmeyer and confirmed that Jewish camps were about to be set up in Riga and Minsk to receive German Jews. Wetzel's draft for Rosenberg concluded that those capable of labor would be sent "to the east" later, but under the circumstances there were no objections "if those Jews who are not fit for work are removed by Brack's device" ("*Brackschen Hilfsmitteln*") in the meantime.

By late October use of "Brack's device" was also planned for the Warthegau. According to Walter Burmeister, the chauffeur of Herbert Lange, the future commandant at Chelmno, Burmeister drove his chief around the Warthegau in the fall of 1941, searching for a suitable site for a camp. Lange then drove to Berlin for consultations and returned to the village of Chelmno in late October or early November to begin construction. His chronology was confirmed by the local *Volksdeutsche Amtskommissar.*[56] According to Jan Piwonski, the station master at Sobibor, a group of SS officers arrived there sometime in the fall of 1941 to measure the track and ramp.[57] And ironically, no one has documented more clearly Nazi plans for a death camp with gassing facilities in Mogilev in the fall of 1941 than Christian Gerlach himself.[58]

In sum, in the fall of 1941, "experimental" gassing of Jews had been undertaken in Auschwitz and the construction of death camps at Belzec and Chelmno was underway. Gassing facilities were also envisaged at

[55] Landgericht Hannover, 2 Ks 2/65, Strafverfahren gegen Pradel und Wentritt: VIII, pp. 221–2 (testimony of Helmut H.); IX, pp. 16–19, and XIV, pp. 118 (testimony of Theodor L.). Matthais Beer, "Die Entwicklung der Gaswagen," VfZ 35/3 (1987), p. 411, dates the Sachsenhausen test to November 3, 1941.

[56] ZStL, 203 AR-Z 69/59, IV, pp. 624–43, and VI, pp. 961–89 (testimony of Walter Burmeister); VII, pp. 1288–93 (testimony of Konrad S.).

[57] ZStL, 298 AR, pp. 643–71 (Staatsanwalt Hamburg, 147 Js 43/69, investigation of Streibel), II, p. 442 (testimony of Jan Piwonski). The forthcoming work of Dr. Bogdan Musial adds additional evidence that preparations for a death camp at Sobibor were already underway in the fall of 1941.

[58] Christian Gerlach, "Failure of Plans for an SS Extermination Camp in Mogilev, Belorussia," HGS, 11/1 (spring 1997), pp. 60–78. See also: Jean-Claude Pressac, "The Machinery of Mass Murder at Auschwitz," *Anatomy of the Auschwitz Death Camp,* pp. 201, 208; Pressac, *Les Crématories d'Auschwitz* (Paris, 1993), pp. 31–40; and Aly, *"Endlösung,"* pp. 342–47. See also: Richard Breitman, *Official Secrets: What the Nazis Planned. What the British and Americans Knew* (New York, 1998), p. 77.

Riga, Mogilev, and Sobibor. Belzec was not an isolated phenomenon. Moreover, three of these sites were near precisely those cities – Lodz, Riga, and Minsk – to which Reich Jews were being transported and from which the reluctant recipients of these transports were assured that the presence of these Jews was temporary and that they would be sent further east next spring. And it was precisely at the one destination to which five transports of Reich Jews were sent but no gassing facilities were planned – Kovno – that all the deportees were murdered immediately upon arrival. Was all this just coincidence? I do not think so.

Indeed, talk of gassing Jews was so widespread at this time among even lower-echelon Nazi planners that on October 23 the Jewish expert of the Foreign Office, Franz Rademacher, could receive a casual note from the foreign editor of *Der Stürmer,* Paul Wurm:

> Dear Party Comrade Rademacher!
>
> On my return trip from Berlin I met an old party comrade, who works in the east on the settlement of the Jewish question. In the near future many of the Jewish vermin will be exterminated through special measures.
> *(In nächster Zeit wird von dem jüdischen Ungezeifer durch besondere Massnahmen manches vernichtet werden.)*[59]

Moreover, the same Rademacher had just learned – presumably from Eichmann's deputy Friedrich Suhr with whom he had traveled to Belgrade – that the interned Jewish women, children, and elderly in Serbia – that is those totally incapable of heavy labor – would be deported to a "reception camp" ("*Auffanglager*") in the east "as soon as the technical possibility exists within the framework of the total solution of the Jewish question"[60] ("*sobald dann im Rahmen der Gesamtlösung der Judenfrage die technische Möglichkeit besteht*"). In such circumstances Gerlach's contentions that the fate of German and west European Jews was still undecided, that Belzec was merely a single test site about whose future role and significance the Nazis were still in the dark, and that the mass murder programs under preparation in the fall of 1941 were manifestations of local and regional initiatives unconnected to the regime's wider vision of a Final Solution strike me as quite untenable.

[59] PA, Inland II A/B 59/3, Wurm to Rademacher, 23.10.41.

[60] PA, Inland IIg, p. 194, Rademacher report, 25.10.41, printed in: *Akten zur Deutschen Aussenpolitik,* D, XIII, pp. 570–2.

Several key documents from November 1941 render Gerlach's contentions even less persuasive yet in my opinion. One of these documents – Rosenberg's remarkable press briefing of November 18, 1941 – Gerlach acknowledges but seriously minimizes. According to Gerlach, Rosenberg's remarks *"could"* be taken to mean that Soviet territory was to be the site of a total extermination of European Jewry but only "in the sense of a slow destruction"[61] ("*Im Sinn einer langsamen Vernichtung*") But is this the most plausible or reasonable interpretation of this document? On November 15, 1941, Himmler had an extraordinarily long 4-hour meeting with Rosenberg, during which they discussed the relationship of the local Jewish experts to the HSSPF and Reich commissars (*Reichskommissaren*) in the east.[62] Three days later Rosenberg gave a "confidential" background report to the German press.[63] Reporters were not to print the details of what was happening in the east, but they needed sufficient background so that the press could give its treatment the proper "color" ("*Farbe*"), he explained. Among the topics Rosenberg dealt with was the Jewish Question:

> At the same time this eastern territory is called upon to solve a question which is posed to the peoples of Europe; that is the Jewish question. In the east some six million Jews still live, and this question can only be solved *in the biological eradication of the entire Jewry of Europe.* [italics mine] The Jewish question is only solved for Germany when the last Jew has left German territory, and for Europe when not a single Jew lives on the European continent up to the Urals. That is the task that fate has posed to us. . . . It is necessary to expel them over the Urals or eradicate them in some other way.

It is this reference to expulsion over the Urals, I presume, that Gerlach would cite as justification for his claim that this document *"could"* mean a total eradication of European Jewry only "in the sense of a slow destruction."

But several other passages of Rosenberg's speech indicate anything but a scenario in which nature would be left to take its gradual course

[61] Gerlach, "Grundsatzentscheidung," p. 43.
[62] MSA, 1372-5-23: Himmler Terminkalendar, 15.10.41; and Nuremberg Document, NO-5329 (Himmler file note of 15.11.41 on conversation with Rosenberg).
[63] PA, Pol. XIII, VAA Berichte, Rosenberg speech, 18.11.41.

in decimating expelled Jews. First, there was a sense of urgency to accomplish the task now: ". . . we must be on our guard that a romantic generation in Europe does not again raise up the Jews." Furthermore, this was a program to be carried out by Germans, not a process to be passively left to nature. "You can imagine that for the implementation of these measures, only those men are assigned who conceive of the question as a historical task, who do not act out of personal hatred, but rather out of this very mature political and historical perspective."

Historians including Gerlach have no doubt that Frank's infamous December 16 speech in the General Government reflected his initiation into the Final Solution. And Gerlach has gone even further to note the degree to which Frank virtually parroted sections of Hitler's speech of December 12.[64] But he resists a parallel and to me equally obvious conclusion that Rosenberg learned of the Final Solution on November 15 and 3 days later gave a speech that represented not only a turnabout from his previous stance but resonated with Himmler-style rhetoric. But such a conclusion, of course, would necessitate Himmler's awareness of a Hitler decision long before Gerlach's date of December 12.

Shortly after his lengthy meeting with Rosenberg, Himmler met with State Secretary Wilhelm Stuckart of the Interior Ministry on November 24, 1942, during which the Reichsführer had insisted: "Jewish questions belong to me."[65] It is probable that Stuckart learned much more than Himmler's jurisdictional ambitions at this time. When a distressed Bernhard Lösener met with Stuckart on December 21, 1941, he relayed graphic reports of the recent massacre of Berlin Jews in Riga. Stuckart replied: "Don't you know that these things happen on the highest orders?"[66] This is yet another indication that Himmler was initiating key personnel in November, weeks before the alleged Hitler *Grundsatzentscheidung* of December 12.

Finally, we must turn to Hitler himself. On November 28, 1941, he met with the grand mufti of Jerusalem. Hitler stated: "Germany was resolved, step by step, to ask one European nation after the other to

[64] Gerlach, "Grundsatzentscheidung," pp. 29–30.

[65] MSA, 1372-5-23: Himmler Terminkalendar, 24.11.41.

[66] Bernhard Lösener, "Als Rassereferent im Reichsministerium des Innern," VfZ, IX (1961), pp. 310–11.

solve its Jewish problem, and at the proper time, direct a similar appeal to non-European nations as well." When Germany had defeated Russia and broken through the Caucasus into the Middle East, Germany would have no imperial goals of its own and would support Arab liberation, Hitler assured the grand mufti. But Hitler did have one goal. "Germany's objective would then be solely the destruction of the Jewish element residing in the Arab sphere under the protection of British power."[67] Is it conceivable that if Hitler were already contemplating the murder of Jews throughout the Middle East, the fate of German and west European Jews was still undecided at this time?

The initial invitations to the Wannsee Conference were sent in late November for a meeting originally scheduled for December 9, 1941, 3 days before Hitler's alleged *Grundsatzentscheidung,* and the meeting eventually held on January 20, 1942, clearly presumed a Hitler decision. Thus Gerlach seeks to establish that the conference as initially planned had a different purpose from the one that was actually held. He claims, on the basis of the November invitation list and text of the invitation, that it was originally planned for the discussion of problems arising primarily from the deportation of German Jews, including the as yet undecided question of their ultimate fate.[68] Yet the reaction of the one invitee that can be documented, the German Foreign Office, was a memorandum outlining eight "desires and ideas" that spanned the continent, including specifically the deportation of Jews from Romania, Slovakia, Croatia, Bulgaria, Hungary, and Serbia.[69] Apparently the Foreign Office thought that the initial conference was to deal with the Jewish question throughout Europe and not only with German Jews. Two officials from the Ostministerium (Alfred Meyer and Georg Leibbrandt) were included in the invitation list, as was Greifelt from Himmler's ethnic German resettlement office. And following a conversation with the HSSPF Friedrich Wilhelm Krüger of the General Government, Heydrich added invitations to Krüger and Frank's state secretary, Josef Bühler, precisely because Krüger had led Heydrich to believe that "the General Governor aspires to completely

[67] *Documents on German Foreign Policy,* D, XIII, No. 515, pp. 882–4.
[68] Gerlach, "Grundsatzentscheidung," pp. 8, 11, 16.
[69] PA, Inland IIg, p. 177, unsigned memorandum "Wünschen und Ideen," and Luther and Rademacher marginalia on Heydrich to Luther, 29.11.41.

monopolize the treatment of the Jewish problem."[70] Thus 6 of the 12 invitees (Luther, Bühler, Krüger, Meyer, Leibbrandt, Greifelt) did not represent agencies narrowly focused on technical issues related to German Jews. And the invitation letter included Heydrich's Göring July mandate to prepare a solution to the Jewish question throughout the German sphere. In short, neither the list of invitees nor the invitation letter convincingly supports Gerlach's speculation that the agenda of the meeting was initially rather narrow and then significantly broadened after Hitler's speech of December 12. And finally, the second invitation list did not change in a way that would suggest the radical change in purpose that Gerlach claims for the rescheduled Wannsee Conference. Here again I find his argument unpersuasive.

Gerlach also argues that no general destruction order could have been given before mid-December because only 6 of 41 transports of Reich Jews were liquidated immediately upon arrival before Hitler's December 12 speech.[71] What Gerlach omits mention of, however, is that only 2 of the next 39 transports between mid-December and the end of April were liquidated upon arrival. A significant *reduction* in the number of transports subject to liquidation following Hitler's speech of December 12 is hardly convincing evidence for the Hitler *Grundsatzentscheidung* that Gerlach has claimed for that date.

Gerlach has provided much new evidence concerning a flurry of activity related to Nazi Jewish policy in December 1941. If the scenario he provides for this flurry of activity is unpersuasive, what did happen that month? I have argued that Hitler solicited the preparation of a plan for the Final Solution in mid-July 1941 and approved the resulting outline in early October. In the following month initial steps were taken: the deportation of Reich Jews and death camp construction began, Jewish emigration came to an end, and various officials of the Foreign Office and Ostministerium joined a widening circle of initiates. Until late November the deported Reich Jews were interned in ghettos in Lodz and Minsk. Then, suddenly, on November 25 and 29, 1941, all five transports from Berlin, Munich, Frankfurt, Vienna, and Breslau

[70] Eichmann note and draft letters, 1.12.41, facsimile in: "A Preparatory Document for the Wannsee 'Conference,'" ed. by Yehoshua Büchler, HGS, 9/1 (spring 1995), pp. 121–5.

[71] Gerlach, "Grundsatzentscheidung," pp. 12–14.

to Kovno were massacred at Fort IX. Did this occur as the result of local initiative, as Gerlach has intimated?[72] Or was it the point at which the Nazi regime officially crossed the threshold between deporting and murdering German Jews not just in conception but also in practice? I would suggest the latter interpretation.

As Gerlach's own research has shown, the deportation and killing of Reich Jews killings in Kovno gave rise to complications and complaints.[73] Therefore, as the first transport of German Jews destined for Riga was arriving on November 30, Himmler telephoned, from Hitler's headquarters, to Heydrich in Berlin with the message: "Jewish transport from Berlin. No liquidation." Such an intervention, I think, suggests that prior to this telephone call both Himmler and Heydrich, as well as HSSPF Friedrich Jeckeln in Riga, understood that these transports of Reich Jews were to be liquidated; there would have been no occasion for a message to the opposite effect if it was not needed to countermand existing policy. This intervention was too late, however, and the Berlin transport that arrived in Riga in the midst of the ghetto liquidation was immediately massacred.[74]

The following day Himmler discussed "executions in Riga" with Heydrich. Moreover, he sent Jeckeln an angry radio message on December 1, 1941, that was intercepted by the British: "The Jews resettled into the territory of the Ostland are to be dealt with only according to the guidelines given by me and the Reich Security Main Office acting in my behalf. I will punish unilateral acts and violations."[75] And on December 4, 1941, Himmler met with Hitler in the morning and Jeckeln, recalled from Riga, in the afternoon.[76] Given Himmler's insistence that German Jews in the east be treated only according to his guidelines and the lack of any repercussions against Karl Jäger for the Kovno massacres (similar to those threatened against Jeckeln), I think this episode and the surviving documentation indi-

[72] Gerlach, *Krieg, Ernährung, Völkermord,* pp. 276–7, in contrast to the cautious discussion in "Grundsatzentscheidung," 13, in which he provides evidence that the SS (Jäger) and the Ostministerium (Kleist) discussed the killing action at least 3 days beforehand.

[73] Gerlach, "Grundsatzentscheidung," pp. 13, 15–16.

[74] David Irving, *Hitler's War,* p. 505; Broszat, "Genesis der Endlösung," pp. 760–1; Raul Hilberg, *The Destruction of the European Jews* (New York: Revised and expanded ed., 1985), p. 353; Andrew Ezergailis, *The Holocaust in Latvia,* p. 253.

[75] Richard Breitman, *Official Secrets,* p. 83.

[76] MSA, 1372-5-23: Himmler Terminkalendar, entry of 4.12.41.

cates that the five Kovno transports were liquidated on Himmler's directive and the first to Riga was liquidated simply because Himmler's new policy was not countermanded in time. Given the complications that emerged, Himmler temporarily retreated from killing German Jews, and thereafter, with just two exceptions, the winter transports to Riga that completed the first wave of deportations were lodged in the recently cleared Riga ghetto or in the nearby camps of Jungfernhof and Salispils.[77] It would appear, therefore, that early December 1941 was not the date of a decision by which the Nazi regime sealed the fate of German Jewry but rather the date at which the murder of German Jewry was briefly postponed when the Himmler-sanctioned executions at Kovno resulted in too many complications.

The Red Army's Moscow counteroffensive on December 5, the Japanese attack on Pearl Harbor on December 7, and the German declaration of war on the United States on December 11 clearly overshadowed the repercussions from the Kovno – Riga massacres. Heydrich postponed the Wannsee Conference on December 8, 1 day before it was scheduled to be held. There would be no "announcement" ("*Bekanntgabe*") to the ministerial bureaucracy at this unpropitious moment. But with all the leading party figures in Berlin for his Reichstag speech, Hitler met with them on December 12 in his apartment and did make his "announcement." For many, like Hans Frank, it was their initiation, but for others like Alfred Rosenberg it was not.

Thus, the flurry of activity in December 1941 did not revolve around a basic Hitler decision for the Final Solution but concerned four other issues. First, Himmler dealt with the unease and uncertainty caused by the massacres of Reich Jews in late November by postponing any further such killing until it could be done more discretely and at a less uncertain time militarily and politically. Second, Hitler affirmed that

[77] The second transport of elderly Czech Jews from Theresienstadt, departing January 15, 1942, was liquidated upon arrival. H. G. Adler, *Theresienstadt*, p. 799. Of the February 10, 1942, transport from Vienna, 700 of 1,000 deportees were killed in the newly arrived gas vans. Safrian, *Die Eichmann-Männer*, pp. 180–1. According to Jeckeln's postwar testimony, Himmler was still wrestling with alternative killing methods for Reich Jews. More transports would come but "he had not yet decided in which way they were to be destroyed . . . to be shot in Salispils or to be chased off somewhere into the swamp" ("*dass er noch nicht entschieden habe, auf welche Weise die zu vernichten seien . . . in Salispils zu erschiessen oder irgendwo auf dem Sumpf zu jagen*"). Helmut Krausnick and Hans-Heinrich Wilhelm, *Die Truppe des Weltanschauungskrieges* (Stuttgart, 1981), p. 568.

the Final Solution would go forward despite the changed military circumstances. This affirmation and clarification was especially necessary because in the fall of 1941, when in my opinion the basic decision had been made, the anticipated timetable had been expressed in two ways – "after the war" and "next spring." In October these were two ways of expressing the same notion. In December, after the Red Army counteroffensive and American entry into the war, however, "after the war" and "next spring" were no longer two different expressions for the same timetable, and the conflict between the two had to be resolved. Hitler's speech made clear that the Final Solution would go forward "next spring" and would not be delayed until "after the war." Third, party leaders like Frank were initiated into a process already underway. And finally, issues of camouflage and rationalization were discussed in the flurry of meetings involving Hitler, Himmler, Rosenberg, and Brandt between December 14 and 18.[78]

On January 8, 1942, Heydrich rescheduled the Wannsee Conference for January 20. As Eichmann later testified, Heydrich "expected considerable stumbling blocks and difficulties."[79] Thus care was taken to minimize the most predictable problems. To preserve the plausibility that Jews were being sent to labor in the east and exclude countless intercessions, Heydrich announced his plan for an old people's ghetto at Theresienstadt. Just months earlier he had envisaged Theresienstadt as a crude transit camp where "the Jews would have to dig their own shelter in the ground" and "would indeed be severely decimated" ("*ja*

[78] When Himmler met with Brandt on December 14, some euthanasia personnel like Josef Oberhauser had already been transferred to the General Government. Himmler did not discuss an alleged Hitler decision but rather his concern about "camouflage" ("*Tarnung*"). When Rosenberg met with Hitler that same day, he noted that "now after the decision" ("*jetzt nach der Entscheidung*") – which Gerlach interprets as a reference to the Final Solution and I see as a reference to the declaration of war on the United States – he would change his remarks and "not speak about the destruction of the Jews" ("*von der Ausrottung des Judentums nicht zu sprechen*"), a standpoint that Hitler approved. After the declaration of war on the United States, deterring "New York Jews" from inciting encirclement of Germany by openly threatening "appropriate consequences against the Jews in the east" was no longer relevant, and in the wake of the November massacres it was not prudent to draw attention to the extermination program. And again when Himmler met with Hitler on December 18, they did not discuss a new, fundamental decision but rather a rationale and possible *Tarnsprache*; the Jews were "to be destroyed as partisans." For Gerlach's arguments, see: "Grundsatzendscheidung," pp. 23–25, including fn 103.

[79] Cited in Raul Hilberg, *Documents of Destruction* (Chicago, 1971), p. 101.

schon stark dezimiert wurden") even before deportation to the east.[80] After the difficulties of late November, now instead an old people's ghetto was cynically to be created, as Eichmann frankly admitted, "to preserve appearances to the outside."[81]

Even when the deportation of Reich Jews resumed in March 1942, the transports were sent to ghettos in the Lublin district but not immediately liquidated. The first Jewish deportees from Slovakia and France in the spring of 1942 were likewise sent to labor camps, not the gas chambers. Only in mid-April did Hitler apparently decide to resume the killing of Reich Jews. Just as Himmler had personally toured the eastern front in late July and early August 1941, helping to disseminate the decision to kill Soviet Jewry, so he and Heydrich personally served as emissaries to the proposed killing sites of Reich Jews. On April 16–17, 1942, following a meeting with Hitler, Himmler traveled to the Warthegau. There he met with Gauleiter Greiser and HSSPF Wilhelm Koppe and ordered the deportation of Reich Jews from Lodz to Chelmno. Between May 4 and 15, 12 trains took over 10,000 Reich Jews to their deaths.[82] Also in April Heydrich personally visited Minsk and told Security Police Commander (KdS) Eduard Strauch that all German and other European Jews were going to be killed. Jewish transports to Minsk would resume, and the deportees were to be killed on arrival. Strauch selected the former collective farm Maly Trostinez as the killing site, and the first transport from Vienna was dispatched on May 5, 1942.[83] Seventeen more transports to Maly Trostinez would follow. The first major deportations from East Upper Silesia that were gassed in Bunker 1 at Birkenau likewise began at this time.

Only in May 1942, therefore, was the mass murder of Reich Jews fully and unequivocally underway. This did not trace to a Hitler decision of December 12, 1941, but was foreseen by Himmler in the fall when he assured reluctant recipients of the first transports that the Jews would be sent further east in the following spring. A brief deviation from this timetable through the immediate liquidation of six

80 H. G. Adler, *Theresienstadt*, pp. 721–2 (protocol of Prague meeting, 10.10.41).

81 ZStL report and document collection, "Judendeportationen aus dem Reichsgebiet," doc. no. 18/1: report on RSHA IV B 4 meeting of 6.3.42, Düsseldorf, 9.3.42.

82 Peter Witte, "Two Decisions Concerning the 'Final Solution,'" pp. 333–6.

83 *Justiz und NS-Verbrechen* (Amsterdam) (JNSV), XIX (Nr. 552: LG Koblenz 9 Ks 2/62), pp. 192–4.

transports of Jews at Kovno and Riga in late November had threatened briefly to breach both the secrecy of and indifference toward the fate of the deportees. Hitler made known his full support for the murder of the Jews to the party leaders; there would be no turning back. A timetable of "next spring" and not "after the war" would be adhered to. But Himmler and Heydrich proceeded with much caution, devising camouflage language and cover stories on the one hand and delaying any immediate liquidation of transports of Reich Jews even when they resumed in March 1942 on the other hand. Only in May 1942 did the Nazi regime begin the systematic mass murder of Reich Jews that Hitler had decided upon the previous fall. A similar fate befell the transports from Slovakia and western Europe soon thereafter. And finally, in mid-July 1942, Hitler reaffirmed his Final Solution decision and demanded rapid and complete implementation, regardless of the looming labor shortage facing the Third Reich.[84]

In short, I would offer the model of an incremental, ongoing decision-making process that stretched from the spring of 1941 to the summer of 1942, with key turning points in the midsummer and early fall of 1941 that corresponded to the peaks of German victory euphoria and sealed the fates of Soviet and European Jews, respectively. Within this extended, incremental decision-making process, decisions were indeed made in December 1941 and January 1942, but not that suggested by Gerlach, Safrian, and Hartog. In December the Nazi regime became aware that killing Reich Jews was a far more delicate proposition than the mass murder of Soviet Jewry. The immediate liquidation of transports of Reich Jews was suspended while Hitler simultaneously informed party leaders – many of them already initiated – of his ultimate intentions during the war. Heydrich's initiation of the ministerial bureaucracy, however, was postponed. When Heydrich finally convened the Wannsee Conference on January 20, 1942, he did not have a new list of invitees or new agenda. What was new was a greater caution concerning the treatment of Reich Jews, as seen in the more clearly articulated labor camp and Theresienstadt subterfuges. Although Heydrich was gratified by the degree of consensus he encountered, in the single most sensitive area concerning the mass

[84] Christopher R. Browning, "A Final Decision for the 'Final Solution'? The Riegner Telegram Reconsidered," HGS 10/1 (spring 1996); pp. 3–10.

murder of Reich Jews he did not prevail, namely, the inclusion of the first-degree Mischlinge (Germans with two Jewish grandparents) and Jewish spouses in mixed marriage.

By mid-April 1942, the regime had survived the winter military crisis, and the prototype death camp at Belzec, despite its limited capacity, had proved itself capable of murdering 74,000 Jews from Lublin and Galicia in one month. At this point, just as the furious killing spree of the most fatal year of the Final Solution was getting underway, Himmler and Heydrich acted as personal emissaries carrying word of the decision that the mass murder of Reich Jews – from which the Nazi regime had temporarily shied away in December 1941 – was now to be resumed in Chelmno and Maly Trostinez. Reich Jews were now included in the Nazi program of systematic and comprehensive mass murder that Hitler had approved and Himmler and Heydrich among others had begun preparing in the fall of 1941. The Final Solution as we now understand it was fully underway.

3

JEWISH WORKERS IN POLAND

Self-Maintenance, Exploitation, Destruction

Historians of the Holocaust have generally accepted that the Nazi regime gave a fundamental priority to racial ideology over economic utility in carrying out the Final Solution.[1] Perhaps the most succinct and emphatic statement in this regard was the cryptic message of December 18, 1941: "In principle, economic considerations are not to

[1] There are a few historians who do not accept the primacy of ideological over economic factors and who have argued in one way or another that the Final Solution was a by-product of economically motivated decisions. For instance, Götz Aly and Susanne Heim have argued at one time that the murder of the European Jews was for the Nazis a "logical" means to solving a problem of overpopulation that blocked the path to economic modernization. Most important among the numerous publications of Aly and Heim in this regard are: "Die Ökonomie der 'Endlösung': Menschenvernichtung und wirtschaftliche Neuordnung," *Beiträge zur nationalsozialistischen Gesundheits-und Sozialpolitik,* vol. V, *Sozialpolitik und Judenvernichtung: Gibt es eine Ökonomie der Endlösung?* (Berlin, 1987), pp. 7–90; "The Economics of the Final Solution; A Case Study from the General Government," *The Simon Wiesenthal Center Annual,* V (1988), pp. 3–48; "Sozialplannung und Völkermord: Thesen zur Herrschaftsrationalität der nationalsozialistischen Vernichtungspolitik" and "Wider die Unterschätzung der nationalsozialistischen Politik: Antwort an unsere Kritiker," *Vernichtungspolitik: Eine Debatte über den Zusammenhang von Sozialpoliitik und Genozid im nationalsozialistischen Deutschland,* ed. by Wolfgang Schneider (Hamburg, 1991), pp. 11–24 and 165–75; and *Vordenker der Vernichtung: Auschwitz und die deutsche Pläne für eine neue europäische Ordnung* (Hamburg, 1991).

For the most recent broad critique of this approach, see: Michael Burleigh, "A 'political economy of the Final Solution'? Reflections on modernity, historians, and the Holocaust," *Ethics and Extermination: Reflections on Nazi Genocide* (Cambridge, 1997), pp. 169–82.

Arno Mayer has argued that the murder of the European Jews (outside the Soviet Union) is to be seen within the context of the economic imperatives of total war and commensurate "hyerexploitation" of labor, in which the intensifying persecution of the Jews was "calibrated in accordance with the productivity-utility precept." Arno Mayer, *Why Did the Heavens Not Darken? The "Final Solution" in History* (New York, 1989).

be taken into account in the settlement of the [Jewish] problem."[2] It is my purpose not to dispute but rather to qualify this axiom of Nazi Jewish policy through an examination of the German exploitation and destruction of Jewish labor in Poland.

I will argue for four points. First, Nazi policy toward the use of Jewish labor in Poland differed in both time and place. Conclusions drawn from a single camp or single phase of occupation are generalized only at the risk of considerable distortion.[3] The story is a complex one. Second, in the German use of Jewish labor in Poland, economic considerations were taken seriously by many Germans but only within and not as a challenge to the parameters set by political and ideological factors. Third, even within these ideological parameters there was no consensus among the Germans over the use of Jewish labor, and productive utilization of Jewish labor often faced opposition and sabotage from both local and higher authorities. In 1942–43, Himmler himself was the driving spirit behind the destruction *of* Jewish labor, apparently finding "destruction *through* labor" an unsatisfactory policy in most circumstances. Fourth, both early in the war when the ultimate goal was Jewish expulsion and later when the ultimate goal was Jewish extermination, there was an initial period of conflict and confusion followed by a period in which advocates for a productive use of Jewish labor were permitted brief and precarious opportunities to pursue their goals. In these brief periods, select Polish Jews were not to be starved or killed systematically. Rather they were to work productively (and intensively) for the moment, though always with the clear expectation that they would be expelled or killed sometime later. In these brief periods, the ultimate ideological goal was never superseded, just temporarily deferred, but this deferral was the difference between life and death for many survivors.

[2] Nuremberg Document PS-3666 (Otto Bräutigam to Hinrich Lohse, 18.12.41), printed in: *Documents on the Holocaust,* ed. by Yitzhak Arad, Yisrael Gutman, and Abraham Margoliot (Jerusalem, 1981), p. 395.

[3] For instance, Daniel Goldhagen – narrowly focusing on two Lublin labor camps during the height of the killing – has argued for a far-reaching consensus among Germans on the use of Jewish labor as a means for not only the destruction of Jewish life but also German psychological gratification derived from the economically wasteful opportunity to inflict punishment and suffering. At the same time he has depicted concerns for a productive use of Jewish labor as an extremely marginal and insignificant phenomenon. See Daniel Jonah Goldhagen, *Hitler's Willing Executioners: Ordinary Germans and the Holocaust* (New York, 1996), esp. Part IV.

I would also suggest that an examination of Nazi policies toward Jewish labor in Poland is necessary in order to understand what in the experience of Polish Jews led them to put so much faith in the strategy of "survival through labor." Why could they not understand the Nazi priorities that seem so self-evident to historians today? There were indeed all too many occasions on which Jewish "work" was organized in an utterly irrational way from the point of view of economic utility and constituted in practice merely another cruel means to imposing additional humiliation and suffering before death. But that is not the whole story. Jewish leaders were not deluded in believing that many local German authorities had a strong interest in the productive exploitation of Jewish labor. They were mistaken, however, in their desperate hope that the fate of their communities lay in the hands of these local authorities and that the combination of their vested interests and the clear demonstration of Jewish productivity on behalf of the German war economy could ultimately save a remnant of the Jewish community. One reason, however, for this mistaken hope placed in the power of local authorities was that frequently the advocates of a productive use of Jewish labor did prevail temporarily over vociferous opposition. An examination of the Nazi exploitation of Jewish labor is also helpful in understanding how a minority of Jews from some labor camps but not others were, contrary to Nazi intentions and against all odds, able to survive.

In the first weeks of the occupation, local German authorities rounded up Polish Jews for forced labor on an ad hoc basis. These razzias frequently became occasions for German amusement and Jewish suffering. Initiatives to bring greater order to the use of Jewish labor came from both sides. In Warsaw, the paralyzing fear and disruption caused by such roundups induced the newly appointed head of the Jewish Council, Adam Czerniakow, to negotiate an agreement in late October 1939 with the Security Police, whereby the Jewish council would supply and pay for a labor battalion on a regular basis,[4] an example that was followed by other Jewish councils.[5] Also

[4] *The Warsaw Diary of Adam Czerniakow* (hereafter cited as WDAC), ed. by Raul Hilberg, Stanislaw Staron, and Josef Kermisz (New York, 1969), p. 84 (entry of 20.10.39).

[5] Isaiah Trunk, *Judenrat: The Jewish Councils in Eastern Europe under Nazi Occupation* (New York, 1972), p. 72.

in late October, the newly appointed head of the General Government, Hans Frank, issued an edict imposing forced labor on all Jews and authorizing implementation through the HSSPF Friedrich Wilhelm Krüger.[6]

Krüger was quite aware that random local roundups constituted a relatively irrational and unproductive use of Jewish labor potential. Particularly in Poland there were many skilled Jewish craftsmen, he noted, and "it would be a pity, if this manpower were not profitably employed." Krüger therefore ordered the Jewish councils to create card files for the systematic registration of all male Jews by profession.[7] Himmler and Heydrich also expressed interest in exploiting Jewish labor, but in a different way. In early 1940 both envisaged vast Jewish forced labor camps to work on border fortifications – a so-called *Ostwall* on the demarcation line – and other construction projects.[8]

For the Germans a number of questions had to be answered. Who would allocate or assign Jewish labor? Were the Jews to be concentrated in vast labor camps or employed selectively according to skill? And how would Jewish labor capacity be maintained over time? After considerable recrimination, especially between the civil administration and SS in the Lublin District and Frank's insistence on a solution,[9] guidelines were announced by the head of Frank's labor division, Max Frauendorfer, in the summer of 1940.[10] In principle, Jewish labor was conceded to be a police matter, but in practice, allocation of Jewish

[6] *Faschismus-Getto-Massenmord* (hereafter cited as FGM) (East Berlin, 1960), p. 203 (decree of 26.10.39).

[7] *Das Diensttagebuch des deutschen Generalgouverneurs in Polen 1939–1945*, ed. by Werner Präg and Wolfgang Jacobmeyer (Stuttgart, 1975), p. 77 (Abteilungsleitersitzung, 8.12.39).

[8] *Biuletyn Glownej Komisji Badania Zbrodni Hitlerowskich W Polsce* (hereafter cited as *Biuletyn*), XII, 66F-75F (NO-5322: Heydrich conference of 30.1.40); Halder, *Kriegstagebuch*, I, 184 (entry of 5.2.40); Rolf-Dieter Müller, *Hitlers Ostkrieg und die deutsche Siedlungspolitik* (Frankfurt/M., 1991), pp. 20–22. Experiments with Jewish forced labor camps had already been undertaken in Germany. Wolf Gruner, *Der Geschlossene Arbeitseinsatz deutscher Juden: Zur Zwangsarbeit als Element der Verfolgung 1938–1945* (Berlin, 1997); for non-German Jews in forced labor camps in, Germany, Wolf Gruner, "Juden bauen die 'Strassen des Führers': Zwangsarbeit und Zwangsarbeitslager für nichtdeutsche Juden im Altreich 1940 bis 1943/44," *Zeitschrift für Geschichtswissenschaft* 9 (1996), pp. 789–808.

[9] *Trials of the War Criminals before the International Military Tribunal* (hereafter cited as IMT), vol. 29, pp. 448–56 (2233-PS: Polizeisitzung, 30.5.40).

[10] Frank, *Diensttagebuch* pp. 230–2 (Wirtschaftstagung, 6–7.6.40); *Documenta Occupationis* (hereafter cited as DO), VI, 568–72 (Frauendorfer circular, 5.7.40).

labor would now take place through the Labor Division and its local labor offices. The use of Jewish labor was "urgently necessary," he wrote, because many Polish workers had been sent to Germany, and in contrast to Reich Jews, many Polish Jews were "good skilled workers and craftsmen." Jews were to be employed in the normal labor market as the best way to utilize their skills. Moreover, as the resources of the Jewish councils were exhausted, and it was in German interest to maintain the strength of these workers, they would have to be paid at 80 percent of the Polish wage. "One could not forget that the Jews, so long as they were there, had to be provided for in some way," he noted. Only Jews who were not employed in the free economy were to be summoned to forced labor, many of them to work in camps along the frontier on large projects. But this was an "experiment" ("*Versuch*"); only the future would show how far one could go in this direction.

There was nothing inherently flawed or economically irrational about Frauendorfer's approach. Precisely such an approach of combining paid Jewish labor on the free market with selective conscription for the labor camps of *Organisation* Schmelt was successfully employed in East Upper Silesia.[11] One result was that Jewish mortality rates remained at the prewar level there for the first 2 years of the war. But there is nonetheless a surreal aspect to reading the documents on Frauendorfer's seemingly rational approach to the use of Jewish labor, for implementation of the plan in the General Government failed in every way.

First, those who had enjoyed the fruits of uncompensated Jewish forced labor were not prepared even to pay cut-rate wages. Frauendorfer continued to insist on the 80 percent wage rate, because "otherwise the maintenance of the strength of the working Jews would not be guaranteed."[12] Such exhortations had little effect. The *Kreishauptmann* of Czestochowa, for example, replied defiantly, "I

[11] For East Upper Silesia, see: Alfred Konieczny, "Die Zwangsarbeit der Juden im Schlesien im Rahmen der 'Organisation Schmelt'," *Beiträge zur nationalsozialistischen Gesundheits und Sozialpolitik*, V (1987), pp. 91–110; Avihu Ronen, "The Jews of Zaglembie During the Holocaust, 1939–1943," Ph.D. thesis, Tel Aviv University, 1989 (abstract in English); and Sybil Steinbacher, "Judenverfolgung im annektierten Osten Schlesiens 1939–1945," German Studies Conference, Washington, D.C., September 1997.

[12] FGM, p. 215 (Labor Division meeting, Cracow, 6.8.40).

assume that this regulation can be lost locally and have acted accordingly."[13] In any case, the issue of employing Jews in the free labor market at whatever wage was increasingly rendered moot by ghettoization, one major effect of which was to severe Jews from employment in the regular economy.

This is an issue to which we shall return. In the meantime, however, the initial experiment in work camps had also failed completely. Labor camps were planned in the Lublin district to house 50,000 Jews working on both military fortifications as well as road construction and water control projects. The Jews were to come from not only the district of Lublin but also those of Warsaw and Radom. Allocation of workers was to be the task of the labor offices, which issued certificates of exemption to Jews already employed in the regular economy.[14]

Reality was otherwise. The SS and police leader (SSPF) in the Lublin district, the notorious Odilo Globocnik, systematically ignored the labor offices and their certificates of exemption, as his men seized Jews at random to fill his own camps.[15] In the end only 13 kilometers of worthless antitank ditches were dug before the military turned its attention to preparing offensive staging areas instead of defensive fortifications.[16] But the human cost was staggering. When Globocnik finally shifted Jewish workers from his own camps to those of water control projects in October 1940, one inspector noted: "The Jews . . . who have been delivered from the Jewish camp at Belzec unfortunately had to be released, because they had been driven to the utmost by those in charge there (SS) and were totally incapable of work."[17] The

[13] Yad Vashem Archives (hereafter cited as YVA), JM 814, Situation report of Czestochowa, 14.9.40.

[14] YVA: JM 2700, Cracow conference on Jewish labor, 6.8.40; and O-53/79/102 (Ramm Vermerk to Jache and Hecht discussion with Globocnik, Wendt, and Hofbauer, 8.8.40).

[15] YVA: O-53/79/197–98 (Hecht Vermerk, 23.7.40); pp. 116–17 (Zamosc labor office report on events of 13–14.8.40); pp. 118–19 (Ramm Vermerk, 15.8.40); pp. 141–42 (Ramm to Globocnik, 19.8.40); p. 137 (Ramm Vermerk to Jache and Hecht, 20.8.40); p. 130 (Labor Division to Globocnik, 20.8.40); p. 136 (Ramm Vermerk to Jache and Hecht, 20.8.40); p. 140 (Globocnik to Labor Division, 23.8.40); and p. 138 (Labor Division to Globocnik, 24.8.40). YVA, JM 2700, Vermerken of 21.10. and 15.11.40.

[16] Müller, *Hitlers Ostkrieg und die deutsche Siedlungspolitik*, p. 22.

[17] YVA, JM 2700, undated note to Labor Division Cracow.

SS was not alone in this regard. Reports on the water control camps also detailed absolutely dreadful conditions.[18]

These labor camps for water control projects were also shut down over the winter months.[19] However, the Lublin water control projects were resumed in the spring of 1941 with Jewish camp labor, and a whole new network of such camps was opened in the Warsaw district as well. These camps became quickly known for terrible food shortages, poor sanitation and medical care, guard brutality,[20] and inadequate pay. Indeed, one camp employer shamelessly announced that, after deductions for food, shelter, salaries for guards, and medical care, his workers owed him money.[21] The camps produced suffering and death but little else. As one German official who inspected the camps calculated, the camps had cost 4.5 times as much to construct as the value of the labor performed there.[22] By late August 1941, when the Germans in Warsaw had finally given up on the water control camps, the head of the labor office for Jews there noted that the use of Jewish labor camps elsewhere in the General Government was also in decline. "The inclination to use Jewish labor in camps is, after many bitter experiences, no longer great. The cost stands in no profitable relation-

[18] FGM, pp. 218–21 (excerpts from reports on the Lublin work camps). Army inspection of the camps produced too very conflicting reports. Major Braune-Krikau, the chief of staff of Oberfeldkommandantur 379 in Lublin, reported very critically on camp conditions, of which the Jews were the victims. In contrast, Lieutenant Börner of the Abwehr blamed the unsatisfactory conditions on the Jews, because "most of the working Jews went around in rags and also showed no interest whatever in cleanliness" ("*die meisten der arbeitenden Juden in Lumpen gehen und für Reinlichkeit auch wohl sowieso kein Interesse haben*"). His suggestion was to assign more guards to enforce camp regulations effectively. National Archives (hereafter cited as NA), T-501/212/634-6 (Anlage 290a: report of Braune-Krikau, Oberfeldkommandantur 379, Lublin, 23.9.40); and pp. 637–42 (Anlage 290: report of Lt. Börner, Abwehrnebenstelle Lublin, 24.9.40).

[19] At least a few Jewish labor camps for water control projects continued in existence in the Lublin district until December 1942. Peter Witte, "Letzte Nachrichten aus Siedliszcze: Der Transport Ax aus Theresienstadt in den Distrikt Lublin," *Theresienstädter Studien und Dokumente,* III/1996, pp. 98–113.

[20] One military report described the treatment of the Jews in the work camps as "bestial" ("*viehisch*") but conveniently implied that this was due solely to the Polish guards. NA, T-501/212/456 (excerpt from the monthly report of Kommandantur Warschau, 16.4–15.5.41).

For another vivid description of conditions in a Jewish work camp at this time, see Yitzhak Zuckerman, *A Surplus of Memory: Chronicle of the Wassaw Ghetto Uprising* (Berkely, CA, 1990). pp. 135–145.

[21] YVA, O-53/105/II/339–41 (Wielikowski report, 10.5.41).

[22] YVA, O-53/105/II/336–7 (Meissner report, 30.6.41).

ship to the labor output."[23] When the idea of reviving the Jewish labor camps for water control projects was broached once again in Warsaw in the spring of 1942, this same man successfully opposed the proposal. On the basis of past experience, he noted, he wanted "no camps of emaciated men, no impossible work demands that even German workers could not surmount."[24] As an experiment in the productive use of Jewish labor, the first generation of Jewish labor camps in the General Government had clearly failed.[25]

Everywhere in German-occupied Poland the Jews faced wholesale confiscation of their property, exclusion from many economic activities, and vast economic hardship. Nowhere did this hardship become so acute as in the two largest Jewish communities in Poland, namely Lodz in the Warthegau and Warsaw, where hermetically sealed ghettoization quickly led to mass starvation. Here a debate over the use of Jewish labor, between factions that I have elsewhere dubbed "productionists" and "attritionists," emerged in the most acute form.

Everywhere German occupation authorities faced two common factors that in retrospect favored ghettoization: first was the dashed expectation of a quick expulsion of Polish Jewry, and second was, in Warsaw ghetto commissioner Heinz Auerswald's words, "the desire to segregate the Jews from the aryan environment for general political and ideological reasons."[26] Nonetheless, there was no uniform policy of ghettoization in Poland, which proceeded in different ways at different times in different regions for different combinations of reasons.[27] Let us examine the Lodz and Warsaw cases more closely.

In the Warthegau in December 1939, Gauleiter Arthur Greiser determined that the Jews had "hoarded colossally" and thus they were

[23] YVA, JM 3462, monthly report of October 1941 for Labor Division branch office of the Jewish district (Hoffmann).

[24] YVA, JM 3462, conference on Jewish labor, 20.3.42.

[25] For greater detail, see my: "Nazi Germany's Initial Attempt to Exploit Jewish Labor in the General Government: The Early Work Camps 1940–1941," *Die Normalität des Verbrechens: Bilanz und Perspektiven der Forschung zu den nationalsozialistischen Gewaltverbrechen,* ed. by Helge Grabitz, Klaus Bästlein, and Johannes Tüchel (Berlin, 1994), pp. 171–85.

[26] YVA, JM 1112, Heinz Auerswald, "Two Year Report," 26.9.41.

[27] Christopher R. Browning, "Nazi Ghettoization Policy in Poland, 1939–1941," *Central European History* 19/4 (1986), pp. 343–68; Philip Friedman, "The Jewish Ghettos of the Nazi Era," *Roads to Extermination: Essays on the Holocaust* (New York and Philadelphia, 1980), pp. 59–87.

to be sealed in ghettos "until what they have amassed is given back in exchange for food and then they will be expelled over the border."[28] In short, a hermetically sealed ghetto in Lodz was initially viewed as a "transition measure" ("*eine Übergangsmassnahme*")[29] for extracting through deliberate starvation the last remnants of Jewish wealth prior to their expulsion, not as a source of productive labor. Little attention was given, therefore, to the initial proposals of the head of the Jewish council, Chaim Rumkowski, to organize ghetto labor and production in order to purchase food for the poor Jews in the ghetto.[30] With the emphasis on extraction, not production, the Germans calculated that the resources of the ghetto would be totally exhausted by July 1940, but deportation of the Lodz Jews was still expected in August.

Two factors then forced the Germans to recalculate. First, the expected August expulsion of Lodz Jews into the General Government was postponed indefinitely,[31] and second, the death rate in the ghetto skyrocketed.[32] The Germans faced a decision. The head of the ghetto administration, Hans Biebow, now argued that every effort had to be made "to facilitate the self-maintenance of the Jews through finding them work."[33] Biebow's rabidly antisemitic deputy, Alexander Palfinger, emphatically opposed the idea of a self-sustaining ghetto. He argued that "especially in the Jewish question, the National-Socialist idea . . . permits no compromise" and that "a rapid dying out of the Jews is for us a matter of total indifference, if not to say desirable . . ."[34] ("*Völlig gleichgültg, um nicht zu sagen, wünschenswert ist uns das rasche Absterben der Juden*"). The local decision went against Palfinger, when in mid-October 1940 "it was established . . . that the ghetto in Lodz must continue to exist and everything must be done to make the ghetto self-sustaining."

A similar pattern of decisions, first to ghettoize and then to harness Jewish labor for self-maintenance, was repeated in Warsaw. The

28 Berlin Document Center, Greiser Pers. Akten, Besuchs-Vermerk of the Staff of the Führer's Deputy, 11.1.40. I am grateful to Dr. Hans Umbreit for a copy of this document.

29 FGM, p. 81 (Rundschreiben of Uebelhoer to party and police officials, 10.12.39).

30 YVA: O-58/78/296–7 (Rumkowski to Marden, 6.4.40); JM 799/209 (Vermerk of conferences of 26 and 27.4.1940). DiM, pp. 74–5 (Oberbürgermeister to Rumkowski, 30.4.1940).

31 Frank, *Diensttagebuch*, pp. 261–3 (entry of 31.7.40).

32 In the brief period between June 16, 1940, and January 31, 1941, nearly 5 percent of the ghetto population perished. *The Chronicle of the Lodz Ghetto 1941–1944*, ed. by Lucjan Dobroszycki (New Haven, 1984), p. xxxix.

33 YVA, JM 798, Activity Report for September 1940.

34 YVA, O-53/78/76–82, Palfinger's "Critical Report," 7.11.40.

Warsaw Jews were hermetically ghettoized in the fall of 1940 after many false starts, including Frank's summer ban on further ghetto construction as "for all practical purposes illusory" in view of the Führer's Madagascar Plan.[35] The demise of this plan in September, combined with dire warnings of German public health doctors in the General Government about the threat of epidemic posed by Warsaw Jews, triggered Frank's decision for their ghettoization.[36]

As in Lodz, the creation of a sealed ghetto cut the Jews of Warsaw off from any employment and business on the outside. All economic relations with the outside world were now to take place through a so-called Transfer Agency (*Transferstelle*), presided over by none other than Alexander Palfinger. Having been bilked of his opportunity to engineer a deliberate mass starvation of the Jews of Lodz, he now controlled the economic lifeline to a Jewish community in Warsaw that swelled to a maximum of 445,000 in the spring of 1941.[37]

Reports reached Cracow in mid-January 1941 that food supplies to the Warsaw ghetto had been stopped entirely.[38] Two months later, in mid-March, Frank went through one his mercurial changes of mood. He cited Göring approvingly that "it is more important that we win the war than implement racial policy." Thus one had to be happy over every Pole or Jew working in a factory, whether he "suits us or not."[39] This burst of pragmatism provided a propitious moment for two of his economic advisers, Dr. Walter Emmerich and Dr. Rudolf Gater, to present an analysis of the economic viability of the Warsaw ghetto and propose an immediate, basic reorientation.[40] Fundamentally, they argued, the Warsaw ghetto was supposed to last five years, but cut off from the outside economy, it consumed far more than it produced. Once the exist-

35 FGM, p. 110 (Schön report, 20.1.41).

36 Christopher R. Browning, "Genocide and Public Health: German Doctors and Polish Jews, 1939–1941," *Holocaust and Genocide Studies,* 3/1 (1988), pp. 147–52.

37 Yisrael Gutman, *The Jews of Warsaw,* p. 63; YVA, JM 814, February Situation Report of Warsaw District, 10.3.41.

38 Frank, *Diensttagebuch,* p. 328 (conference of 15.1.41).

39 Frank, *Diensttagebuch,* p. 337 (Regierungssitzung, 25.3.41).

40 YVA, JM 10016, "Die Wirtschaftsbilanz des jüdischen Wohnbezirks in Warschau." The entire document has now been published in: *Beiträge zur Nationalsozialistischen Gesundheits und Sozialpolitik,* vol. 9, *Bevölkerungsstruktur und Massenmord: Neue Dokumente zur deutschen Politik der Jahre 1938–1945* (Berlin, 1991), ed. by Susanne Heim and Götz Aly, pp. 74–138. For a very different interpretation of the Gater memorandum and the events surrounding it, see: Susanne Heim and Götz Aly, "Die Ökonomie der 'Endlösung': Menschenvernichtung und wirtschafliche Neuordnung," *Beiträge zur Nationalsozialistischen Gesundheits und Sozialpolitik,* vol. 5 (Berlin, 1987), pp. 7–90.

ing wealth of the ghettoized Jews was exhausted, the Germans would face one of four choices: (1) subsidize the ghetto; (2) accept the consequences of inadequate provisioning; (3) harness the Jews to productive labor; or (4) loosen the seal around the ghetto to allow the resumption of direct economic ties with the surrounding population. Gater and Emmerich accepted the impossibility of the first and fourth options, which is to say that they did not challenge the wider ideological parameters. Thus the choice was simple; one could either view the ghetto "as a means to liquidate the Jews" ("*als ein Mittel . . . das jüdische Volkstum zu liquidieren*") or as a source of productive labor, and Emmerich and Gater clearly supported the later option.

Rather than openly arguing for a deliberate policy of mass starvation for its own sake, Governor Ludwig Fischer of the Warsaw district and his minions in reply consistently denied any impending hunger crisis. Emmerich brushed such claims aside as mere fantasy. As the ghetto had been created for the long haul, economic planning had to be done accordingly. "The starting point for all economic measures concerning the ghetto has to be the idea of maintaining the capacity of the Jews to live. The question is whether one can succeed in solving this problem in a productive manner. . . ."[41]

Frank sided with the Cracow "productionists" over the Warsaw "attritionists." In May 1941, on the very eve of Germany's "war of destruction" against the Soviet Union, a change of personnel in the Warsaw ghetto administration ensued. Heinz Auerswald, a lawyer who at least on one occasion could not remember when he had joined the Nazi Party,[42] was made the new commissioner, and a Viennese banker, Max Bischof, whose wife was half Jewish,[43] took over the Transfer Agency in place of the odious Palfinger, with the explicit task of creating a self-sustaining ghetto economy.

One point should be clearly made. The ghettoized Jews of Lodz and Warsaw were not to be kept alive in order to work; rather they were to be put to work in order to be kept alive by their own efforts and at their own expense. The Germans did not yet perceive themselves facing a serious labor shortage, and Jewish labor was thus not viewed as

[41] Frank, *Diensttagebuch*, pp. 337 and 343–6 (entries of 25.3.41 and 3.4.41).
[42] YVA, O-53/49/103–4, personnel questionnaire of Auerswald's.
[43] Götz Aly, *Vordenker der Vernichtung*, p. 324.

essential to the war effort. But the local Germans who had improvised ghettoization without direction from Berlin were now left to improvise solutions to the dilemma posed by ghettoization once expulsion was indefinitely postponed and mass starvation loomed. They were neither philo-Semitic nor humanitarian, but they were concerned about public health and public aesthetics. Starving Jews threatened to spread epidemic, and even the "attritionist" governor of the Warsaw district, Ludwig Fischer, conceded "that the corpses lying in the street create a very bad impression."[44] The military commandant in Warsaw was more blunt: "The ghetto was developing into a cultural scandal, a center of disease. . . ."[45] Local ghetto administrators assumed that in accordance with central policy, one day the Jews would disappear. Left to themselves in the meantime, they conceived of the creation of self-sufficient ghetto economies harnessing productive Jewish labor as being in Germany's interest and hence their patriotic and professional duty.

To create ghetto economies, the ghetto managers had to operate under many constraints. The ideological parameters had already made impossible either a loosening of the ghetto seal or feeding the Jews at German expense. The ghettos were temporary phenomena destined to be emptied at some point in the future and thus ranked low in any claim on priorities. Most importantly, the incarcerated Jews were at the bottom of the Nazi racial hierarchy with the least claim to scarce resources. Thus the ghetto managers were free to improvise ghetto economies only as long as they worked with marginal resources not claimed by others. What they could not do was to achieve a reallocation of scarce resources, especially food, to benefit Jews at the expense of anyone else.[46]

Operating under such constraints, the ghetto managers were only partially successful. Hunger and disease continued to haunt Warsaw and Lodz, and the skyrocketing death rates were only gradually and precariously stabilized. Yet, in the end, Jewish labor in both ghettos became productive, though along different organizational models.

44 WDAC, p. 239 (entry of 21.5.41).

45 NA, T-501/roll 212/456 (Monthly report of the Warsaw commandant, 16.4–15.5.41).

46 In this regard, the reactions of Greiser in the Warthegau and Frank in the General Government to requests for an increased food supply to the Lodz and Warsaw ghettos were identical. DiM, III, p. 248 (Ventzki Aktenvermerk, no date); YVA, JM 112 (Frank Tagebuch, 15.11.41).

In Lodz Hans Biebow was determined to keep all strings of the ghetto economy in his own hands. He set about collecting all of the unused machinery in the Warthegau and then machinery that had been confiscated from Jews in Germany. He also toured Germany in search of new contracts that would allow him to add new workshops and new products.[47] After the terrible winter of 1940, employment began a steady rise in the spring of 1941. By the summer of 1941, 40,000 Jews were working in the Lodz ghetto; by the following spring the figure was 53,000; by the spring of 1943, it stood at 80,000. Chief among the contractors was the Wehrmacht. Though initially "dubious" about the quality of goods that would be produced in the ghetto, it was soon ordering military supplies of all kinds.[48] Ghetto productivity was not increased only by procuring new machinery and contracts, however. Biebow ordered the work week extended from 54 to 60 and finally to 72 hours and imposed draconian factory discipline. The result – in Isaiah Trunk's words – was "the most industrialized ghetto in all of Eastern Europe."[49]

In contrast to the controlled economy in Lodz, a decentralized, laissez-faire economy gradually emerged in Warsaw, though it turned the corner toward economic viability quite belatedly, only in the spring of 1942. The initial attempts of Auerswald and Bischof in the summer of 1941 to increase employment within the ghetto failed miserably. The Jews were reluctant to register with the labor office, for fear that they would be sent to the notorious labor camps. And the Wehrmacht was reluctant to place orders.[50] More success was obtained when the Transfer Agency got out of the business of trying to run workshops and allowed private firms to create their own shops in the ghetto, procure their own contracts, import their own raw materials, and deliver their own products outside the control of the Transfer Agency.[51]

47 YVA: O-53/78/137–8 (Gettoverwaltung memorandum, 24.3.43); JM 798 (Activity report, February 1941); JM 800/148 (Aktennotiz, 10.3.41). DiM, III, 114–16 (Biebow to Treuhandstelle Posen, 26.3.42).

48 YVA, O-53/78/137–9 (Gettoverwaltung memorandum, 24.3.43); DiM, III, 177–9 (Marder to Uebelhoer, 4.7.41) and 243–5 (Biebow to Fuchs, 4.3.42).

49 Isaiah Trunk, *Judenrat,* pp. 84, 91.

50 YVA, JM 3462 (Hoffmann reports of October and November 1941).

51 WDAC, p. 401 (appended document: Auerswald to Medeazza, 24.11.41); Gutman, *The Jews of Warsaw,* p. 75; Trunk, *Judenrat,* p. 78–81.

As late as mid-October 1941, a discouraged Bischof confessed that the ghetto economy was a "field of ruins"[52] ("*Ruinenfeld*"). However, in early 1942 a significant change in the ghetto economy began to occur. German employers in Poland began to appreciate the potential of Jewish labor as awareness of a major labor shortage spread through the war economy. As laborers were taken from Poland back to the Reich, the ghetto increasingly was seen as a reservoir of replacement labor essential to the local economy.[53]

In April, May, and June 1942, demands for Jewish labor rose dramatically, new firms opened operations in the ghetto and others expanded their operations there, and production figures skyrocketed. And in May 1942 the monthly death rate fell below 4,000 for the first time in 12 months.[54] The destruction of the Warsaw ghetto that commenced in late July 1942 did not occur because the Warsaw Jews had stubbornly survived a policy of deliberate starvation or because "impossible circumstances" deliberately engineered by cynical local authorities compelled a radical solution; rather, the local experiment in a self-sufficient ghetto economy in Warsaw was just beginning to bear fruit when basic changes in policy fashioned in Berlin rendered such local experiments obsolete.

As the idea of murdering all the Jews of Europe had crystallized within the Nazi leadership in the fall of 1941, Reinhard Heydrich had quickly perceived a major threat to the comprehensive nature of the emerging plan. In a discussion of the Jewish Question with officials of Alfred Rosenberg's Ostministerium (Konrad Meyer and Georg Leibbrandt) on October 4, 1941, he observed: "There is in any case the danger that above all, those in the economic sector will in numerous cases claim their Jewish workers as indispensable and no one will make the effort to replace them with other workers. But this would undo the plan for a total

[52] Archivum Panstwowe m. St. Warszawy, Der Kommissar für den jüdischen Wohbezirk in Warschau, Nr. 132, speech of Max Bischof, 15.10.41.

[53] Ulrich Herbert, *Fremdarbeiter: Politik und Praxis des 'Ausländer-Einsatz' in der Kriegswirtschaft des Dritten Reiches* (Bonn, 1985), esp. pp. 137–49; YVA, JM 3462, Conference on labor, 20.3.42.

[54] YVA: JM 3462 (Hoffmann reports of April and May 1942, and Czerniakow report, May 1942); O-53/101 (Hummel's monthly reports to Bühler, January through May, and bi-monthly report of June/July 1942).

resettlement of the Jews from the territories occupied by us."[55] Heydrich's fears in this regard could only have been intensified during the month of October, as evidence of a severe labor shortage in the German war economy inexorably mounted, and on October 31, Hitler gave in to economic realism and ordered the large-scale labor exploitation of Soviet POWs on Reich territory.[56] Berlin stuck to the hard line concerning Jewish labor, however, even into December. When officials of the Ostland inquired whether all Jews should be liquidated regardless of age, sex, and economic interest, Berlin replied "economic interests are to be disregarded in principle" in solving the Jewish Question.[57]

Several factors brought about a change in this hard-line policy in winter of 1941. The mirage of solving Germany's current labor shortage through the exploitation of Soviet POWs evaporated when the staggering mortality and debilitation they had suffered became apparent.[58] And after the Soviet counteroffensive and Pearl Harbor in the first week of December, it was clear that the demands of the war economy for labor would only intensify. The Nazi regime accepted the necessity of importing vastly increased numbers of civilian forced laborers from the east, especially Russians, Poles, and Ukrainians.[59] At the same time, Himmler and Heydrich altered the SS position on the use of Jewish labor. More as the exception than the rule, Himmler had

[55] Nuremberg Document NO-1020 (Meeting of Heydrich, Meyer, Schlatterer, Leibbrandt, and Ehlich, 4.10.41). Philippe Burrin, *Hitler and the Jews: The Genesis of the Holocaust* (London, 1994), p. 123.

[56] Ulrich Herbert, *Fremdarbeiter,* pp. 137–43. In his article "Labour and Extermination: Economic Interests and the Primacy of Weltanschauung in National Socialism," *Past and Present,* No. 138 (February 1993), pp. 153 and 168, Herbert suggests that the decisions over the fate of the Jews and over the use of Soviet labor were made by the same people at the same time and were inherently interrelated – that is, the decision to use Soviet POW labor freed the Germans to exterminate potential Jewish labor. I am not convinced of the causal connection. First, I think the key concluding decision for the Final Solution was made by Hitler in early in October at the height of victory euphoria, and the change in attitude toward Soviet labor came in the following weeks as both the evidence of labor shortage and an unconcluded war mounted. Second, the notion of using Jewish labor does not seem to have been brought into the discussion until the following January.

[57] Nuremberg Document 3663-PS (Ostministerium, Berlin, to RK Ostland, 18.12.41).

[58] Christian Streit, *Keine Kameraden: Die Wehrmacht und die sowjetischen Kriegsgefangen* (Stuttgart, 1978), pp. 9, 136. According to Herbert, *Fremdarbeiter,* p. 149, by March 1942 only 5 percent – some 167,000 – of the 3.35 million Soviet POWs captured in 1941 were capable of labor.

[59] Herbert, *Fremdarbeiter,* pp. 144–5, 152–61.

already approved two local systems of SS controlled Jewish labor camps: first those of *Organisation* Schmelt in East Upper Silesia in the fall of 1940, and second, the so-called D-4 camps to provide Jewish labor for road construction in Galicia in the fall of 1941.[60] When Heydrich voiced the intention to use Jewish labor on a large scale for the first time at the Wannsee Conference, he annunciated what has become known as the doctrine of "destruction through labor." This was already the policy in practice in the D-4 camps, if not in those of *Organisation* Schmelt, and indeed, Heydrich's specific reference at Wannsee to decimating the Jews through road construction might well have been a quite concrete reference to them.[61]

Five days later Himmler informed the head of the concentration camp inspectorate, Richard Glücks, "now that Russian prisoners of war cannot be expected in the near future," he could expect that 150,000 Jews would be sent to the camps for "large economic missions and tasks."[62] As Oswald Pohl informed his camp commanders, the camps were to be "as productive as possible" and prisoner employment was to be, "in the true meaning of the word, exhaustive."[63] The official SS vision for the use of Jewish labor was, therefore, quite clear. Jews capable of labor were to work productively and die in the process.

The totality and clarity of this murderous vision was not fully and immediately comprehended by Germans in Poland, nor did Himmler remain content with it for long. When the vastly increased numbers of civilian workers began to be sent from Poland to the Reich in the spring of 1942, local authorities responded with a policy of substitution, in which Jewish labor would fill the void. The first planned act of substitution of Jewish for Polish laborers seems to have taken place in the course of the expulsion of the Jews from Mielec to the Lublin district on March 9, 1942. Those Jews selected as capable of work were not expelled but sent instead to a nearby airplane factory. The military deemed the experiment a success.[64] Indeed, so much so that in early

[60] Hermann Kaienburg, "Jüdische Arbeitslager an der 'Strasse der SS,'" *1999*, 1/96, pp. 19–20; Thomas Sandkühler, "Judenpolitik und Judenmord im Distrikt Galician, 1941–1942," *Nationalsozialistischen Vernichtungspolitik*, p. 136.

[61] Kaienburg, "Jüdische Arbeitslager an der 'Strasse der SS,'" *1999*, pp. 13–14.

[62] Nuremberg Document NO-500 (Himmler to Glücks, 25.1.42).

[63] IMT, vol. 38, pp. 365–6 (Nuremberg. Doc. R-129: Pohl circular, 30.4.42).

[64] YVA: JM 3462, Warsaw labor conference, 20.3.42; O-53/130/601–2, quarterly report of Rü Kdo Krakau, 1.10.-21.12.42.

May 1942, the Armaments Inspectorate endorsed the employment of a further 100,000 skilled Jewish workers, thus freeing Polish and Ukrainian workers to be sent to the Reich.[65]

At the same time, just prior to the first deportations from Lublin to Belzec, the ghetto was divided into A and B sections for nonworkers and workers. Though not always honored in the chaos and brutality of the ensuing ghetto-clearing operation, certificates of exemption were given to essential workers who were to be resettled in a temporary "work ghetto" of Majdan Tatarski. And Globocnik's deputy, Hermann Höfle, informed the civil administration concerning incoming transports from Slovakia and the Third Reich that the trains would stop in Lublin for a selection of able-bodied Jews before the others were sent to Belzec to "never again return."[66] Höfle then proceeded to enlist the local officials of the Lublin district to take a census of working and nonworking Jews, one of whom replied emphatically: "In these deportations only old people, incapable of work, women and children may be seized, and such men who are not employed by German agencies. Craftsmen must under all circumstances remain here for the moment."[67] Frank himself remained in a pragmatic mood: "If I want to win the war, I must be an ice-cold technician. The question what will be done from an ideological-ethnic point of view I must postpone to a time after the war."[68]

In Poland, indeed, anti-Semitic ideology and economic pragmatism seemed quite compatible at this point. The initial argument of the ghetto managers had been that Jews had to be put to work so that they might live, not that they should be allowed to live so that they might work. But this gradually changed. In their attempt to justify greater food supplies for the malnourished and starving ghetto inhabitants, the ghetto managers increasingly reversed the terms of the argument. Because these Jewish workers were making a significant contribution to the war economy, they should be better fed to enhance their pro-

[65] NA, T-501/219/347 (Kriegstagebuch, Oberquartiermeister, entry of 8.5.42). For an pioneering analysis of the pertinent military documents, see: Hanns von Krannhals, "Die Judenvernichtung in Polen und die 'Wehrmacht,'" *Wehrwissenschaftliche Rundschau,* 15 (1965), pp. 571–81.

[66] DiM, II, pp. 32–3 (Türk note, 17.3.42).

[67] DiM, II, p. 54 (Lenk to SSPF Lublin, 9.5.42).

[68] Frank, *Diensttagebuch,* p. 489 (entry of 14.4.42).

ductivity. The corollary, of course, was that nonworking Jews were a burden not deserving of food. The ghettos had never been viewed as permanent; now that Berlin had decided finally to "evacuate" the ghettos, relief from the burden of nonworking Jews was welcomed by all.[69] This widespread view was expressed by Frank's state secretary, Josef Bühler, at Wannsee, when he had urged that the Final Solution begin in the General Government, since most of the Jews there were already incapable of work.

The only critical concern voiced in the General Government, therefore, was not about the deportation of nonworking Jews but about whether labor of the working Jews left behind would be properly exploited. On May 5, 1942, Bühler told his division heads that:

> According to the latest information, there are plans to dissolve the Jewish ghettos, keep the Jews capable of work, and to deport the rest further east. The Jews capable of work are to be lodged in numerous large concentration camps that are now in the process of being constructed.

Bühler feared that using Jewish labor in large camps would destroy the existing organizational forms within which Jews were working and damage their "multifaceted use" ("*Mehrfaches des Nutzes*").[70] Labor Department head Max Frauendorfer, perhaps fearing a repeat of the 1940 camps, urged that the Jews "should be maintained capable of work for the duration of the war." He was convinced that with so many Polish workers in the Reich, the General Government was "for the time being absolutely dependent upon the use of Jewish labor," and he was also convinced that Himmler, Albert Speer, and Fritz Sauckel all increasingly valued the use of Jewish labor as well.[71]

Indeed, even into the summer of 1942 the dominant tone among Frank's officials was not fear over the possible loss of Jewish labor (whose continuing presence they took for granted) but impatience that they had not yet been fully relieved of the burden of their nonworking Jews. HSSPF Krüger did nothing to disabuse them of their assumptions about working Jews in late June when he stated that

[69] For the emergence of the distinction between working and nonworking Jews, see also: Götz Aly, "*Endlösung*," pp. 263–8.

[70] Frank, *Diensttagebuch*, p. 495 (entry of 5.5.42).

[71] Frank, *Diensttagebuch*, p. 516 (Hauptabteilungsleitersitzung, 22.6.42).

not only would Jewish workers in the armaments industries be retained but their families would be also.[72] The situation then abruptly changed in late July, when Himmler issued a December deadline for clearing the General Government "of the entire Jewish population." This included all Jewish labor "except in internment camps." Massively accelerated deportations ensued, which threatened to leave behind only a fraction of the number of Jewish workers earlier envisaged.[73]

The German historian Christian Gerlach has now brilliantly analyzed a hitherto neglected dimension to our understanding of this concerted assault upon Jewish labor in the summer of 1942.[74] Perhaps owing to the all-too-frequent use of transparently formulaic rationalizations in German documents of the period, many historians – myself included, I must emphasize – have simply read past the many references to the Nazi perception of a looming food crisis in 1942 in connection with the Final Solution. But Gerlach convincingly demonstrates that these references were not formulaic but instead reflected an obsession gripping many leading Nazi officials at the time. In my opinion, Himmler's determination to liquidate the "work Jews" stood independent of the "food crisis." It began before and continued long after the crisis was at its most acute stage. But the widespread concern over food shortages – constantly associated with so-called Jewish blackmarketeering – contributed greatly to Himmler's leverage, as the near-total liquidation of the Jews could now be seen as offering immediate economic advantages to offset the economic disadvantages related to loss of scarce labor.

The reaction among the civil administration and military to this decimation of the "work Jews" differed, but in general complaints were minimal. In Warsaw, Bischof chronicled the total collapse of the ghetto economy.[75] But other officials in this stronghold of erstwhile "attritionists" expressed no doubt about either their priorities or the fate of

[72] Frank, *Diensttagebuch,* pp. 507–9 (Polizeisitzung, 18.6.42).

[73] Nuremberg Document NO-626: Himmler to Berger, 28.7.42. Christopher R. Browning, "A Final Hitler Decision for the 'Final Solution'? The Riegner Telegram Reconsidered," *Holocaust and Genocide Studies* 10/1 (spring 1996), 3–10.

[74] Christian Gerlach, "Die Bedeutung der deutschen Ernährungspolitik für die Beschleunigung des Mordes an den Juden 1942," *Krieg, Ernährung, Völkermord* (Hamburg, 1998), pp. 167–257.

[75] YVA, O-53/105/II/220–30 (*Transferstelle* reports of 5.8, 5.9, and 8.10.42).

the deported Jews. "These economic disadvantages must . . . be put up with, because the extermination of the Jews is unconditionally necessary for political reasons."[76]

In the end only certain elements of the German military in the General Government openly broke with the consensus and tried to impede, however temporarily, Himmler's designs. On July 17, 2 days before Himmler issued his end-of-the-year deadline to clear the General Government of Jews, Krüger met with Generalleutnant Maximilian Schindler, head of the Armaments Inspectorate, and announced that all previous arrangements between Schindler and the SS concerning Jewish labor were now null and void. Krüger announced a new arrangement, whereby the SS would build conveniently located labor camps in which Jewish workers necessary for military production would be incarcerated. Moreover, Krüger assured Schindler, the Jewish ghettos would only be dissolved in agreement with the Armaments Inspectorate.[77]

Quickly, however, the military was literally flooded with reports that production at firms with which they had contracted for supplies had been disrupted owing to the seizure without notice of Jewish workers.[78] The military then sought the assurance of the SS that "Jewish actions" would take place only after the military had been informed and had approved because, "with the complete combing-out of Polish workers for the Reich, Jews are the sole available labor manpower."[79]

At a following meeting, Krüger's representative announced flatly that the plan of substituting Jewish for Polish workers – so in vogue just months earlier – had been given up. He then invoked Göring, often an advocate of economic pragmatism in the past:

> In the opinion of the Reich Marshal one must give up the notion that the Jew is indispensable. Neither the Armaments Inspectorate nor any other agencies

[76] YVA, O-53/113/348–61 (Bimonthly report for August/September, 1942, from the district of Warsaw to the State Secretary, General Government, 15.10.42).

[77] NA, T-501/216/927 (Krüger account of meeting with Schindler, 17.8.42). Excerpts from many of the documents pertaining to the military-SS negotiations have been printed in: Helge Grabitz and Wolfgang Scheffler, *Letzte Spuren* (Berlin, 1988), pp. 306–15.

[78] NA, T-501/219 (Kriegstagebuch of Oberquartiermeister): pp. 380 (entry of 20.6.42), 412 (entry of 5.8.52), 414 (entry of 8.8.42), 422 (entry of 17.8.42), 434 (entry of 2.9.42), 442 (entry of 13.9.42). NA, T-501/216/966 (Oberquartiermeister to MiG, 5.8.42).

[79] NA, T-501/216/927 (Forster to GenQu, 5.8.42).

in the General Government would retain Jews until the end of the war. The orders that had been issued were clear and hard. They were valid not only for the General Government but also for all occupied territory.[80]

The SS position was quickly supported by Wilhelm Keitel and the Armed Forces High Command (Oberkommando der Wehrmacht, or OKW), which on September 5 ordered that Jewish workers were now to be replaced with Poles.[81] Having planned in the spring of 1942 to replace Polish workers sent to the Reich with Jewish workers, Germans in the General Government were now being told that the Jewish workers were only temporary substitutes who were to be replaced yet again with Poles!

On September 18, 1942, Kurt Freiherr von Gienanth, the military commander in the General Government, composed and sent to the OKW the only unequivocal denunciation of the economic absurdity being perpetrated in the General Government, though not of course even mentioning the much greater moral outrage being committed in the death camps.[82] Twelve days later, the "war diary" of the senior quartermaster noted succinctly, "General of the Cavalry, Freiherr v. Gienanth, has been retired, effective immediately."[83] His successor was explicitly ordered to comply with SS labor policies,[84] and an incensed Himmler also threatened harsh consequences for anyone else who opposed him "with alleged armaments interests" but "in reality merely wanted to support the Jews and their business."[85]

Himmler's policy distinguished between "so-called" armaments workers who "merely" worked on such things as clothing and footwear on the one hand, and "actual" armaments workers who produced weapons and munitions on the other hand. Those in the former category were to be collected immediately in SS camps, where they would fulfill military orders. Those in the latter were to be held in closed barracks at their factories, which in effect would become "concentration-camp enterprises" ("*Konzentrationslager-Betriebe*"), which

[80] NA, T-501/216/923–6 (meeting on Jewish labor, 14.8.42).
[81] Grabitz/Scheffler, *Letzte Spuren,* p. 310.
[82] NA, T-501/216/350–2 (Gienanth to OKW, 18.9.42). Printed in: FGM, pp. 444–6.
[83] NA, T-501/219/452 (entry of 1.10.42).
[84] YVA, O-53/130/575–6 (copy of telegram of OKW, circulated by Forster, 10.10.42).
[85] FGM, pp. 446–7 (Nuremberg Document NO-1611: Himmler to Pohl, Krüger, Globocnik, Reichssicherheitshauptamt [Reich Security Main Office, or RSHA], and Wolff, 9.10.42).

paid the SS per head for the use of these laborers.[86] Even these work Jews were eventually to be transferred to large SS camps in eastern Poland. Then they, too, Himmler insisted, "will also disappear some day in accordance with the wish of the Führer." The only concessions gained by the military were the temporary sparing of the "so-called" armaments workers producing uniforms alongside the "actual" armaments workers and the promise of sufficient time to sort out those truly essential workers who were to remain.[87]

If the Jewish workers most essential to military production were temporarily spared, their families usually were not. Nor were the Jews in other sectors of the economy even when vital to replacing Poles taken to Germany or working in ways at least indirectly important to the war economy. For example, in December 1942, Frank belatedly regretted the loss of Jewish workers that brought numerous railway construction projects to a halt:

> In our time-tested Jews we have had a not insignificant source of labor manpower taken from us. It is clear that the process of mobilizing labor is rendered more difficult when in the midst of this wartime labor program the order comes that all Jews are to be left to their destruction.[88]

Himmler's triumph in 1942 was nearly total. The civil administration in the first half of the year had expected to be rid of the nonworking Jews but still enjoy the widespread use of Jewish labor, especially to replace Polish workers sent to the Reich. This expectation had been totally dashed in July 1942. Of all the employers in the General Government, only the military had been granted a temporary reprieve for essential armaments workers, but only if they were turned over to the SS by their former employers, incarcerated in either SS or factory camps, and rented back at 5 Zloty per head per day. For Himmler this was a brief political concession to remove the chief pretext for military opposition, not a recognition of the indispensability of Jewish labor to the war economy. Well into 1943, Himmler

[86] The payment arrangement was first worked out in Warsaw by SSPF Sammer-Frankenberg. Anordnungen of 14.9.42, facsimile in: Grabitz/Scheffler, *Die Letzte Spuren*, pp. 172–3.

[87] NA, T-501/216/776–7 (Forster to WiG, 20.10.42); YVA, O-53/130/573 (Forster memos, 14 and 15.10.42).

[88] Frank, *Diensttagebuch*, p. 588 (Regierungssitzung, 9.12.42).

would push for both ever greater control over the still-living Jewish armaments workers and their even more total destruction, regardless of economic considerations and the disastrous German defeats in the Russian and Mediterranean theaters. Owing to Himmler's relentless pursuit throughout 1943, far more Jews – classified as essential workers the previous year – would be murdered outright than would die through an exhaustive "destruction through labor." In his zeal to murder the remaining work Jews, Himmler far outstripped even the most murderous henchmen he had employed for the destruction of Polish Jewry – namely Odilo Globocnik and Friedrich Wilhelm Krüger.

In the last half of 1942, when the bulk of Polish Jewry had been deported to death camps, usually a remnant of some 10 percent to 20 percent of each community had been granted the treasured work exemption and left behind. Since large SS camps to hold such numbers did not exist, these remnants of work Jews were incarcerated either in factory camps or fenced-in areas of the Jewish quarters now renamed *Arbeitsghettos* or *Restghettos*. These "work ghettos" or "remnant ghettos" served not only as improvised forced labor camps (*Zwangsarbeitslager* or ZAL) but also as illusory sanctuaries to lure Jews out of hiding.

Himmler had no intention of allowing the situation to stabilize. In January 1943 he descended upon Warsaw and was furious to discover that no further progress had been made in shifting Jewish workers out of the ghetto to SS camps. He ordered that under Globocnik's supervision the work Jews were to be transferred to SS camps in Lublin, after which the ghetto was to be torn down completely. In a fit of pique, he also ordered that the factory proprietors who had allegedly arrived in Poland with nothing and made themselves wealthy on "cheap Jewish labor" be sent to the front.[89] While the liquidation of the Warsaw ghetto led to the great uprising in April 1943, the liquidation of the *Restghettos* elsewhere was driven forward. This process amounted to yet another mass selection, in which some Jews (now a remnant of a remnant) were sent to work camps and the others were either shot on the spot or deported to a death camp.

[89] Nuremberg Document NO-1882 (Himmler to Krüger, 11.1.43); NO-2514 (Himmler to Pohl, 16.2.43); NO-2494 (Himmler to Krüger, 16.2.43). FGM, pp. 449–50 (Sammern-Frankenegg to Himmler, 2.2.43). For the transfer of the Schultz firm from Warsaw to Trawniki, see: Grabitz/Scheffler, *Letzte Spuren*, pp. 179–210, 318–27.

Unlike in Warsaw, SSPF Julian Scherner in Cracow had already ordered the transfer of his work Jews to Plaszow as soon as the construction of the enlarged camp was complete.[90] The liquidation of the Cracow ghetto followed on March 13–14, 1943, and 14,000 Jews were sent to Plaszow for labor, whereas 3,000 were deported to Auschwitz and nearly as many were shot on the spot.[91] In March, April, and May the *Restghettos* of the Lublin district (Piaski, Cholm, Wlodawa, Izbica, Leczna, Miedzyrzec, and Lukowa) were liquidated, with at least some of the Jews sent to Majdanek for labor but many others to their immediate deaths in Sobibor and Treblinka.[92] From April through June, SSPF Fritz Katzmann launched the final savage assault on the remaining ghettos in Galicia – by far the largest contingent of Jews still alive in the General Government.[93] On June 30, 1943, Katzmann proudly informed Himmler that over 434,000 Jews had been "deported" ("*ausgesiedelt*") from Galicia, and all ghettos there had now been dissolved. The remaining 21,000 Jews were in camps under the control of the SS and their numbers would be steadily reduced.[94] The Radom district was no exception. The *Restghettos* of Kielce and Tomaszowa–Mazowiecki were cleared in late May, with the surviving remnants of worker groups sent to nearby work camps.[95] In late June the so-called little ghetto of Czestochowa was also liquidated, with only a minority of the work Jews left alive.[96]

[90] FGM, doc. nr. 357, p. 448 (Scherner circular to factory managers, 14.12.42).

[91] Staatsanwaltschaft StA Hanover, 11/2 Js 481/69 (indictment of Körner, Heinemeyer, and Olde), p. 116 (Zentral Stelle der Landesjustizverwaltungen [hereafter cited as ZStL], II 206 AR 641/70, vol. 13).

[92] Dieter Pohl, *Von der "Judenpolitik" zum Judenmord: Der Distrikt Lublin des Generalgouvernements 1939–1944* (Frankfurt/M., 1993), pp. 165–6. For the liquidation of Miedzyrzec and Lukow, see: Christopher R. Browning, *Ordinary Men: Reserve Police Battalion 101 and the Final Solution in Poland* (New York, 1992), pp. 133–4.

[93] Dieter Pohl, *Nationalsozialistische Judenverfolgung in Ostgalizien 1941–1944* (Munich, 1996), pp. 246–65; Thomas Sandkühler, *"Endlösung" in Galizien: Der Judenmord in Ostpolen und die Rettungsinitiativen von Berthold Beitz 1941–1944* (Bonn, 1996), pp. 194–8.

[94] IMT, vol. 37, p. 401 (Nuremberg Document 018-L (Katzmann report to Himmler, 30.6.43).

[95] For Kielce: StA Darmstadt 2 Js 1721/64 (indictment of Wollschläger), pp. 88–89. For Tomaszow-Mazowiecki: Landgericht Darmstadt, 2 Ks 1/69 (judgment against Böttig, Fuchs, and Reichl), p. 49 (YVA, TR-10/861).

[96] Landgericht Lüneburg 2 a Ks 2/65 (judgment against Degenhardt), pp. 31–35 (YVA, TR-10/585).

This ongoing drive to liquidate the "work ghettos" and vastly reduce the number of Jewish workers left alive traced clearly to Himmler, though with declining support from his key SS men in Poland. Indeed, a new factor now weighed on Himmler that made him even more determined. The Warsaw ghetto uprising that began in April 1943 clearly shook Himmler. In addition to his inveterate suspicion that virtually every claim about the indispensability of Jewish labor to the war economy was both a pretext for personal profit and manifest evidence of the insidious temptation to corruption that the Jews – if left alive – represented, his ideologically conditioned obsession with the Jews as a security risk and the cause of all unrest behind the lines was now also fully activated. On May 10, 1943, Himmler discussed police reinforcements to the General Government and particularly the use of SS units, "as for example in street fighting in the Warsaw ghetto." He then declared:

> I will not slow down the evacuations of the rest of the some 300,000 Jews in the General Government, but rather carry them out with the greatest urgency. However much the carrying out of Jewish evacuations causes unrest at the moment, to the same degree they are the main precondition for a basic pacification of the region after their conclusion.[97]

The repercussions were quickly felt in the General Government, where Krüger stated before Frank and Heydrich's successor Ernst Kaltenbrunner among others that he had "just recently again received the order to carry out the removal of the Jews in a very short time." They were to be taken out of armaments factories and other businesses producing for the military and placed in large concentration camps, from which they would be made available to the armaments industry. "But the Reichsführer wishes that even the employment of these Jews ceases." Krüger then voiced open disagreement. These work Jews were "Maccabeans, who work wonderfully" ("*Makkabäer, die ausgezeichnet arbeiten*"). He did not think that Himmler's wish could be fulfilled,

[97] FGM, p. 355 (Himmler Aktennotiz, 10.5.43). Greifelt recorded Himmler's comments two days later: "It is an urgent task in the General Government to remove the 3–400,000 Jews still present there" ("*Eine vordringliche Aufgabe im Generalgouvernemnt sei es, die dort noch vorhandenen 3–400,000 Juden zu entfernen*"). FGM, p. 356 (Nuremberg Document NO-3173: Greifelt note on Himmler presentation of 12.5.43).

because among the Jews were skilled workers who could not be replaced. He asked Kaltenbrunner to explain the situation to Himmler and "beseech him to refrain from taking away this Jewish manpower"[98] ("*ihn zu ersuchen, von der Wegnahme dieser jüdischen Arbeitskräfte Abstand zu nehmen*).

Himmler was clearly not swayed by economic arguments, however, and in this regard received full support from Hitler. As Himmler noted after a meeting on June 19, 1943, once again devoted to security concerns: "To my presentation on the Jewish question, the Führer spoke further, that the evacuation of the Jews was to be carried out radically and had to be seen through, despite the unrest that would thereby arise in the next 3–4 months"[99] ("*Der Führer sprach auf meinen Vortrag in der Judenfrage hinaus, dass die Evakuierung der Juden trotz der dadurch in den nächsten 3 bis 4 Monaten noch entstehenden Unruhen radikal durchzuführen sei und durchgestanden werden müsste*").

The assault on the work Jews continued along two lines. Targeted were both Jews already in work camps who were not deemed essential to military production on the one hand and Jews in the few still-existing major "work ghettos" throughout eastern Europe on the other hand. Beginning in late June and culminating in two days of coordinated, multiple massacres on July 22–23, 1943, the Galician D-4 labor camps for road construction were systematically liquidated.[100] And four *Restghettos* that had been converted into labor camps in the eastern Cracow district (Przemysl, Tarnów, Bochnia, and Rzeszów) were closed down simultaneously in the first 3 days of September, with only a portion of their workers distributed to work elsewhere.[101]

The bigger targets for Himmler, however, were the remaining major "work ghettos" of Bialystok, East Upper Silesia, and Lodz as well as the

98 Frank, *Diensttagebuch*, p. 682 (Arbeitssitzung, 31.5.43).

99 YVA, O-53/130/438–9 (Himmler note on his meeting with Hitler at the Obersalzberg on 19.6.43).

100 Pohl, *Nationalsozialistische Judenverfolung in Ostgalizien*, pp. 348–55.

101 For Przemysl: StA Hamburg 147 Js 39/67 (indictment of Stegemann, Benesch, et al.), pp. 152–87 (YVA, TR-10/945). For Rzeszow: Landgericht Memmingen Ks 5 a-d/68 (judgment against Schusster, Dannenberg, Lehmann and Öster), pp. 22–3 (YVA, TR-10/687). For Tarnow: Landgericht Bochum 16 Ks 2/70 (judgment against Baach and Wunder), pp. 99–101 (YVA, TR-10/751). For Bochnia: Landgericht Kiel 2 Ks 4/66 (judgment against Müller), pp. 45–50, 63 (YVA, TR-10/725).

remaining ghettos even further east, such as Minsk. For Bialystok and Lodz, as in Warsaw the previous spring, he enlisted the services of Odilo Globocnik, who hoped to pillage both manpower and machinery for his own growing empire in Lublin. At this point, at least, both Himmler and Globocnik viewed the SS camps of Lublin as the last repository of the remnant of a remnant of work Jews, who in turn would work in SS-controlled industries rather than private firms. The model for this was the transfer of the Többens and Schultz firms, along with their machinery and workers, from Warsaw to camps in Poniatowa and Trawniki.[102] Here they were slated to be taken over by a SS firm known as Osti (Ostindustrie) created specifically to utilize Jewish workers and property as well as the machinery of ghetto firms.[103]

The Lublin camp conglomerate thus included the concentration camp at Majdanek (under the Wirtschafts-und Verwaltungshauptamt [WVHA], the Economic and Administrative Main Office of the SS), the two Lublin work camps at Lipowa and the "old airport,"[104] a Heinkel factory at Budzyn, Globocnik's private workshop at Krasnik, and the new work camps at Poniatowa and Trawniki. Globocnik boasted of 45,000 Jewish workers, most of whom had recently come from Warsaw. Furthermore, he expected this number to increase "significantly more in the coming months" ("*in den nächsten Monaten noch bedeutend*") because of a similar windfall of workers and machinery from Bialystok. He also proposed the same fate for Lodz.[105] And in August Himmler ordered additionally that Jews of Minsk were to be taken to Lublin as well.[106]

Globocnik's staff did indeed help carry out the liquidation of the Bialystok ghetto in mid-August 1943 and received the bulk of the workers not gassed at Treblinka.[107] However, the transfer of Jews from

[102] Grabitz/Scheffler, *Letzte Spuren*, pp. 179–210, 318–23.

[103] Enno Georg, *Die wirtschaftlichen Unternehmungen der SS* (Stuttgart, 1963), pp. 90–9; *Trials of the War Criminals before the Nürnberg Military Tribunals* (hereafter cited as TWC), V, pp. 512–24 (NO-1271: Fischer report, 21.6.44).

[104] Daniel Goldhagen, *Hitler's Willing Executioners*, pp. 283–316.

[105] Nuremberg Document NO-485 (Globocnik to Brandt, 21.6.43, and Vermerk), printed in: Grabitz/Scheffler, *Letzte Spuren*, pp. 322–7.

[106] TWC, XIII, p. 1206 (Nuremberg. Doc. NO-3304: Brandt to Berger, 20.8.43).

[107] Landgericht Bielefeld 5 Ks 1/65 (judgment against Altenloh et al.), pp. 297–310; StA Dortmund 45 Js 1/61 (indictment of Zimmermann), pp. 121–4; StA Hamburg 147 Js 24/72 (indictment of Michalsen et al.), pp. 157–63.

Minsk to Lublin never materialized, except for one small contingent of Jews from Minsk selected at Sobibor.[108] And the great prize of Lodz, moreover, eluded Globocnik entirely. Though Himmler approved the transfer in principle in September 1943,[109] the scheme came to naught as the entire Globocnik empire collapsed precipitously in the fall of 1943 with fatal consequences for the Jewish workers.

Globocnik had been useful to Himmler in carrying out the liquidation of the work ghettos while providing the cover, however implausible, that war production would not be impaired. But Himmler's obsessive suspicions about the seductive lure of wealth produced by Jews must have made him uneasy about Globocnik's growing ambitions for the Lublin labor camp empire. In any case, with the last work ghettos liquidated, Himmler transferred Globocnik to Trieste in September 1943. Then came the event that inflamed Himmler's other obsessive suspicion about the Jews as a dangerous security risk, when on October 14, the inmates of Sobibor staged a successful revolt and outbreak. This followed upon the Treblinka breakout and unsuccessful resistance at Bialystok.

The Germans had already shown a well-grounded fear that to begin a gradual elimination of work camps would give warning and invite resistance among desperate prisoners who had nothing to lose, once the last hope of survival through labor was dashed. Thus the elimination of entire labor camp systems – the D-4 camps in Galicia on July 22–23 and in eastern Cracow district on September 1–3 – had been coordinated, simultaneous operations. In the former case, at least, outside killing units were brought in and even German camp personnel were not warned ahead of time. Himmler now ordered that this same scenario be played out in Lublin on a much vaster scale. Police and SS units were brought in from all over Poland and even the Protectorate, and on the 2 days of November 3 and 4, some 42,000 Jews – virtually the entire Jewish labor force in Lublin – were massacred in what was cynically dubbed Operation *Erntefest*, or "harvest festival."[110]

[108] Grabitz/Scheffler, *Letzte Spuren*, p. 266.

[109] FGM, 369 (Nuremberg Document NO-519: Pohl to Himmler, 9.2.44).

[110] On the *Erntefest* massacres, see: Grabitz/Scheffler, *Letzte Spuren*, pp. 262–72, 328–34; Jozef Marszalek, *Majdanek; The Concentration Camp in Lublin* (Warsaw, 1986), pp. 130–4; Browning, *Ordinary Men*, pp. 135–42; Pohl, *Von der "Judenpolitik" zum Judenmord*, pp. 170–4.

The assault on the labor camps did not end there, however. One day after *Erntefest,* on November 5, the labor camp at Szebnia in the Cracow district was liquidated, when its nearly 4,000 workers were shipped to Auschwitz.[111] And on November 19, the 4,000 inmates of the last major Jewish labor camp in eastern Poland – the Janowska Road camp in Lwów where thousands of Jews had already perished under what was perhaps the most terrifying and murderous regime of all the Jewish labor camps – were also massacred.[112]

In the entire region of Galicia, Lublin, Bialystok, Warsaw, and Cracow, only the major labor camp at Plaszow and a few minor camps such as the Heinkel plane factory at Budzyn and the oil refinery at Drohobycz remained in existence.[113] In March 1943 before Himmler's assault on the work ghettos and labor camps, more than 300,000 Jews had been temporarily spared as "work Jews" in these regions.[114] At the end of November 1943, perhaps 25,000 were still alive.[115] The overwhelming majority of fatalities had not been caused by "destruction *through* labor." Instead, they had been victims of a Himmler-driven campaign for the "destruction *of* labor" through outright massacre.

November 1943 was a turning point, however. The work camps of Plaszow, the Radom district, and East Upper Silesia were not liquidated in turn. Himmler even permitted Lodz to continue as a work ghetto, rejecting Oswald Pohl's bid to turn it into a concentration camp.[116] And in the Radom district, in contrast to Plaszow and East Upper Silesia, the camps also remained "factory camps" distantly supervised by the SSPF but not incorporated into the concentration camp system (of the WVHA). These camps continued in operation until the approach of the

[111] StA Munich 116 Js 15/67 (indictment of Unterhuber), p. 16 (YVA, TR-110/717).

[112] Pohl, *Nationalsozialistische Judenverfolgung in Ostgalizien,* pp. 332–8, 359–60.

[113] For the survival of a remnant of work Jews of Drohobycz, see in particular: Sandkühler, *"Endlösung" in Galician,* pp. 290–406.

[114] Nuremberg Document NO-5193 (Korherr report, 19.4.43), printed in: *The Holocaust: Selected Documents in Eighteen Volumes,* ed. by John Mendelsohn (New York, 1982), vol. 12, pp. 212–19; Nuremberg Document NO-5194 (Korherr report, 23.3.43), excerpts printed in: *Documents on the Holocaust,* ed. by Yitzhak Arad, Yisrael Gutman, and Abraham Margoliot (Jerusalem, 1981), pp. 332–4.

[115] For a similar estimate, see: Frank Golczewski, "Polen," *Dimension des Völkermords: Die Zahl der jüdischen Opfer des Nationalsozialismus,* ed. by Wolfgang Benz (Munich, 1991), pp. 479–81.

[116] Nuremberg Document 519 (Pohl to Himmler, 9.2.44; and Greiser to Pohl, 14.2.44), printed in FGM, pp. 369–70.

Red Army forced closure, and even then the inmates were not killed on the spot but rather evacuated westward. Moreover, within at least some camps, the murderous regimen was significantly moderated over time.[117] The massive selections and gratuitous killings were curtailed, and death from exhaustion, malnutrition, and disease dropped significantly as well. Compared with the horrendous conditions within the Jewish labor camps and their near total liquidation further east by November 1943, a new period of precarious stability began. With the war clearly lost and the labor shortage clearly insurmountable, a weak glimmer of economic pragmatism was belatedly tolerated. At least in some camps neither a regimen of "destruction of labor" nor a regimen of "destruction through labor" characterized this period. Rather, it was "work now, destruction later" until the chaotic period of evacuations and death marches set in, and the fate of the surviving remnant of Polish "work Jews" was inextricably mixed with that of other slave laborers being driven westward in the closing months of the war.

In summary, German attitudes toward the exploitation of Jewish labor in Poland were mixed and changing, though always within the parameters of the Nazi regime's ideology and ultimate political priorities and goals. During the period when expulsion was envisaged as the ultimate goal and no overall labor shortage was perceived, the Nazi exploitation of Jewish labor was as wasteful and inefficient as it was cruel. When expulsion stalled and local authorities were left to deal with the large concentrations of impoverished Jews cut off from employment in the regular economy, at least in the two largest ghettos of Lodz and Warsaw advocates of a productive use of Jewish labor prevailed over advocates of attrition through starvation. Precarious ghetto economies were established for the purpose of maintaining the ghettoized Jews at their own expense. Though death rates soared and hunger and suffering remained immense, the Jews of Lodz, Warsaw, and the rest of Poland did not suffer the same fate as the Soviet POWs who died by the millions in the first 9 months after Operation Barbarossa.

The situation in Poland was fundamentally altered by two decisions in Berlin in the fall of 1941, one calling for a massive increase in the

117 Felicya Karay, *Death Comes in Yellow: Skarzykso-Kamienna Slave Labor Camp* (Amsterdam, 1996), pp. 125–6.

use of foreign labor and the other substituting extermination for expulsion as the goal of Nazi Jewish policy. Local authorities assumed that they would reconcile these conflicting policies by exploiting Jewish labor to replace deported Polish labor while simultaneously ridding themselves of what they considered the unwanted burden of the nonworking Jews. This time, however, Berlin did not leave local authorities to themselves. Himmler intervened consistently and savagely from July 1942 through November 1943 to force the destruction of the working Jews in Poland, a goal that he achieved throughout the districts of Galicia, Bialystok, Warsaw, Lublin, and most of Cracow.

Local authorities of the SS, military, and civil administration all saw this as a clear conflict between political and economic goals. Despite their full awareness of the damage to the war economy, however, they almost without exception conceded priority to the regime's political goal of the Final Solution. For Himmler and Hitler, however, no such conflict existed. All claims of Jewish indispensability to the economy were dismissed as invalid. Indeed, such claims were seen as evidence that the Jewish spirit of profiteering was still threatening to infect the Germans, and hence inspired an even more fanatical determination to exterminate Jewish labor. Jewish workers clung desperately to the strategy of survival through labor, until Himmler's policy left no option but hopeless resistance. The Warsaw ghetto uprising in turn activated another Himmler obsession that the Jews stood behind all resistance to the Germans and their total removal was the prerequisite for pacification. To Himmler's ideologically driven delusion about Jews and the economy was now added a mechanism of self-fulfilling prophecy concerning Jews and resistance.

Then in November 1943 came the last turn. With the war lost and German labor shortage insurmountable, Himmler's obsessive campaign to destroy Jewish labor slackened. The surviving Jews of Radom, Lodz, and East Upper Silesia did not suffer the same fate as those further east, and local authorities were once again left to make their own decisions. As a result, they treated their Jewish captives once again as slave laborers to be exploited mercilessly and draconically but not as objects to be destroyed immediately and totally. Unlike further east, from these camps there would be a surviving remnant, and it is to their story and their testimony that we turn next.

4

JEWISH WORKERS AND SURVIVOR MEMORIES

The Case of the Starachowice Labor Camp

Between early December 1941, when the Nazis opened the first death camp at Chelmno in the Warthegau, and mid-February 1943, when the ghetto-clearing units had completed the last stage of their initial sweep of the Polish ghettos, the vast bulk of Polish Jewry was destroyed. Aside from those who had made good their escape to the east, about 300,000 Polish Jews remained alive under German control in various work camps and so-called remnant or work ghettos. The temporary survival of this remnant of Polish "work Jews," while mollifying to those primarily concerned with German war production and the growing shortage of labor, was not pleasing to Heinrich Himmler. Between the spring and fall of 1943, he labored furiously and with considerable success to murder the Polish "work Jews" as well. By late November 1943 the remnant ghettos of eastern Poland, especially Warsaw and Bialystok, as well as the labor camps of the districts of Galicia and Lublin, had, with minuscule exceptions, all been destroyed.

This elimination of these "work Jews" was not, I must emphasize, achieved through what the Nazis euphemistically termed "destruction through labor." For the most part, the victims were not gradually worked and starved to death. Rather, the workers in these camps and remnant ghettos were killed in a relentless campaign of systematic mass murder, exemplified above all by the great *Erntefest* or "harvest Festival" massacre of 42,000 "work Jews" in the Lublin district in a mere 2 days on November 3–4, 1943.

When this campaign to murder the Polish "work Jews" came to a halt in late 1943, only a remnant of a remnant of Polish Jewry still survived. They were incarcerated within one of three systems: first, the myriad camps of the vast Auschwitz complex in Silesia and the Plaszow camp near Cracow, all of which had been incorporated into the SS concentration camp system; second, the Lodz ghetto under the regional party leader of the Warthegau; and third, a group of factory camps in the Radom district in west central Poland. Included in this last category was a complex of four relatively small camps in the city of Starachowice.

The Starachowice labor camps were untypical in a number of ways. First, the systematic liquidation of Jewish work camps in Poland stopped barely short of the Starachowice camps in 1943. Second, these factory camps were not subsequently incorporated into the more deadly SS concentration camp system. And third, when Starachowice was evacuated on July 28, 1944, the Jewish prisoners were transferred into Birkenau en bloc without further selection on the ramp. Because of these fortuitous German decisions, of the 2,300 Jews interned in the Starachowice camps, up to 75 percent might still have been alive in August 1944,[1] before they suffered the deadly ravages of Auschwitz and the death marches.

[1] Two witnesses provided very precise and quite similar figures for the Starachowice labor camps. According to Alan N., Zentral Stelle der Landesjustizverwaltungen (hereafter cited as ZStL 206 AR-Z 39/62 (Hamburg StA 147 Js 1312/63, investigation of Walter Becker [hereafter cited as Becker]), p. 732, about 1,200 men and 400 women were taken from Starachowice. Added to the camp population were 150 from Cracow, 200 from Majdanek, 150 from Radom, 150 from Tomaszowa, and 100 from nearby. According to Simcha M., who gave a very early testimony in June 1945, about 1,500 Jews from Starachowice were interned in the labor camps, and were joined by 36 Jews from Tomaszowa-Mazowiecki, 260 from Wolanow (near Radom), 100 from Radom, 150 from Cracow, and 200 from Majdanek. Yad Vashem Archives (hereafter cited as YVA), M-49E/155. Thus both estimate that about 2,300 Jews entered the camp.

Danuta Czech, *Kalendarium der Ereignisse im Konzentrationslager Auschwitz-Birkenau 1939–1945* (Reinbek bei Hamburg, 1989 [hereafter cited as Czech]), p. 832, notes the arrival of a transport from the Jewish work camps in the district of Radom on July 30, 1944, from which 1,298 male and 409 female Jews were registered. The number of Jews killed upon arrival, if any, is not stated.

There are three survivor estimates of the number of Jews who were evacuated from Starachowice: 1,200 (Alan N., in Becker, p. 732), 1,900 (Moses W., in YVA, O-2/319); and 2,000 [Israel A., in Fortunoff Archives, Sterling Library, Yale University (hereafter cited as FA), T-91].

Simcha M. (YVA, M-49E/155) said that 700–800 of the Starachowice Jews perished in the camps there. An estimated 100 prisoners perished during the trip to Auschwitz. Becker, p. 500 (Helen S.).

If we accept 2,300–2,400 as the number of Jews who entered the camp, 100 as the number of Jews who died in transit to Auschwitz, and approximately 1,700 as the number registered upon arrival in Auschwitz with no significant selection beyond the 100 deaths in transit, then the death toll in the Starachowice camps comes to 500–600 out of 2,300–2,400, or between 21 percent and 26 percent.

Thus, in contrast to many Jewish labor camps, from which only a handful – if any Jews – survive, the history of the Starachowice camps can be studied through a significant body of survivor testimony. My study of Starachowice is based primarily on 134 survivor testimonies, 57 by women and 77 by men. Most of these testimonies can be placed in one of three categories: immediate postwar testimonies collected in Poland, 1960s testimonies taken by German judicial investigators, and 1980s testimonies videotaped for the Fortunoff Archives. The Shoah Foundation in Los Angeles is in the process of cataloging an additional 35 testimonies filmed in the 1990s, so the final number will reach at least 169.

Several general comments must be made about the nature of this considerable body of survivor testimony. There are no literary giants among the survivors of Starachowice – no Primo Levi, Elie Wiesel, or Charlotte Delbo. In fact, the survivors virtually did not write at all. Their testimony was given orally and either transcribed or videotaped. It is for the most part straightforward and factual, spontaneous and unreflective.

The testimonies, not surprisingly, frequently contradict one another concerning chronology, dates, persons, and events. Nothing made the Starachowice survivors more infallible in their memory than other human beings. Indeed, 134 witnesses cannot be expected to have seen, experienced, and remembered the same events in the same way even in far less traumatic circumstances than a Nazi slave labor camp. It is no offense to survivor memory to accept their fallibility as witnesses; they often openly admit to failing memory themselves. And it is no act of disrespect to subject survivor testimonies to the same critical analysis that we would the conflicting and fallible testimony of other historical witnesses, even as we recognize that the survivors have lived through events that we cannot even remotely imagine on the basis of our own personal experiences.

If a collection of 134 testimonies makes clear the contradictions among survivor accounts, it also reveals a firm core of shared memory. In this regard, it is important to note what – contrary to expectation – I did not discover in the collective testimony. Given that the testimonies clustered in three periods – immediate postwar, the 1960s, and the 1980s – and that the survivors clustered geographically in three places – Israel, the Toronto area of Canada, and the Boston–New York region of the U.S. northeast – I had expected to find patterns of changing and diverging memory. I had expected that as time passed the survivors would speak less and less about sensitive topics like the role of the

Jewish camp council and camp police and the resulting tensions within the prisoner community and that they would increasingly cast their narratives in the less ambiguous terms of generic perpetrators and generic victims. I had also expected that as the survivors periodically met with one another regionally and retold their stories to one another, three geographically separate "memory communities" would take shape, increasingly homogeneous within but increasingly divergent from one another. These expectations were not realized. I did not find Israeli, Canadian, and American memory communities with identifiably different oral traditions of Starachowice. And I did not find that certain topics had become taboo over time in favor of a simpler, less ambiguous narrative. In short, survivor memories proved to be more stable and less malleable than I had anticipated.

What then can the historian learn about the Starachowice Jewish labor camps from this core of shared memory? I would like briefly to touch on three topics: first, the general phases of the camp history and mortality pattern; second, the underground economy and politics of the prisoner community; and third, the prisoner perception and categorization of German perpetrators.

Prewar Starachowice was composed of two parts: a new factory complex and modern residential area of Starachowice proper and two kilometers away the old town of Wierzbnik, where the Jewish community of 3,000 lived. In the memories of three witnesses who addressed the question, Poles and Jews lived fairly well together in Starachowice in comparison to other parts of Poland, though Polish–Jewish relations did begin to deteriorate sharply just before the war.[2]

In the fall of 1939, the steel and munitions factories of Starachowice were quickly claimed by the Hermann Göring Werke. The conquering Germans also immediately inflicted the entire spectrum of persecutive measures upon the Jews, from burning down the synagogue and cutting the beards of orthodox men to the increasingly systematic policies of marking, forced labor, confiscations, and ghettoization. The Germans also killed individual Jews in the early years of occupation,[3] but such killing still had limits. For example, the daughter of the rabbi remem-

[2] FA, T-955 (Gutta T.); YVA, O-3/8476 (Meir G.) and O-8231 (Jakov H.).

[3] Becker, p. 814 (Alter W.); p. 854 (Israel C.); p. 1290 (Anna G.); pp. 1384, 1386 (Pinchas H.); p. 1425 (Naftula K.).

bered that one day "Gestapo officials" came to her house with orders to kill her father, but the family successfully begged for his life. "I had the impression that the people were not yet used to killing," she concluded.[4]

The most memorable killing of the early period was not of Jews but rather the public hanging of 16 or 17 Polish hostages in the town square in June 1941, orchestrated by the chief of the Security Police branch office in Starachowice, *Kriminalkommissar* Walter Becker. This carefully planned "theatrical" event took place on a Sunday morning in the sealed-off main square, and Poles leaving church were forced to watch. The bodies were left hanging for several days, and in a transparent attempt to stir up Polish hatred against the Jews, the Germans had forced the Jewish council to provide young Jewish men wearing masks to serve as hangmen.[5]

In Starachowice the Jewish council adopted the same defense strategies as appeared elsewhere in Poland. To mitigate the fear and disruption of random labor roundups, the Jewish council organized its own "Jewish division" in the German Labor Office to allocate labor assignments.[6] The Jewish council also followed the standard practice of bribing German officials.[7] The police in particular exhibited an insatiable appetite for payoffs and an unusual inventiveness in extortion.[8] Most onerous in this regard was the frequent arrests of propertied Jews, who were held against payment of ransom,[9] and the sending of Starachowice Jews to the terrible labor camps in the Lublin district and arranging for their release in return for hefty payments.[10] As a result, the Jewish council was left with the onerous task of assessing quotas on propertied

[4] Becker, p. 514 (Ruth W.).

[5] At least 24 witnesses described this event, including: Becker, pp. 82 (Mendel M.), 368 (Chaim R.), 370 (Moshe R.), 764 (Howard S. C.), 822–3 (Ben Z.), and 875 (Adrian W.); and FA, T-1884 (Regina N.).

[6] Becker, pp. 405 (Fred B.) and 866 (Anna W.).

[7] Becker, pp. 1006 (Mendel M.) and 1021 (Simcha G.).

[8] The Germans frequently descended upon the Jewish council with ever-escalating demands for new "contributions" and deliveries, and they carried out relentless searches for "illegal" possessions to confiscate. Becker, p. 508 (Dina T.), p. 789 (Leib R.), p. 808 (Helen W.), pp. 879 and 1265 (Morris Z.), p. 938 (Zvi Hersh F.), p. 978 (Josef U.), p. 1409 (Abe F.).

[9] Becker, pp. 775 (Fay G.), 822 (Ben Z.), and 1197 (Helen W.).

[10] Becker: pp. 879, 1269 (Morris Z.); p. 1295 (Irene L.). FA, T-1683 (Meyer K.). For a Starachowice Jew whose return was not purchased but who nevertheless survived: YVA, M-1. E/1742 (Solomon B.).

Jews to help meet German demands. When necessary, it enforced these assessments through arrest by the Jewish police.[11] In contrast to the German police, trustees of confiscated Jewish businesses, who stood to gain more from a productive rather than a predatory approach, were remembered more positively by the survivors.[12]

By the fall of 1942, the Jewish population of Starachowice had nearly doubled. First came refugees produced by Nazi ethnic cleansing in the territories of western Poland incorporated into the Third Reich.[13] Then in 1942, as ghetto after ghetto in the Radom district was cleared, Jews from nearby towns flocked to Starachowice in hope that factory employment would protect them from deportation.[14] In the early morning of October 27, 1942, the unwalled ghetto was surrounded, and the Jews of Starachowice were driven to the marketplace for selection and deportation. The old, ill, and frail were shot on the spot.[15] Families were torn apart, as 3,748 Jews judged unfit to work were deported to Treblinka,[16] and about 1,200 men and 400 women were kept for labor.[17]

[11] Becker: p. 405 (Fred B.); pp. 460, 1290–2 (Anna G.).

[12] The large Jewish bakery was assigned to Otto Bastian of Saarbrücken, whom the former owners got along well with and visited in Germany after the war. Becker, p. 780 (Rosa H.). The German trustee who took over the Jewish lumber mill would take no money himself from the former owner and treated his family kindly; eventually, as we shall see, the lumber mill became a sanctuary for Jewish workers within the Starachowice camp system. FA, T-955 (Gutta T.). And the Pole who was assigned by the Germans to manage a confiscated construction and fuel supplies company found a hiding place in a Christian orphanage for the former owner's son, who thereby survived the war. Becker, pp. 903, 905 (Mordka M.).

[13] From Lodz in 1940: Becker, pp. 418 (Celia N.), 1129 (Anna A.), 1142 (Sam L.), and 1310 (Gutta W.). From Plock in 1941: FA, T-1884 (Regina N.). Becker: pp. 21, 1136 (Mach A.); pp. 25, 1123 (Israel A.); pp. 637, 1359 (Chaim A.); p. 752 (Leonia F.); p. 829 (Ben L.); pp. 1296 (Arthur A.).

[14] Becker: p. 86 (Kalman C.); pp. 423, 1244 (Jack S.); pp. 504, 1249 (Max S.); p. 736 (Toby W.); p. 1317 (Emil M.); p. 1378 (Toby S.). Some 200 Jews were forced into Starachowice from the nearby town of Wachock just days before the deportation. Becker, p. 1024 (Natan W.).

[15] At least 40 Jews killed at this time were identified individually by name in the survivor testimony. Staatsanwaltschaft Hamburg, 147 Js 37/67, Anklageschrift, pp. 28–33. According to those involved in the cleanup and burial details, the total number of Jews killed in the clearing action was between 40 and 60. Becker, pp. 797 (Abraham G. R.), 937 (Zwi Hersch F.), 955 (Israel E.), and 996 (Nathan G.).

[16] Landgericht Hamburg, Urteil (50) 35/70 in der Strafsache gegen Walter Becker, p. 17. According to a letter kept by the German Gendarme Max Strasser, this figure was written in chalk on the side of the train.

[17] According to Alan N. (Becker, p. 732), about 1,200 men and 400 women were taken from Starachowice. According to Simcha M., who gave a very early testimony in June 1945 (YVA, M-49E/155), about 1,500 Jews from Starachowice were interned in the labor camps.

In most towns in the Radom district, about 10 percent of the Jewish population was selected for labor. The much higher percentage in Starachowice – nearly 30 percent – was probably due to two factors. First, the key steel and munitions industries in Starachowice that had been taken over by the Hermann Göring Werke were producing directly for the military. And second, the factory management had already constructed its own special labor camps for Jewish workers even before the deportation, thus meeting the terms upon which Himmler was insisting in the fall of 1942 for the preservation and use of Jewish labor.

Initially, there were two large camps – Strelnica and Majowka – and two small camps – the lumbermill and the electricity works – to which the Jewish slave laborers were distributed. The camp at Strelnica was constructed in a clearing in the forest outside of town that had initially served as a firing range and lacked virtually any sanitary facilities; it lodged Jews who worked in the munitions factory. The camp at Majowka backed onto a stone quarry and lodged Jews who worked in the blast furnace and rolling mill of the steel works.[18] In the late summer of 1943, Majowka was enlarged to accommodate the prisoners from Strelnica, which was closed down. In April or May 1944 the entire Majowka camp was moved again to a new site directly on the grounds of the munitions factory.[19] It was from this camp that the surviving prisoners were evacuated to Birkenau on July 28, 1944.

Four phases or periods emerge from the testimony of the survivors. First was the traumatic day of October 27, 1942, in which they experienced the roundup, selection on the marketplace, the run from town under the blows and gunshots of the Ukrainian factory guard, and entry into camp, where they were stripped of all their possessions. It was the day on which virtually every prisoner saw many of his or her closest family for the last time.

The killing of prisoners began immediately, though still on a scale by which the victims could be remembered individually. On the run to the camp, the guards fired blindly or into the ground at the feet of the prisoners, wounding many in the legs with stone splinters.[20] At least three young men were killed on the way, one of whom struggled to

[18] Becker, pp. 1414, 1417 (Akiva R.).
[19] Becker: pp. 94–5 (Cwi Hersz U.); p. 372 (Moshe R.); pp. 730, 734 (Alan N.).
[20] Becker, pp. 956 (Israel E.) and 1201 (Dina T.).

keep up while trying to carry a large packet.[21] At least four men were shot during the collection of valuables, either for trying to hide a few coins or as a "demonstration" to frighten others into surrendering hidden valuables.[22] And one young man who broke down completely and began to sing and scream was shot immediately.[23]

In the second phase, from the fall of 1942 through the spring of 1943, the prisoners lived under a reign of terror and killing indelibly associated in the memories of the survivors with the handsome and well-dressed factory security chief and camp commandant, Willi Althoff. He descended upon the terrified prisoners virtually every night and invariably left dead Jews in his wake. Many of his killings were theatrically staged for his greater personal amusement[24] or even to entertain invited guests.[25] The crazed and "sadistic trance" in which he undertook in his killing led at least two prisoners to assume that he was a drug addict.[26]

Though Althoff's obvious "pleasure" in killing remained foremost in the memories of the prisoners, it must not obscure the fundamental policy of the factory that lay behind it. Quite simply, the factory direc-

[21] For the death of Josef Rosenberg, see Becker: p. 99 (Rachmiel Z.); pp. 461, 1294 (Anna G.); pp. 510, 1201 (Dina T.); pp. 785 (Max N.); p. 790 (Leib R.); p. 964 (Sarah p.); p. 974 (Rachmiel Z.); p. 1015 (Lea G., who claimed seeing Becker himself shoot Rosenberg); p. 1023 (Riwka G.); p. 1065 (Luba B.); p. 1152 (Leib R.); p. 1191 (Abe F.); pp. 1219–20 (Ben Z.); p. 1241 (Eva Z.); p. 1288 (Fred B.). For the death of Leib Spagat, who struggled with his packet, see Becker: pp. 780, 1175 (Rosa H.); p. 785, 1180 (Max N.); p. 790 (Leib R.); pp. 804, 1213 (Syma R.); pp. 824, 1219 (Ben Z.); p. 876 (Adrian W.); p. 1152 (Leib R.); p. 1226 (Howard S. C.). For an otherwise unidentified "Emil from Wachock," see Becker, p. 1168 (Israel C.).

[22] For Strelnica, they were identified as Mikulki by Fred B. (Becker, pp. 407, 1228) and Finkelstein by Max N. (Becker, p. 785). For the killing of two young men from Plock at the saw mill, see Becker: p. 887 (Frymeta M.); p. 946 (Avracham S.); pp. 1185, 1426 (Naftula K.); p. 1196 (Helen W.); p. 1283 (Mania K.); p. 1360 (Chaim A.); p. 1393a (Hil K.).

[23] For the death of Abe Kumec, see Becker: p. 83 (Mendel M.); p. 100 (Rachmiel Z.); p. 431 (Hersz T.); p. 790 (Leib R.); p. 798 (Abraham G. R.); p. 1153 (Leib R.); pp. 1191, 1409 (Abe F.); p. 1208 (Toby W.); p. 1386 (Pinchas H.).

[24] Some killings were arranged as target practice; see Becker, pp. 866 (Eva Z.) and 896 (Anna B.). More often, he conducted runs or stair-climbing competitions and shot those who fell behind; see Becker, pp. 417 (Celia N.), 436 (Toby W.), 503 (Helen S.), 732 (Alan N.), 778 (Fay G.), 792 (Leib R.), and 840 (Zelda W.), 860 (Eva Z.), 868 (Anne W.), 875 (Adrian W.), and 896 (Anna B.).

[25] Becker, pp. 792 (Leib R.) and 831 (Ben L.).

[26] Becker, pp. 675 (Meyer H.) and 759 (Mina B.).

tors preferred to kill sick and weak Jews rather than pay the SS the required 5 Zloty per day per head for all Jewish workers, including unproductive ones. On the day the Jews were first incarcerated in the factory camps, a Jewish nurse asked Leopold Rudolf Schwertner, the director in charge of recruiting all non-German workers for the Hermann Göring Werke in Starachowice, if a hospital barrack would be constructed. He merely replied that in case of illness, "You will be immediately shot."[27] And "amusement" killings aside, the bulk of Althoff's victims were the sick and weak. In addition to conducting notorious running and stair races to select the weak, Althoff twice entered the isolation barracks for typhus patients and killed every single person. On the second such occasion he also proceeded through some of the men's and women's barracks and shot sick people in their beds.[28] One prisoner who worked as a nurse in the camp calculated that Althoff singlehanded killed 120 Jews in his various "visits to the sick" ("*Krankenbesuchen*") apart from all his other killings.[29]

The factory management of the Hermann Göring Werke in Starachowice was not alone in its calculation that sick and exhausted Jews were not worth the payment of 5 Zloty per day. In a rare case where the internal correspondence has been preserved, we can see that a similar conclusion was reached by the factory management using Jewish camp labor in Rozwadow near Jaroslaw in the Cracow district. Its response was to report Jews deemed incapable of productive work to the Gestapo each month for "resettlement."[30] What distinguished Starachowice, therefore, was the willingness of the factory management to employ its security chief to kill its sick Jewish prisoners immediately rather than wait and request the Gestapo to do it for them on a monthly basis.

The climax of Althoff's bloodletting came in the first week in March 1943. Twenty young men were sent to the Bugaj forest to dig a mass

[27] Becker, p. 798 (Abraham R.).

[28] Among the numerous references to the hospital barracks massacres, see Becker, pp. 29 (Israel A., the sole escapee from the hospital barracks), 83 (Mendel M.), 407 (Fred B.), 435 (Toby W.), 631 (Mania B.), 749 (Leonia F.), and 896 (Anna B.). FA, T-91 (Israel A.).

[29] Becker, p. 791 (Leib R.).

[30] Nürnberg Documents NG-5690, NG-5693, NG-5694: Abwehrbeauftragte Schulte-Mimberg to Industriebeauftragte Major Schmolz, 29.10.42, 25.2.43, and 29.3.43.

grave, and several days later 120 prisoners were selected by Althoff, loaded on trucks, and taken to the forest, where they and the gravediggers were all shot. One young boy escaped and returned to the camp to tell the tale.[31] Polish workers reported that for days the earth over the grave moved – an image that still haunted many survivor memories years later.[32]

Shortly after the Bugaj selection and massacre, the factory directors in Starachowice apparently realized that murdered Jews could no longer be replaced but recuperated Jews could return to work. In these circumstances, even temporarily unproductive prisoners were worth 5 Zloty per day. Thereupon Leopold Schwertner came to Strelnica and announced that henceforth sick prisoners would no longer be shot.[33] Moreover, the instrument of the factory's previous policy, Willi Althoff, was removed from his position and sent away. His removal was attributed by several survivors to a division manager of the munitions factory, Kurt Otto Baumgarten, who simultaneously took over Althoff's duties as head of factory security.[34]

After the departure of the murderous Althoff, a third period of relative stability set in, punctuated by one major selection and mass killing on the one hand and an identifiable number of individual killings on the other. Althoff's eventual successor as camp commandant was the extremely obese Walter Kolditz. He closed the notorious Strelnica camp, which had been Althoff's chief killing site,[35] and moved the prisoners from there to the newly enlarged and slightly less unsanitary Majowka camp.[36] On November 8, 1943,[37] Kolditz conducted a campwide selection in Majowka, after which 150–160 Jews

[31] Becker: pp. 83–4 (Mendel M.); p. 425 (Jack S.); p. 491 (Ralph C.); p. 505 (Max S.); p. 509 (Dina T.); p. 515 (Ruth W.); p. 732 (Alan N.); pp. 859, 1239 (Eva Z.); p. 865 (Anna W.); p. 897 (Anna B.); p. 1388 (Pinchas H.). YVA, M-49E/155 (Simcha M.).

[32] Becker: pp. 83–4 (Mendel M.); p. 425 (Jack S.); p. 491 (Ralph C.); p. 505 (Max S.); p. 509 (Dina T.); p. 515 (Ruth W.); p. 732 (Alan N.); pp. 859, 1239 (Eva Z.); p. 865 (Anna W.); p. 897 (Anna B.); p. 1388 (Pinchas H.). YVA, M-49E/155 (Simcha M.).

[33] Becker, pp. 818 (Faye G.) and 828 (Ben Z., according to whom it was Becker, not Schwertner, who made this announcement).

[34] Becker, pp. 65 (Rywka G.), 84 (Mendel M.), 406 (Fred B.), and 759 (Mina B.).

[35] Becker, p. 815 (Alter W.).

[36] Becker, pp. 776 (Arnold F.), 1390 (Chaim H.).

[37] Many survivors placed this selection in the spring of 1944. For the most precise and reliable dating, see: Becker, pp. 470 (Adam G.) and 1364 (Rachiel P.).

were taken away in three or four trucks to Firlej near Radom and killed. The trucks soon returned with only the clothing of the victims, which was redistributed among the prisoners.[38]

It is unlikely that this selection was initiated by the factory management in Starachowice, however, for similar selections and deportations to Firlej, where SS men did the killing, were carried out in many other camps in the Radom district at the same time. It came just days after the great *Erntefest* massacre in the neighboring Lublin district.[39]

Aside from the great selection of November 8, 1943, the survivors remembered a number of other individual killings as well, for as one survivor put it, killing was no longer an "everyday" ("*alltäglich*") event.[40] At least seven prisoners were shot individually during the Kolditz period prior to the great November selection,[41] with at least two marked by extraordinarily sadistic cruelty.[42] Thereafter Kolditz was replaced by Baumgarten as camp commandant, and at least another 27 killings between November 1943 and July 1944 were remembered by the survivors.[43] In their testimony, the killings of the Baumgarten period were related to some specific cause, such as attempted escape, refusal or inability to work, or faulty production, and were not characterized as amusement killings. The two chief killers identified by the survivors in

[38] A large number of survivors remember this major selection. Some detailed accounts are found in Becker: pp. 470 (Adam G.), 714 (Ida G.), 859 (Eva Z.), 1328 (Alan N.), 1364 (Rachiel P.), 1369 (Max R.). Also: YVA, M-49/1172 (anonymous).

[39] Adam Rutkowski, "Die Hitlerischen Arbeitslager für Juden im Distrikt Radom," *Biuletyn Zydowskiego Instytutu Historycznego.* Nr. 17/18 (1956), p. 19, for the "reduction" of camps in Radom on the same day, November 8, 1943. Willi Schroth, who accompanied the trucks to Firlej, testified that Jews were also brought there from other places. ZStL, II 206 AR 298/68 (hereafter cited as Schroth), vol. I, p. 41. The camp at Skarzysko–Kamienna seems not to have been included, however. Felicja Karay, *Death Comes in Yellow: Skarzysko-Kamienna Slave Labor Camp* (Amsterdam, 1996), p. 61.

[40] Becker, p. 1382 (Adam K.).

[41] Becker: pp. 411, 413 (Hanna A.); p. 420 (Celia N.); p. 793 (Leib R.).

[42] On one occasion Kolditz ordered a prisoner to beat his brother, which he did. Kolditz thereupon ordered the prisoner to kill his brother. When the prisoner refused, Kolditz shot both brothers. Becker, p. 869 (Anna W.).

[43] There are numerous witnesses for the killing of Jadwiga Feldman and Mala Szuch, Toby and Szmul Waisblum, Marysia and Roma Lefkowitz, Brenner, and a hostage shooting of eight Jews from the blast furnace and two sick Jews. For six additional killings with only one or two witnesses each, see: Becker, pp. 647 (Leo B.), 873 (Adrian W.), 1369 (Jankiel C.), and 1397 (Salomon B.), and StA Dortmund 45 Js 19/67, Anklageschrift gegen Willi Schroth, in ZStL 206 298/68, vol. I, pp. 102–3.

this period were the chief of the Ukrainian factory guard, Willi Schroth, and one of the deputies of factory security, Gerhard Kaschmieder.

The final phase of the camp was a tumultuous period in July 1944 characterized by rising fear, mass escape attempts, and ultimately the dissolution of the camp through evacuation to Auschwitz – Birkenau. The tremendous rise in fear actually began in the spring of 1944, when some 150–200 Jewish prisoners from Majdanek – called the "Lubliners" – arrived in Majowka and told the other prisoners what they knew of the death camps and gas chambers. Individual escape attempts increased, and a warning was issued that for each escape, coworkers of the same group would be shot. When 10 Jews from the blast furnaces escaped, 10 coworkers were indeed selected and executed.[44] For greater security against partisan attacks which aimed at seizing weapons from the Ukrainian guards, the Germans closed Majowka and moved the prisoners to a new camp directly on the munitions factory grounds in May or June.[45] In July the sound of Russian artillery in the distance heightened anxiety that all the prisoners would be shot before the Red Army arrived.[46] When some of the Lubliners recognized Majdanek personnel among a visiting commission of SS officers, fear turned to panic.[47]

On July 26, 1944, a train arrived at the factory camp, and loading began. Surprisingly, the loading was abruptly stopped and the prisoners were sent back to their barracks.[48] That night a minority of prisoners attempted to break out. Some did not know of the imminent attempt, and others judged it too risky. The attempt was in fact discovered just as the second line of the double wire fence was being cut. The searchlights came on, machine guns opened fire, and the head of the camp guard, Willi Schroth, threw hand grenades that stopped the breakout in its tracks. By one account, 64 prisoners were killed, many were left lying badly wounded between the wires, and the others ran back to the barracks. Almost no one escaped.[49]

44 Kaschmieder: pp. 49 (Edward S.) and 64–5 (Schmul L. L.). Becker, p. 646 (Leo B.).

45 Becker, p. 772 (Arnold F.).

46 Becker: pp. 647 (Leo B.), 726 (Bella W.), and 1416 (Akiva R.). FA, T-955 (Gutta T.).

47 YVA, M-49/1172 (anonymous).

48 Becker, pp. 79 (Pinchas H.), 513 (Ruth W.), 787 (Max N.), 805 (Syma R.), 816 (Alter W.), 819 (Faye G.), 826 (Ben Z.), and 1380 (Toby S.).

49 Among the many accounts of the breakout attempt, see Becker: pp. 437 (Toby W.), 470 (Adam G., who gave the figure of 64 dead), 654 (Mayer G., who testified that he was one of five who managed to escape during the breakout attempt), 714–15 (Ida G.), 726 (Bella W.), and 1329 (Alan N.); FA: T-91 (Israel A.) and T-1884 (Regina N.); YVA: O-2/319 (Moses W.), M-49E/1742 (Lena W.), and O-3/8489 (Chaim G.).

The following morning Baumgarten appeared in camp. Though one fatally wounded leader of the escape attempt was immediately shot[50] and other wounded prisoners by the fence were denied medical aid and left to die, no further retaliatory shootings occurred. Baumgarten assembled the prisoners and gave a speech in which he expressed his "disappointment" that the Jews whom he had treated so well should have tried to escape. He assured them that they were being sent to a better camp and had nothing to fear. Even as he spoke, however, many Jews broke from their ranks and attempted to scale the fences and escape in broad daylight. Once again most were shot down. The Jews were then forced to surrender their shoes in an attempt to discourage further escapes.[51] In addition, the Ukrainian guard around the camp was reinforced by military police.[52]

Another train arrived on July 28, and after standing for hours in the hot sun, the Starachowice prisoners were packed into overloaded cars, without food, water, toilet facilities, or even enough air to breath. Except for a few lucky ones who were put in open cars at the end of the train, most experienced the slow trip of 2 days and 2 nights to Auschwitz as a hell that made arrival in Birkenau seem a "huge relief" ("*Riesenerlösung*"). Over 100 Jews died from suffocation and heat prostration in the closed train cars.[53] Though some prisoners remembered a selection on the ramp,[54] more said that the Starachowice prisoners entered into the camp as a group of already proven workers.[55]

[50] This was a policeman named Moshe Herblum, whom Jeremia Wilczek, the camp elder, had identified as the ringleader. A minority of accounts state that he was left to die; according to one, he slit his wrists to end his suffering.

[51] In addition to the testimonies of the previous two footnotes, see: Becker, pp. 95 (Cwi Hersz U.), 495 (Ralph C.), 648 (Leo B.), 742 (Mendel T.), 1365 (Rachela P.), 1369 (Max R.), 1397 (Salomon B.), and 1416 (Akiva R.); and YVA, M-19/1172 (anonymous). Typical of the conflicting memories concerning the actions of individual Germans, some accounts attribute the speech to either Becker or the long-departed Kolditz.

[52] Becker, p. 866 (Anne Wilson).

[53] Becker, pp. 500 (Helen S.), 767 (Howard S. C.). Another survivor estimated that 400 died on the transport: FA, T-91 (Israel A.). For other descriptions, see: Becker, pp. 416 (Matys F.), 494 (Ralph C.), 506 (Max S.), 511 (Dina T.), 518 (Ruth W.), 591 (Maurice W.), 643 (Arthur H. A.), 742–43 (Mendel T.), 787 (Max N.), 819 (Faye G.), 827 (Ben Z.), 870 (Anne W.), 1370 (Max R.); FA, T-91 (Israel A.), T-442 (Sarah W.), T-1884 (Regina N.); and YVA, M-1/E.2469 (Josef K.), O-3/8489 (Chaim G.).

[54] FA, T-91 (Israel A., who claimed Josef Mengele conducted the selection), T-1683 (Meyer K.), T-442 (Sarah W.).

[55] YVA, O-3/9394 (Ruth Z.). FA, T-1884 (Regina N.), T-955 (Gutta T.). Becker, p. 462 (Anna G.).

The Starachowice Jews were then placed in quarantine in one part of the "Gypsy camp," where they could hear the dreadful sounds of the liquidation of the remaining "Gypsies" in Birkenau on August 2.[56] After quarantine, the Starachowice Jews were dispersed to various work sites and merged with the rest of the Auschwitz prisoner population.

The collection of Starachowice survivor testimonies provides ample evidence for both the course of events and mortality pattern of the labor camps and the immense suffering of the prisoners. Somewhat rarer in this collection is testimony that provides insight into the internal governance and underground economy of the camps. The topic of internal governance is particularly sensitive. To avoid the impression or suggestion that discussion of such a topic is equivalent to blaming the victim and exculpating the perpetrator, it is important to draw upon the depressing wisdom of Primo Levi.

Levi reminds us that despite our natural desire for simplification and clarity, "the network of human relationships inside the Lagers [camps] was not simple; it could not be reduced to the two blocs of victims and persecutors. . . . It is naive, absurd, and historically false," he continues, "to believe that an infernal system such as National Socialism sanctifies its victims; on the contrary, it degrades them, it makes them resemble itself."[57]

To facilitate both control over and the degradation of the prisoners, the designers of the camp system perfected the use of *kapos* and other privileged functionaries – a method that turned the "space" between persecutors and victims into a "gray zone" or "zone of ambiguity" that was "studded with obscene or pathetic figures."[58] As Levi noted, "if one offers a position of privilege to a few individuals in a state of slavery, exacting in exchange the betrayal of a natural solidarity with their comrades, there will certainly be someone who will accept. . . . The more power that he is given, the more he will be consequently hateful and hated."[59]

The development of this technique of control had occurred, of course, within the concentration camp system in Germany long before Jews were a major contingent of the prisoner population, and initially

[56] FA, T-1683 (Meyer K.), T-91 (Israel A.). YVA, M-49E/1669 (Leon W.), O-2/319 (Moses W.). For the date of the liquidation of the "Gypsy" camp (BIIe), see: Czech, p. 838.

[57] Primo Levi, *The Drowned and the Saved* (Vintage Edition: New York, 1989), pp. 37, 40.

[58] Levi, *The Drowned and the Saved,* pp. 39–40.

[59] Levi, *Survival in Auschwitz,* p. 83. (New York: Collier Books Edition, 1961)

convicted criminals and then eventually also political prisoners comprised the bulk of the privileged camp elites. Subsequently the Nazis also exploited the technique of using Jewish councils and Jewish police within the ghettos of Poland. In Starachowice, a labor camp where all the prisoners were Jews, these two methods of control and manipulation – the kapo system of the concentration camps on the one hand and the council and police system of the ghettos on the other – were merged, which by necessity involved the creation and partial empowerment of a Jewish camp elite. All the ambiguities and torments of Levi's "gray zone" unfortunately followed.

When the Jews selected for labor were taken to the Starachowice camps on October 27, 1942, the Starachowice *Judenrat,* or Jewish council, was not transferred and reestablished as the institution for internal governance. Instead a new *Lagerrat,* or camp council, was set up in its place, along with a new camp police. By virtually everyone's account, the most powerful prisoner within the camps was Jeremia Wilczek. According to one survivor, Wilczek had already ingratiated himself with the Germans in the predeportation period, when he served as the middleman who collected money and valuables for the release of Jews who had been arrested by the police for the purpose of extorting ransom.[60] In Majowka, Wilczek surrounded himself with a coterie of people related to him by blood or marriage and placed them into key positions to control the police, kitchen, and allocation of labor assignments.[61] Most of Wilczek's coterie came from four large and important families of the prewar Jewish community – the Wilzceks, Herblums, Rubensteins, and Koguts.[62]

[60] Becker, p. 370 (Moshe R.).

[61] Wilczek's son-in-law, Chaim Kogut, and possibly Kogut's father as well, served on the police force. Becker, pp. 499 (Helen S.), 655 (Mayer G.), 807 (Syma R.), 825 (Ben Z.). Chaim Kogut's brother-in-law was also a policeman. Becker, pp. 872, 876 (Adrian W.). A Wilczek cousin, Jacob Rubenstein, was head of the kitchen and controlled the allocation of food. In turn, Rubenstein's brother-in-law, Moshe Herblum, served in the police. Becker, pp. 511 (Dina T.), 721 (Rywka S.), 728 (Bella W.), 768 (Howard S. C.), 1334 (Morris P.). YVA, M-49/1172 (anonymous). Another Herblum also worked in the kitchen. Becker: pp. 674, 1344 (Meyer H.); p. 772 (Arnold F.); p. 777 (Fay G.). Wilczek's son Abraham was a policeman, and according to one witness was also in charge of work. Becker, pp. 717 (Ida G.), 872 (Adrian W.); FA, T-91 (Israel A.). His wife, the elder Wilczek's daughter-in-law, served as camp secretary. Becker, p. 864 (Anna W.). Virtually all the other wives of the prisoner elite worked in the kitchen. YVA, M-49/1172 (anonymous).

[62] Becker, p. 1410 (Abe F.).

And the camp council did retain three members of the old Jewish council.[63] Thus the Wilczek regime represented only a partial displacement of traditional leaders rather than a social revolution within the Jewish community.

The camp elite enjoyed a number of privileges that the other prisoners did not. They lived in separate housing together with their wives and in some cases with their children whom they had been allowed to bring into camp.[64] They were also able to maintain contact with people outside the camp and even visit them in town when accompanied by guards, in order to conduct business or have access to valuables hidden with friends.[65]

A number of accusations made against Wilczek and the camp elite in the postwar testimony concerned inequity and stealing. They were accused of living and eating well, in effect stealing from the common food and clothing supply while the rest of the camp suffered hunger and malnourishment and dressed in rags. Jacob Rubenstein, in charge of the kitchen, was a particularly hated figure in this regard.[66]

Wilczek was also personally accused of abusing his position of power to extract sexual favors from many women in the camp. Only one survivor voiced this accusation, but she was quite explicit. Wilczek "became the rooster of the camp" and had lots of girls available to him, even though he lived with his wife. When the survivor in question refused to go to him, he made her life miserable.[67]

Two survivors accused the camp council of participating in selections. According to one testimony of August 1945, one of the very earliest, the Firlej selection of November 8, 1943, was based on a list prepared by the camp council.[68] According to the Jewish barber who shaved Kolditz every day, during which time the commandant often received members of the camp council, there was intensive coopera-

[63] Moshe Birenzweig, Rachmiel Wolfowicz, and Szlomo Enesman. Becker, pp. 636 (Mania B.), 896 (Anna B.), 1006 (Mendel M.), 1051 (Pinchas H.), 1292 (Annie G.), 1335 (Moshe P.), 1382 (Adam K.), 1390 (Chaim H.); Kaschmieder, p. 75 (Arnold F.); YVA, M-49/1172 (anonymous).

[64] Becker, p. 1335 (Moshe P.). FA, T-1884 (Regina N., who said that Wilczek had three children in camp).

[65] FA, T-955 (Gutta T.). YVA, O-3/9394 (Ruben Z.). Becker, p. 652 (Mayer G.).

[66] YVA, M-49/1172 (anonymous). Becker, pp. 652 (Mayer G.), 728 (Bella W.). YVA, O-3/9394 (Ruben Z.).

[67] FA, T-1884 (Regina N.).

[68] YVA, M-49/1172 (anonymous).

tion, including working together on selections. "This latter I know exactly," the barber emphasized.[69]

Although no testimonies praised either Wilczek or the camp police as a whole, some explicitly did credit the intervention of individual policemen with saving their lives.[70] Included in the list of good policeman was Wilczek's son. According to one survivor: "He helped us a great deal." She immediately added: "His father, however, was not a good man."[71]

The camp council was involved in two kinds of power struggles, the first against dissident prisoners challenging its policies and privileges, and a second between German rivals for external control of the camps. Most disenchanted with the camp council were latecomers to the camp from outside Starachowice. When prisoners from the Wolanow camp near Radom, where the Jewish camp leaders had imposed a strict but honest and egalitarian regime, were transferred to Starachowice in the fall of 1943, they were dismayed by the rampant inequality at Starachowice. The newcomers' possessions were taken from them under the guise of disinfection; these possessions were never returned but were instead sold to Poles on the black market. Rare items like meat and sugar that they had received as occasional rations at Wolanow were in Starachowice sold to those who could pay, with the camp council pocketing the proceeds. When the Wolanow newcomers protested indignantly, they were branded as rebels, discriminated against even more in terms of being assigned the worst jobs, and dispersed among different barracks so they could not act in concert.[72]

When the remnant of Lubliners arrived in the spring of 1944, these scarred and tested survivors of the camp system openly challenged the Starachowice elite for control of the camp. Temporarily, they won out and one of their own became chairman of the council. In the end, the old elite bribed its way back into power, though it was careful thereafter not to steal quite so openly as before.[73] Another survivor testified concerning the mistreatment of the Lubliners by the camp council:

69 Becker, pp. 654–5 (Mayer G.).

70 Becker, pp. 425 (Jack S.), 804 (Syma R.), 896 (Anna B).

71 Becker, p. 717 (Ida G.). Another survivor, however, held Wilczek's son responsible for a beating she suffered for missing the departure of her group for work. FA, T-91 (Regina N).

72 YVA, M-49/1172 (anonymous).

73 YVA, M-49/1172 (anonymous).

"They were persecuted by our people, not so much by Germans. Everything was blamed on them."[74]

The other challenge to the camp council seems to have ensued from a rivalry between camp commandant Kolditz and chief of factory security Baumgarten. When Kolditz arrived, he brought with him two of his own Jewish policemen from his previous assignment. Kolditz then "forced" another prisoner to take the position of commandant of the camp police, though the reluctant prisoner wanted nothing to do with the "shady intrigues" of the camp council. Not willing to impose additional forced labor on workers returning from the factory shifts to improve the camp's sewage system, the newly appointed police chief offered extra bread rations for volunteer workers. By his own account, he was then denounced by the camp council to Baumgarten for "wasting" bread and barely escaped summary execution. This showed, his wife concluded, that "no decent human being" could be Jewish police commandant in Starachowice.[75]

The contest between Baumgarten and Kolditz over control of the camp council and police continued. During the November selection, Kolditz found a prisoner hiding in a barracks that the Jewish policeman Chaim Kogut had been responsible for searching. Kolditz thereupon shot Kogut, who was Wilczek's son-in-law, in full view of the other prisoners. This execution of one of the camp elite was a singular event remembered by many survivors, one of whom explained that Kolditz did not like Wilczek, and that the killing of the son-in-law was Kolditz's way of attacking him.[76]

It is likely that this indirect attack on Wilczek was also an indirect attack on Wilczek's German sponsor and chief recipient of bribes, Kurt Baumgarten. Citing Kolditz's drunkenness, sexual relations with Polish women, and the shooting of the Jewish policeman Kogut,[77] Baumgarten, who had already replaced the dismissed Althoff as head of factory security, now obtained Kolditz's dismissal as camp commandant and took that position for himself as well. The head of the Ukrainian camp guard, Willi Schroth, who had reported Kolditz's order to shoot two Polish women with whom he had been unable to achieve satisfactory sexual

[74] FA, T-1884 (Regina N.).
[75] Becker, pp. 750–1 (Leonia F.), 770–1 (Arnold F.).
[76] Becker, p. 824–5 (Ben Z.).
[77] ZStL, II 206 AR 125/68 (hereafter cited as Baumgarten), p. 23 (Kurt Baumgarten). Becker, p. 692 (Paul F.).

consummation,[78] was rewarded with the day-to-day supervision of the camp, his own Polish mistress and child notwithstanding.[79] When Kolditz then physically attacked Baumgarten in the factory canteen,[80] the dismissed commandant was sent away from Starachowice and assigned to the Waffen-SS.[81]

The alliance and triumph of Baumgarten and Wilzcek in parallel struggles for supremacy against their respective rivals was fueled by an underground camp economy based on a dizzying network of bribes and black market trading that involved Jews, Germans, and Ukrainian guards. It was only the last chapter in a strategy of bribery that Jewish leaders had employed from the beginning of the German occupation. The initial focus of the Jewish council's bribery attempts was the head of the Security Police branch office in Starachowice, Walter Becker. A career member of the Criminal Police (Kripo), Becker had joined the German Socialist Party (SPD) in the 1920s and consequently had been suspended from the police force for a few weeks in the spring of 1933. Reinstated, Becker joined the National Socialist German Workers' Party (NSDAP) in 1937, though his SS application of the same year was never officially completed and approved.[82] In Starachowice, Becker was less feared than several notorious members of the Order Police.[83] Moreover, he displayed an insatiable appetite for Jewish

78 Schroth, p. 32 (Willi Schroth).

79 Becker, p. 615 (Otto T.).

80 ZStL, II 206 AR 298/68, vol. 2 (Judgment, Düsseldorf 8 Ks 2/70), p. 34.

81 National Archives/Berlin Document Center microfilms, SS Lists 5479 and 6487. According to Willi Schroth, Koldtiz was assigned to a "punishment company." Becker, p. 457.

82 Becker, pp. 1106–7 (Walter Becker). National Archives/Berlin Document Center (hereafter cited as NA/BDC): Ortskartei, Zentralkartei, and RuSHA file.

83 Two members of the Gendarmerie stood out in particular: Ertel, simply known as Näsel because of the comical shape of his nose, and Schmidt. In the early period, Näsel was considered the "worst of all." Becker: pp. 431 (Hersz T.), 727 (Bella W.), 742 (Mendel T.), 764 (Howard S. C.), 774–5 (Fay G.), 785 (Max N.), 796 (Abraham R., who is the only witness to claim that Näsel set his dog on people by crying "Bite the man," as the notorious Kurt Franz of Treblinka did with his dog Barry), 809 (Helen W.), 814 (Alter W.), 935 (Zwi Hersh F.), 1042 (Riwka G.), 1049 (Pinchas H.), and 1384 (Pinchas H.). Also notorious was the head of the *Schutzpolizei,* Rudolf Angerer, a man of well-muscled body and dark complexion. He was known as Tarzan by the younger Jews who had seen the movie, and as Tiger or Schwarze by the older generation who had not. He was notorious for the beatings he inflicted. Becker, pp. 782 (Rose H.), 785 (Max N.), 822 (Ben Z.), 856 (Israel C.), 877 (Adrian W.), 999 (Mendel M.), 1273 (Irene L.), and 1323 (Alan N.). His proclivity for beating eventually was his downfall; he committed suicide when he came under investigation for beating to death a ethnic German during an interrogation. Schroth, pp. 389 (Heinrich E.) and 398 (Otto M.).

property.[84] The Jewish council resolved to give him everything he wanted in the hope that Becker would protect the source of his material gains out of sheer greed.[85] Becker's berserk rampage on the day of deportation – when he ran about like a "wild animal"[86] ("*wildes Tier*") shooting and beating people – came as a surprise to Jewish leaders.[87] Becker coped with the strain of beating, killing, and deporting Jews all day in the same way as so many other Germans in occupied eastern Europe. That night an acquaintance found him very drunk and stammering: "I can't stand it anymore" and "it's only bearable when [I'm] drunk."[88] Clearly, with Becker the strategy of bribery was a total failure, both in terms of a mistaken estimate of his character and an incorrect assumption about his power to decide the fate of the ghetto.

The desperate Jews had more success with Leopold Schwertner, who was in charge of recruiting non-German workers at the Hermann Göring Werke. In the accounts of many survivors, Schwertner took money for the precious work cards that they hoped would save them when deportation became imminent.[89] Moreover, he took money directly from the Jewish council in Starachowice and from other Jewish communities to create as many jobs as possible. His motives for doing this mattered little to the Jews. As one survivor commented: "He thereby saved the lives of these people."[90] Nor did Schwertner select workers solely on the basis of bribes. On the marketplace during the deportation, in civilian clothes and without a gun, he chose many Jews for work who did not have a work card.[91] In December 1943, Jewish valuables were found in Schwertner's apartment, and he was arrested for corruption. He was released from prison in April 1944 but banned

84 Becker, pp. 400 and 1291 (Annie G.), 789 (Leib R.), 795 (Abraham R.), 809 and 1193 (Helen W.), 879 and 1265 (Morris Z.), and 1409 (Abe F.).

85 Becker, pp. 508 (Dina T.) and 1021 (Mendel M.).

86 Becker, p. 411 (Anna A.).

87 Becker, pp. 824 (Ben Z.) and 1021 (Mendel M.).

88 Becker Indictment, StA Hamburg 147 Js 37/67, p. 44.

89 Becker, pp. 736–7 (Toby W.), 796 (Abraham R.), 938 (Zwi Hersh F.), 961 (Sarah P.), and 970 (Rachmiel Z.).

90 Becker, pp. 956 (Israel E. for the quotation), 1053 (Pinchas H.).

91 Becker, pp. 425 (Jack S.), 765 (Howard S. C.), and 995 (Nathan G.). Schwertner was described by two survivors as "proper" ("*ordentlich*"). Becker, pp. 425 (Ralph C.) and 501 (Helen S.). One survivor accused him of beating and kicking prisoners in the factory. Becker, p. 877 (Adrian W.).

from residing in the eastern occupied territories because his behavior had "badly damaged German prestige" and he was "not suited for a responsible assignment in the east."[92]

Once incarcerated in the labor camps of Starachowice, the camp council shifted the focus of bribery from Becker and Schwertner to Kurt Otto Baumgarten, a division manager in charge of grenade production in the munitions factory since 1941. With the dismissal of Althoff, Baumgarten became chief of factory security, and with the dismissal of Kolditz, the commandant of the Jewish labor camps as well. Baumgarten himself claimed credit for only the Kolditz dismissal, but a number of survivors also credited him with some role in the dismissal of Althoff.[93]

A member of the Nazi Party since 1932 and the SS since 1933, Baumgarten was easily remembered by survivors for his costume – leather Bavarian shorts and suspenders and a Tyrolean hat. But survivor judgments of Baumgarten were very mixed. Several extravagantly praised him for allegedly writing a letter that saved the Starachowice Jews from the gas chambers at Birkenau.[94] Others granted that the period of Baumgarten's control was the "most peaceful," and that in comparison to his predecessors Baumgarten was "not so bad" and "not so feared."[95] Still others, however, did not forget the killings that occurred under his regime. As one survivor noted, Baumgarten never shot anyone personally but nonetheless caused numerous shootings.[96]

In his own postwar testimony, Baumgarten took credit for dismissing Kolditz, cutting out middlemen who were siphoning off food allocated to the camp, building a camp bakery, permitting Jewish leaders to live in private rooms with their wives and to keep their children, and finally allowing them occasionally to leave camp and visit the town. He claimed that he had done this both for humanitarian reasons and to

92 Becker, pp. 1090–1 (Leopold Rudolf Schwertner). NA/BDC microfilms: SS-enlisted men file.

93 Becker, pp. 65 (Rywka G.), 84 (Mendel M.), 406 (Fred B.), 592 (Mina B.).

94 Becker, p. 462 (Annie G.). FA, T-955 (Gutta T.). The latter even claimed that Baumgarten had been an English spy, occasionally treating the prisoners roughly to avoid suspicion!

95 Becker: p. 518 (Ruth W.); p. 753 (Leonia F.); p. 771 (Arnold F.); p. 814 (Alter W.); p. 873 (Chaim H.); and p. 1396 (Salomon B.).

96 Becker, p. 592 (Maurice W.).

enhance production.[97] What he did not admit, of course, was that he received large payments from the camp council.[98]

How did the Jews, forced to surrender their remaining valuables upon entry into the camp, finance large-scale bribery? This brings us to the complex nature of the underground economy in Starachowice. Within Starachowice, as in other camps, virtually every prisoner sought to "organize" materials from the work site that could be made into marketable goods. In Starachowice, such goods were then smuggled out of camp when the more well disposed of the Ukrainian guards were on duty and sold to Poles on the black market.[99] Much of this income then flowed to the camp council through the purchase of both extra food and lighter work assignments.[100] Within the camp the Germans had collected a group of skilled craftsmen, such as tailors and shoemakers, to work for them.[101] Another layer of the underground economy was based on the production of these same craftsmen for the camp council, which sold these goods to the Polish workers at the factory or smuggled them to the outside by bribing susceptible Ukrainian guards. For instance, when a shipment of 2,000 pairs of shoes was sent from Majdanek to Starachowice, the camp council distributed only 100 pairs to the ill-shod prisoners. The rest were cut up, and the craftsmen used the materials to make tops for wooden-soled shoes that were sold on the black market to Poles.[102] Some money was smuggled in from outside organizations.[103] But the most unusual feature of the Starachowice underground economy owed to the fact that many of the prisoners were still in their hometown. Some of the wealthier and more assimilated Starachowice fam-

97 Becker, pp. 447–8 (Baumgarten).

98 Becker, pp. 868 (Anne W., Wilzcek's daughter-in-law) and 873–4 (Adrian W., Wilczek's son). YVA, M-49/1172 (anonymous). According to Wilczek's son, Baumgarten's chief of the Ukrainian camp guard, Willi Schroth, was also a well-paid and "willing tool" ("*Willfähriges Werkzeug*") of the camp council.

99 FA, T-955 (Gutta T.).

100 YVA, M-49E/1669 (Leon Wolf) and M-49/1172 (anonymous). Conversely, those in disfavor with the *Lagerrat* were assigned the worst jobs as punishment. FA, T-1884 (Regina N., whose husband turned down the offer to be a policeman and was promptly sent to a terrible job in a different camp).

101 Becker, p. 492 (Ralph C.).

102 YVA, M-49/1172 (anonymous). FA, T-955 (Gutta T.) and T-1884 (Regina N.).

103 For funds received from Dr. Weichert's Jewish-Self Help in Cracow, see: YVA, O-2/319 (Maurice W.) and O-3/624 (Nathan S.).

ilies, with whom Wilzcek was allied, had both business and social contacts in the Polish community. On some occasions they were permitted to go into town to conduct business and retrieve valuables; on other occasions money was smuggled into the camp from their local sources.[104]

In the case of bribing first Schwertner and then Baumgarten, the entire camp received some benefits, such as the unusually high percentage of "work Jews" exempted from the ghetto-clearing deportation, the dismissal of Kolditz, and minor improvements in the Majowka camp. But clearly the members of the camp council and police were the major beneficiaries, both in the privileges they enjoyed and the backing they received against their rivals. As one sharp critic noted, there was no appeal beyond the camp council to Baumgarten because he was in the council's pocket.[105]

Relatively few survivors chose to give details about the tensions and conflict between the camp elite and the other prisoners, which is probably a reflection of what they deemed suitable for public rather than private memory. Many survivors, however, did allude to one key event, namely the fate of Wilczek and his coterie. Virtually none of the camp elite, riding in the first car, survived the terrible transport to Auschwitz. For four survivors, the explanation for the death of Wilczek, Rubenstein, and other members of the camp elite was simply the suffocation and heat prostration that claimed over 100 lives. [106] Two witnesses noted that cyanide was available in the first car and that at least some had taken it.[107] But a total of 10 survivors, none of them actual witnesses, testified that they had heard from others that Wilczek and many others of the camp elite had been killed on the way to Auschwitz by fellow prisoners who took revenge on them.[108]

[104] FA, T-955 (Gutta T.). YVA, O-3/9394 (Ruben Z.).

[105] YVA, M-49/1172 (anonymous).

[106] Becker, pp. 416 (Matys F.), 430 (Hersz T.), 742 (Mendel T.), and 833 (Ben L.). However, three of these four survivors also thought that at the loading, German police chief Becker had intentionally sought out the camp elite and placed them in the especially overcrowded first car. One survivor surmised that Becker wanted to bring about the death of those "who had given him gifts" and were thus potential witnesses to his corruption.

[107] Becker, p. 767 (Howard S. C.). FA, T-955 (Gutta T.).

[108] Becker, pp. 511 (Dina T.), 518 (Ruth W.), 655–6. (Meyer G.), 728 (Bella W.), 787 (Max N.), 819 (Fay G.), and 827 (Ben Z.). FA, T-1889 (Regina N.). YVA, M-49/1172 (anonymous). Statement of Emil N. to author, November 1, 1998.

Survivor testimony from all three periods – the late 1940s, the 1960s, and the 1980s – mentions the fate of the camp elite, and this is one area in which a change in attitude over time can be detected. In the very earliest testimony of August 1945, one survivor displayed vehement satisfaction over the fate of the camp elite, exclaiming that "they were punished with the death they deserved."[109] In the very last testimony to mention Wilczek, the videoptaped survivor briefly hesitated to broach the topic and then sighed that this, too, was a part of history and should be told.[110]

If survivor testimony provides insight into the internal governance, underground economy, and tensions between prisoners within the camp, it also provides the major source of evidence concerning the German perpetrators. Indeed, one unusual characteristic of the testimonies concerning Starachowice is that 116 of 134, or 87 percent of them, were gathered by German judicial investigators seeking evidence about specific crimes and specific suspected perpetrators. Prosecution for murder under the German criminal code of 1940 required evidence concerning the "malicious" or "cruel" manner in which the crimes were committed, or the "base motives" behind the crimes. Thus, far more than unguided or free-form survivor testimonies, this particular body of evidence offers a *concentrated focus from the perspective of the victims* on both the behavior as well as the attitudes and mind-set of the German personnel in Starachowice. For the prisoners, the ability to discern differences between German perpetrators was one key to survival.

Felicja Karay, herself both a survivor and historian of the nearby Jewish labor camp of Skarzysko – Kamienna, concluded that for the perpetrators in that camp, the "primary aim was thievery and not extermination as such, so that their methods took on the nature of business negotiations."[111] Although this element of "business negotiations" was certainly not lacking in Starachowice, the collective testimony points to a somewhat wider spectrum among the perpetrators. Aside from the many nondescript Germans whose behavior did not imprint itself on survivor memory in any particular way, three rough categories of Germans emerge. The first category was composed of what the survivors referred to as the "dangerous" ("*gefährlich*")

[109] YVA, ML-49/1172 (anonymous).
[110] FA, T-1889 (Regina N.).
[111] Karay, *Death Comes in Yellow*, p. 97.

Germans, such as Althoff, who killed often and with personal zeal and obvious pleasure. The second category was composed of "corrupt" ("*bestechend*") Germans, susceptible to bribes, like Schwertner and Baumgarten, with whom business-like deals could be made. The third category, certainly the rarest, were the "decent" ("*anständig*") Germans, with whom Jewish prisoners found refuge and protection.

Most remarkable in this regard was a man named Fiedler, who had taken over the Jewish-owned lumbermill that produced munitions crates. On the day of deportation, his deputy in the marketplace rescued not only his current employees but selected other Jews as well, bringing the total to some 150. Over the 21 months of the lumbermill camp's existence, 8 prisoners were killed there, but none of these killings were attributable to Fiedler. The German policemen who escorted the Jews to the lumbermill killed four prisoners – two for trying to conceal money, as well as a young mother and the newborn child she had unsuccessfully tried to bring into the camp hidden in her pack.[112] Then in January 1943, when Fiedler was on leave, his malevolent secretary Fräulein Lutz reported the outbreak of typhus, and 4 sick prisoners were immediately shot.[113] Between January 1943 and July 1944, there were no further killings at the lumber mill camp.

The survivors uniformly condemned Fräulein Lutz as "very dangerous."[114] In contrast, Fiedler, who apparently shared his secretary's bed[115] but not her attitude toward Jews, was held in high regard.[116] He was deemed "exceptionally decent" ("*hochanständig*")[117] and a "pacifist" incapable of killing.[118] Reportedly, he provided his workers with flour for unleavened bread at Passover.[119] The workers at the lumbermill were not only safer but also much better fed and clothed than in

[112] Becker, pp. 708 (Lea G.), 799 (Abraham R.), 945 (Avraham S.), 1185 and 1426–28 (Naftula K.), 1196 (Helena W.), 1393a (Hil K.), 1430–1 (Rozia L.).

[113] Becker, pp. 781 (Rosa H.), 800 (Avraham R.), 810–11 (Helen W.), 881 and 1270–1 (Morris Z.), 887–8 (Frymeta M.), 1314 (Gutta W.), 1361 (Chaim A.), and 1427 (Naftula K.).

[114] Becker, p. 904 (Mordka M.).

[115] Becker, p. 1271 (Morris Z.).

[116] Becker, pp. 781–2 (Rosa H.), 804 (Syma R.), 810–11, (Helen W.), 887 (Frymeta M.), and 904 (Morka M.). Fiedler's only partial detractor claimed that he took the prisoners' money and butter and sugar rations but kept them relatively well fed and well dressed and killed no one. Becker, pp. 799–800 (Avraham R.).

[117] Becker, p. 996 (Nathan G.).

[118] Becker, p. 849 (Ruth R.).

[119] Becker, pp. 996 (Nathan G.d) and 1266 (Morris Z.).

Strelnica and Majowka. Indeed, the lumbermill camp under Fiedler was such a sanctuary for Jews, in comparison to not only the other Starachowice camps but the outside as well, that it had no guards.[120] There was in fact no place to go to that was safer. Prisoners not only did not attempt to escape but they even paid to get themselves or their relatives transferred there.[121] Above all, Fiedler assured the prisoners that nothing would happen to them as long as he was there. When he left, they could leave, too, he noted in open reference to the lack of guards. True to his word, he left a half hour before the police arrived to evacuate the Starachowice Jews to Auschwitz–Birkenau.[122]

In survivor memories, the Starachowice camps stood apart from other camps by virtue of their excessive filth and ubiquitous lice. Auschwitz in comparison was clean! These camps were also unusual for the conjuncture of fortuitous factors that led to a relatively large body of survivor testimony. I know of no other Nazi camps, aside from Oskar Schindler's factory camp in Cracow, for which the historian has access to testimony by more than 7 percent of all Jews who were interned there. Unlike Schindler's camp, however, there is no reason to believe that many of the insights gathered from the collected Starachowice testimonies do not reflect conditions typical of other Jewish labor camps in western Poland: a mortality pattern that declined between 1942 and 1944; the existence of an underground camp economy; the Germans' cynical and manipulative use of privileged prisoners to facilitate control of the camp; the resultant internal tensions between prisoners and revenge taking; and the rough division of the Germans into the dangerous, the corrupt, and the all too few decent. The density of Starachowice testimony gives added weight and confirmation to other, more fragmented survivor testimony to the same effect.

Ironically, the very density of Starachowice testimony did not help the German judicial investigators who collected the bulk of it. The worst of the perpetrators, Willi Althoff, lived under a false name until his death in 1964, and Kolditz died before he came to trial. Baumgarten and Schwertner were not indicted because there was insufficient evidence

[120] Becker, pp. 810 (Helen W.) and 1271 (Morris Z.). YVA, O-3/2860 (Chava F.) and M-1E. 2469 (Josef K.).

[121] YVA, M-49/1172 (anonymous); pp. 800 (Avraham R.) and 880–1, 1271 (Morris Z.).

[122] YVA, M-1E.2469 (Josef K.). FA, T-1682 (Mania K.).

that they had personally killed. In the case of Becker and other defendants accused of individual killings, the large number of witnesses virtually guaranteed that for every specific crime investigated, there were conflicting memories about the individual perpetrators from which each defense counsel could successfully plead reasonable doubt concerning the guilt of his particular client. After years of investigation and numerous trials, exactly one Starachowice guard – Willi Schroth – was convicted for exactly one murder. But if the collective testimony of the Starachowice survivors did not achieve justice, it can still serve history.

5

GERMAN KILLERS

Orders from Above, Initiative from Below, and the Scope of Local Autonomy – The Case of Brest–Litovsk

Both the Nürnberg Trial prosecutors, who sought to convict so-called criminal organizations as well as the major Nazi leaders, and the pleas of the defendants, which invariably cited binding orders, created an image of Hitler's dictatorial "SS state" as the engine driving the Final Solution from above. One of the great contributions of Raul Hilberg's magisterial work, first published in 1961, was to portray a much more extensive "machinery of destruction" that "was structurally no different from organized German society as a whole." Indeed, "the machinery of destruction *was* the organized community in one of its specialized roles."[1] Moreover, the cadres of bureaucrats that staffed this machinery of destruction were not merely passive recipients of orders from above. Inspired by a Faustian sense of *Erlebnis,* the intoxicating experience of making history, on the one hand and armed with a series of rationalizations and language rules on the other hand, the bureaucratic perpetrators were innovators and problem solvers. With "uncanny pathfinding ability," he concluded, they "found the shortest road to the final goal."[2]

In the revised edition Hilberg's work in 1985, the far-flung components of Hilberg's machinery of destruction became even more autonomous and the decision-making role of Hitler and the top leadership less central. Hilberg was clearly more concerned with how the system worked at the local level than with the chronology of decision making and policy evolution at the top. Over time, he argued, a formal

[1] Raul Hilberg, *The Destruction of the European Jews,* rev. ed. (New York, 1985), p. 994.
[2] Ibid., p. 9.

structure of public laws and written regulations dissolved into an increasingly opaque network of secret directives, vague authorizations, oral communications, and "basic understandings of officials resulting in decisions not requiring orders or explanations." In such a shapeless regime, Hilberg concluded:

> A middle-ranking bureaucrat, no less than his highest superior, was aware of currents and possibilities. In small ways as well as large, he recognized what was ripe for the time. More often it was he who initiated action. . . . In the final analysis, the destruction of the Jews was not so much a product of laws and commands as it was a matter of shared comprehension, of consonance and synchronization.[3]

Even as Hilberg was producing his revised edition, the intentionalist/functionalist controversy was at its height and many scholars were focusing on precisely that which Hilberg was somewhat deemphasizing, namely the chronology of decision making and policy evolution at the center, and the role of Hitler and his ideology therein – an important topic in my opinion to which I have devoted the first two lectures of this series. But now many young scholars – particularly in Germany – are producing important new regional studies, based upon extensive use of the newly opened archives in eastern Europe and hitherto neglected German court records, that return to Hilberg's themes: the importance of local initiatives, and the unspoken consensus among and broad participation of the entire occupation apparatus in the killing process. To the above they have added an emphasis on a striking variation from region to region that seems to diminish the centrality of policies uniformly imposed by orders from above.[4]

3 Ibid., pp. 54–55, 995–8.

4 For example: Christian Gerlach, *Krieg, Ernährung, Völkermord* (Hamburg, 1998) and "Deutsche Wirtschaftsinteressen, Besatzungpolitik und der Mord an den Juden in Weissrussland, 1941–1943," *Nationalsozialistische Vernichtungspolitik 1939–1945: Neue Forschungen und Kontroversen,* ed. by Ulrich Herbert (Frankfurt, 1998), pp. 263–291; Christoph Dieckmann, "Der Krieg und die Ermordung der litauischen Juden," *Nationalsozialistische Vernichtungspolitik,* pp. 292–329; Thomas Sandkühler, *"Endlösung" in Galizien: Der Judenmord in Ostpolen und die Rettungsinitiativen von Berthold Beitz, 1941–1944* (Bonn, 1996); Dieter Pohl, *Von der "Judenpolitik" zum Judenmord: Der Distrikt Lublin des Generalgouvernements 1939–1944* (Frankfurt/M., 1993); and *Nationalsozialistische Judenverfolgung in Ostgalizien 1941–1944* (Munich, 1996).

These regional studies are making a major contribution to Holocaust scholarship, in both their detailed empirical research and insightful interpretations. But I would offer a word of caution. Local initiatives were indeed important, but so were exhortations, instigations, and explicit orders from above. Consensus among a plethora of local German occupation authorities – the SS, civil administration, the Wehrmacht, and economic managers – on the killing of Jews was often present, but so was discord among rival German agencies and conflict between competing German priorities. In the end, however important local factors were for local variations in carrying out the Final Solution, the policies of the Nazi regime set not only the goals that local German authorities were expected to pursue but also the parameters within which they were free to operate. And in the end, one way or another, the Jews were murdered. One case in which we can explore the interaction of local initiative and orders from above, as well as the scope of local autonomy and its limits, is Brest–Litovsk, a city situated immediately across the 1939 demarcation line from German-occupied Poland at the crossroads of Polish, Byelorussian, and Ukrainian populations with a plurality of Jews.

The destruction of the Jews of Brest went through three phases. Brest was the site of some of the earliest and largest massacres in the first 2 months of Operation Barbarossa, in which 15 percent of the population of Brest, disproportionately Jews, were murdered outright. This was followed by a 13 and one-half-month period of harsh deprivation and repression but relative stability, in the course of which over 40 percent of the Jewish population became employed in German economic projects. Then on October 15–16, 1942, with terrible suddenness, the entire Jewish population, including *all* workers, was murdered.

Brest was attacked and occupied on the opening days of the war, and Einsatzkommando 7b briefly carried out unspecified "security police measures" in the city on June 26–27 before departing on June 28.[5] However, the first massacre of Brest Jews was perpetrated not by the notorious Einsatzgruppen but rather by Police Battalion 307 with Wehrmacht support, in mid-July, on the orders of Himmler's chief of

[5] Einsatzgruppe B Tätigkeitsbericht 23.6–13.7.41, printed in: *Die Einsatzgruppen in der besetzten Sowjetunion 1941/42: Die Tätigkeitsberichte des Chefs der Sicherheitspolizei und des SD,* ed. by Peter Klein (Berlin 1997), p. 337.

Order Police, Kurt Daluege, and the commander of the Rear Army Area Center, General Max von Schenckendorff.

Police Battalion 307 was composed of rank-and-file who had applied for a professional career in the police in 1939 and early 1940. Their average age was approximately 30 years old, and they had trained extensively as a unit in Lübeck for 6 months before being sent to the General Government in October 1940. Training there had continued (in Biala Podlaska) in the Lublin district across the Bug River from Brest–Litovsk until Operation Barbarossa.[6] In contrast to Reserve Police Battalion 101, about which I have written previously, these were not randomly selected "ordinary" Germans, therefore, but a well-trained group of young men who were self-selected for a police career in a police state.

Police Battalion 307, under the command of Major Stahr, arrived in Brest on July 2, and 2 days later, Major General Stubenrauch established himself as local military commandant (Feldkommandantur 184).[7] On July 5, both Stahr and Stubenrauch sent alarming reports concerning the very insecure situation in and around Brest. There were many Soviet soldiers still roaming the area, the citadel and city still had to be cleared of weapons and ammunition, and both warehouses and some 500–600 train cars in the railyard were loaded with valuable goods that needed to be guarded. Extra manpower was desperately needed.[8] The initial reaction of Security Division 221, the nearest military unit, was that the military commandant would simply have to make do with the manpower he had, though it advised using Jewish

[6] I have based this characterization of Police Battalion 307 on the statistics and testimonies of 23 former members, as found in: ZStL, 204 AR-Z 82/61 (hereafter cited as PB 307). I have not included in the calculations the three more elderly policemen who held administrative positions on the battalion staff. Unlike Reserve Police Battalion 101, this was not a battalion of poorly trained, middle-aged, conscripted reservists. However, some reserve battalions, like Reserve Police Battalion 45 in the Ukraine, were used in the opening months of Operation Barbarossa to carry out mass killings. On the composition of the police battalions, see also Peter Longerich, *Politik der Vernichtung: Eine Gesamtdarstellung der nationalsozialistischen Judenverfolgung* (Munich, 1998), pp. 305–310.

[7] National Archives (hereafter cited as NA) Microfilm, Series T-315/roll 1667/frame 11, Sicherheitsdivision 221, report of Ib to Ia, 4.7.41; and T-315/1667/43, Befehlshaber des rückwärtigen Heeres-Gebietes 102, Korpsbefehl Nr. 22, 2.7.41, signed by chief of staff Rübesamen.

[8] T-315/1667/358-9 and 374-6: Stahr report, 5.7.41, and Stubenrauch report, 5.7.41.

labor to consolidate the valuable materials found strewn about the city into a few more easily guarded central storage areas.[9]

But Schenckendorff and his chief of staff Rübesamen of Rear Army Area Center thought otherwise. On July 9 they ordered the motorized portion of Infantry Division 162 to Brest, with a quite specific task. "Pure guard duty is not the task of this unit, rather it is advisable to employ it for special actions ["*besondere Aktionen*"]. There are thus no objections, for example, if the unit of Infantry Division 162 is employed for cordon measures in police search actions[10] ("*Durchsuchungsaktionen der Pol*"). At the same time, Schenckendorff informed the Army High Command (OKH) that with the help of the Order Police and Security Service (SD) at his disposal, a systematic search of the large cities in his jurisdiction, especially Bialystok and Brest, was now underway.[11]

The general nature of what these military documents euphemistically referred to as "search actions" is revealed in one report of the head of Economic Inspectorate Center, General Wiegand, who wrote candidly on July 22: "In large numbers that go into the thousands, Jews suspected of sedition have been shot"[12] ("*in grossen Massen, die in die mehrere Tausend gehen, sind der Aufwieglung verdächtigte Juden erschossen worden*"). How exactly these events played out in Brest is illuminated by the better-documented course of events in nearby Bialystok.[13] Following the first search action in Bialystok on July 8, Heinrich Himmler and HSSPF Erich von dem Bach-Zelewski arrived and met with General von Schenckendorff and his staff, Colonel Max Montua of Police Regiment Center, and the commanders of Police Battalions 322 and 316. The following day, July 9, Himmler's chief of

[9] T-315/1667/314, SD 221 to FK 184, 8.7.41.

[10] T-315/1667/357, Befehlshaber des rückwärtigen Heeres-Gebietes Mitte (hereafter BdrHGM), to Sicherheitsdiv. 221, 9.7.41, signed Rübesamen.

[11] T-501/1/497-9, BdrHGM to OKH, 9.7.41.

[12] T-501/2/319-27, report of Wirtschaftsinspekteur Weigand, 22.7.41.

[13] This is due above all to the survival of the war diary of Police Battalion 322 in the Prague Military Archives. See in particular: Andrej Angrick, Martina Voigt, Silke Ammerschubert, and Peter Klein, "'Da hätte man schon ein Tagebuch führen müssen': Das Polizeibattalion 322 und die Judenmorde im Bereich der Heeresgruppe Mitte während des Sommers und Herbstes 1941," *Die Normalität des Verbrechens: Bilanz und Perspektiven der Forschung zu den nationalsozialistischen Gewaltverbrechen,* ed. by Helge Grabitz, Klaus Bästlein, and Johannes Tuchel (Berlin, 1994), pp. 325–85; Konrad Kwiet, "From the Diary of a Killing Unit," *Why Germany? National Socialist Anti-Semitism and the European Context,* ed. by John Milfull (Providence, 1993), pp. 75–93.

the Order Police, Kurt Daluege, arrived as well and addressed the police regiment. They could be "proud" of their role in the "final" destruction of Bolshevism, he proclaimed. Not coincidentally, starting on the night of July 8, the assembled police in Bialystok began shooting thousands of Bialystok Jews. This was clearly an action specifically instigated by Himmler and his close associates Daluege and Bach-Zelewski in conjunction with the military commander Schenkendorff. It can also not be coincidental that it was just one day after his meeting with Himmler on July 8 that Schenckendorff dispatched parts of Infantry Division 162 to assist Police Battalion 307 – also part of Montua's Police Regiment Center – in a "special action" in Brest.

Immediately following his speech to Police Battalions 316 and 322 in Bialystok, Kurt Daluege must have traveled to Brest–Litovsk. There he gave a speech to the men of Police Battalion 307 on their tasks in the east, including the Jewish Question, and how they must fulfill their soldierly duties.[14] Immediately thereafter, a so-called retaliation action (*Vergeltungsaktion*) was ordered against the Jews of Brest, allegedly for attacks on German soldiers. The action lasted several days, beginning before and ending after Sunday, July 13.[15] Each morning male Jews between 16 and 60 years old were rounded up by the policemen, who surrounded different sections of the Jewish quarter in Brest in succession. With intended deception, the assembled Jews were explicitly told that they were being sent to Germany for work.[16] Instead, they were loaded onto trucks and driven south of Brest to a sandy region, where the first Jews sent out had been forced to dig large open pit graves.[17]

In this initial killing action by Police Battalion 307, the form of a court-martial firing squad was preserved. The shooters stood in

[14] PB 307, testimony of members of Police Battalion 307. On the contents of Daluege's speech: Max K., I, p. 188, and III, p. 471; Kuno K., I, p. 194, and III, p. 521. On his presence in Brest immediately preceding the shooting of Jews: Friedrich S., I, p. 130; Heinrich S., I, p. 135; Wilhelm E., I, p. 170; Julius T., I, p. 227; Günther B., II, p. 246; Hans M., II, p. 286. That Daluege was in Brest after Bialystok is indicated by the testimony of Max K. that Kaiser was involved in checking security arrangements for Daluege's trip from Brest eastward toward Slusk.

[15] PB 307: Hans S., I, p. 121, and Hans M., II, p. 286; both remember distinctly that the shooting continued through a Sunday

[16] PB 307: Friedrich N., I, p. 18; Wilhelm E., I, p. 169; Heinz H., I, pp. 179–80; Kuno K., I, p. 194, and III, p. 524; Heinrich M., II, p. 227; Rudolf O., III, pp. 554–6.

[17] PB 307: Johanness E., I, p. 79; Paul H., I, p. 93; Erich S., I, p. 115, and III, p. 511; Heinz H., I, p. 179; Walter J., I, p. 185, and III, p. 567.

double, staggered rows, with those in the first row assigned to shoot at the head and those in the second at the body. Driven by blows, the Jews were forced to stand at the edge of the pit and face the shooters. When struck by two bullets from a firing squad only 5 to 10 meters away, the bodies of the victims usually tumbled into the pit.[18] Some women, who refused to be separated from their husbands, were shot at their husbands' sides in the same way.[19]

On the first night of the mass killings, the shooters were rewarded with an unusual treat of strawberries and cream.[20] Thereafter they got a more mundane meal of smoked ham, canned milk, bread and butter, and Schnaps.[21] A small number of policemen testified that volunteers had been requested for the firing squads.[22] Other witnesses suggested that only the toughest and strongest had been selected for this duty.[23] No one could remember a single policeman in the firing squads who refused to shoot, though one claimed that he had informed his noncommissioned officer beforehand that he would not be able to shoot. Thereafter he had not been selected for a firing squad and allegedly was scorned by his commanding officer as "weak."[24] Some of the men in the firing squads got sick and had to be replaced,[25] but only one case of a nervous breakdown was reported.[26]

18 PB 307: Johannes E., I, p. 79; Heinrich H., I, p. 183; Max K., I, p. 187, and III, p. 475; Kurt K., I, 209, and III, p. 537; Erich S., III, p. 528; Rudolph O., III, p. 554; Walter J., III, pp. 569–71. Only one witness testified to a different procedure, in which the Jews were forced to lie facedown with their head over the edge of the pit and the German police, using fixed bayonets as aiming guides, gave "neck shots." Heinrich M., II, p. 227; and his testimony cited in Paul Kohl, *Der Krieg der deutschen Wehrmacht und der Polizei 1941–1944: Sowjetische Überlebende berichten* (Frankfurt/M. 1995), pp. 224–5.

19 PB 307: Walter J., I, p. 185, and III, pp. 568, 571; Rudolph O., III, p. 556; Johannes M., III, p. 619.

20 PB 307: Kuno K., I, p. 191, and III, p. 526.

21 PB 307: Walter J., III, pp. 568 and 574; Rudolf O., III, p. 554; and Friedrich S., I, p. 130.

22 PB 307: Friedrich N., I, p. 18; Paul H., I, p. 93; Günther B., II, p. 247.

23 PB 307: Hans S., I, p. 123; Rudolph O., II, p. 288.

24 PB 307: Erich S., III, p. 529. Kuno K., II, p. 195, confirmed that he had learned on the evening of the first day of shootings that policemen could get out of shooting.

25 PB 307: Max K., I, p. 189; Hans S., I, p. 123.

26 PB 307: Otto M., II, p. 279. In a recent, as yet unpublished study, Yehuda Baver relates the story of a survivor that two naive young Jewish men, not wanting to be left behind, raced after a departing truck full of Jewish men and were warned by Germans who shouted: "Go back, go back!"

The mood in the battalion during and after the killings was characterized in different ways by different witnesses. Some reported that the men did not want to talk about the mass shootings and took refuge in silence.[27] Several others said the mood was sufficiently depressed that Major Stahr gave a speech, reaffirming that they had acted on orders and "that the entire action against the Jews had to be"[28] ("*dass die ganze Aktion gegen die Juden sein musste*"). The spectrum of emotions was most fully described by one policeman as follows:

> When I am asked about the mood of these comrades, then I must say that actually I observed nothing special, that is the mood was not especially bad. Many said that they never again wanted to experience something like that in their entire lives, while in contrast others were content with saying an order is an order. With that the matter was settled for them.[29]

On July 17, Police Battalion 307 moved on from Brest to Baranovichi, and the following day Brest was shifted from the jurisdiction of Rear Army Area Center to the military commander in the General Government.[30] The new military commandant was Lieutenant General Walter von Unruh, previously commandant in Warsaw. He set about confiscating Jewish property, forming the Jews into large work parties, and – as he put it – "putting an end to Jewish swindling" ("*den Juden das Handwerk des Gaunerns zu legen*"). He also strove to maintain close cooperation with what he called the "commissar for security"[31] ("*Sicherheitskommissar*").

Who was this so-called commissar for security? Before the invasion, the commander of Einsatzgruppe B, Artur Nebe, had recommended that reinforcements of Security Police from Warsaw and Lublin fill in behind the advancing Einsatzgruppen to continue pacification measures, and Heydrich approved such "cleansing actions" ("*Reiniungsaktionen*") in the border regions of the newly occupied territories on July 4. Thus, 15

[27] PB 307: Erich S., I, p. 116; Kurt K., III, p. 340.

[28] PB 307: Johannes K., II, p. 516, and III, p. 261; Otto M., II, p. 279.

[29] PB 307: Walter J., III, 568.

[30] T-501/1/326, Tagesmeldung, 18.7.41, and T-501/2/167-9, BdrHGM, Korpsbefehl Nr. 30, 17.7.41.

[31] T-501/214/622-23, Kommandantur Brest, Schlussbericht über Tätigkeit in Brest–Litowsk, 1.9.41

Security Police from Lublin under SS-Untersturmführer Schmidt were assigned to Brest.[32]

What was the total impact on Brest of Police Battalion 307 and the subsequent Security Police units from Lublin? The Einsatzgruppen report of July 24 credited the "police" with killing 4,435 people, more than 4,000 of them Jews, in Brest.[33] Then from late July until early September, the Security Police unit was credited with "liquidating" 4,403 people in Brest (though without any indication as to how may were Jews, much less a breakdown between men, women, and children).[34] If the details of the Security Police killings as opposed to those of Police Battalion 307 have never been clarified, the cumulative magnitude of 2 months of German occupation is clear. In 1931 Brest had a population of some 50,000, of which 43 percent (21,400) were Jews.[35] In September 1939, the population of Brest had risen to 59,600. In November 1941, after Brest had been placed in the Reichskommissariat Ukraine, the newly installed civil administration reported the population of the city as slightly under 50,000, of whom only 17,500 were Jews.[36] In a brief period of several months, therefore, some 15 percent of the city's population (at least 8,838 by German count) had been murdered outright, and among the various ethnic groups, including Poles, Ukrainians, and White Russians, the Jews had suffered the most severe decimation.

Brest had the unfortunate distinction of drawing the malevolent attention of an unusually high number of Nazi leaders, who contributed to the Nazi terror in the summer of 1941. Daluege's visit to Brest, directly following his meeting with Himmler in Biaylstok, triggered the mass killing by Police Battalion 307.[37] Then at the suggestion of Nebe and approval by Heydrich, an Einsatzkommando of Lublin Security Police quickly followed with a sustained campaign of

[32] Einsatzgruppe B activity report, 23.6-13.7.41, and Heydrich's Einsatzbefehl Nr. 6, 4.7.41, printed in: Klein, *Die Einsatzgruppen in der besetzten Sowjetunion 1941/42*, pp. 329, and 376–7.

[33] Ereignismeldung Nr. 32, 14.7.41.

[34] Ereignismeldungen Nr. 43, 5.8.41 (1,280 victims); Nr. 47, 9.8.41 (510 victims); Nr. 56, 18.8.41 (1,296); Nr. 66, 28.8.41 (769), and Nr. 78, 9.9.41 (548).

[35] Hilberg, *The Destruction of the European Jews*, p. 292.

[36] For the 1939 and November 1941 estimates, see: Bundesarchiv Berlin, R 94/6, report of Stadtkommissar Burat, 21.11.41.

[37] As Richard Breitman has shown in his recent book, *Official Secrets* (New York, 1998) this was no exception. Daluege's itinerary throughout the summer closely coincided with ensuing police battalion massacres.

mass killing there that lasted until the end of the summer. At this point one can hardly speak of local initiatives and local factors. Brest was at the crucible of killing actions explicitly ordered by the highest authorities of the Third Reich to implement their vision of a "war of destruction," though not yet the Final Solution.

But if the historian looks back one step from events in Brest itself, the importance of local initiative and improvisation reemerges. From where did Himmler, Daluege, and Heydrich derive the notion of using police battalions and ad hoc units of Security Police from the General Government as a crucial manpower supplement to the Einsatzgruppen for mass killing that proved so fatal in Brest and then elsewhere? Before Himmler and Daluege had ordered the police battalion killings in Bialystok and Brest in mid-July, Police Battalion 309 had already carried out a deadly pogrom upon its entrance into Bialystok on June 27. And the acquiescence of the military had been demonstrated graphically. When Jewish emissaries begged General Pflugbeil of Security Division 221 to intervene, he turned his back while a member of Police Battalion 309 unzipped his trousers and urinated on the kneeling Jews.[38] Just 11 days later, Himmler had his meeting with General Schenckendorff and his Order Police chief, Kurt Daluege, that resulted in the police battalion massacres in Bialystok and Brest of mid-July.

And further north, the Tilsit Security Police had crossed the border and executed over 500 male Jews between June 24 and 27 on the pretext that Jews had aided the Red Army resistance and then killed and mutilated wounded German soldiers. Firing squads were initially provided by the Schutzpolizei or urban units of the Order Police. And both the army and air force (in the latter case, young recruits still in basic training) provided contingents of shooters when more men were needed for the firing squads. The commander of Einsatzgruppe A, Franz Stahlecker, arrived after the first massacre and "declared himself in basic agreement with the action." And on June 30, Himmler and Heydrich had themselves briefed,

[38] Christopher Browning, *Ordinary Men: Reserve Police Battalion* 101 *and the Final Solution in Poland* (New York, 1992), pp. 11–12. For a contrasting interpretation, that sees the Bialystok pogrom as "the emblematic initial killing operation of a formal genocide" based on an "explicit genocidal order," see: Daniel Jonah Goldhagen, *Hitler's Willing Executioners: Ordinary Germans and the Holocaust* (New York, 1996), pp. 188–91. For the most recent analysis of the June 27 massacres in Biaylstok, see Peter Longerich, *Politik der Vernichtung*, pp. 345–48.

and both "approved unreservedly of the measures" taken by the Tilsit commando.[39] Immediately thereafter, Heydrich issued his order approving Nebe's suggestion to have Security Police from the General Government – that is, units analogous to the Tilsit commando – carry out "cleansing actions" in the border regions farther south as well. It was one of these ad hoc *Einsatzkommandos,* following on the Tilsit model, that continued the summer massacres in Brest.

Thus, in the first week of Operation Barbarossa, Major Max Weis of Police Battalion 309 and Sturmbannführer Hans-Joachim Böhme of the Tilsit commando seemed to have better intuited the vision of the Nazi leadership for a war of destruction than did the commanders of any other of the myriad units invading the Soviet Union. The alacrity with which Himmler, Heydrich, and Daluege seized upon what Konrad Kwiet has called "rehearsals" for mass murder and institutionalized them would indicate that they were eagerly looking for appropriate and feasible models. And Brest was one of the sites where both of these now institutionalized killing methods were first carried out on the basis of orders from above.

As an initial conclusion to the first phase in the destruction of Brest Jewry, therefore, I would suggest that the Final Solution on Soviet territory should not be seen either as the product of some "autonomous conception" in the minds of top Nazi leaders from above or as the product of "spontaneous generation" from below. Rather the killings, as exemplified in Brest, were the product of an interaction between local and central authorities. The Nazi leadership sketched out a vision and issued guidelines for a war of destruction against the Soviet Union. Local authorities interpreted these guidelines in different ways. Himmler, Heydrich, and Daluege seized upon those initiatives and improvisations that best suited their purposes and institutionalized them as policies and methods to be implemented elsewhere.

Let us now turn to the second phase in the destruction of Brest Jewry. In early September 1941 much of the Baltic, Byelorussia, and

[39] Jürgen Matthäus, "Jenseits der Grenze: Die ersten Massenerschiessungen von Juden in Litauen (Juni–August 1941)," *Zeitschrift für Geschichtswissenschaft,* 44/2 (1996), pp. 101–17; Konrad Kwiet, "Rehearsing for Murder: The Beginning of the Final Solution in June 1941," *Holocaust and Genocide Studies,* 12/1 (1998), pp. 3–26. For the key new document for understanding the first Tilsit killings, see: Böhme, Staatspolizeistelle Tilsit, 1.7.41, to Reichssicherheitshauptamt [Reich Security Main Office] (hereafter cited as RHSA), now printed in: Klein, *Die Einsatzgruppen in der besetzten Sowjetunion,* pp. 372–5. See also: Peter Longerich, *Politik der Vernichtung,* pp. 326–31.

the Ukraine passed from the zone of military operations to the civilian administration of Alfred Rosenberg's Reich Ministry of the Occupied Eastern Territories or so-called Ostministerium. Brest was allotted to the Reichskommissariat Ukraine under Erich Koch. Brest became somewhat of a backwater and the fate of Brest Jewry fell increasingly into the hands of newly installed local authorities.

I have argued that in the late summer of 1941, the total and systematic mass murder of Soviet Jews – including specifically women and children – was getting underway, and that by the early autumn of 1941, the Nazi regime envisaged a similar fate for the European Jews, even though it was not yet in a position to implement such a policy systematically and immediately. Nonetheless, the green light was now on, and the killing intensified rapidly in many parts of the Nazi empire. In some cases the intensified killing was the result of direct orders from Berlin, such as Himmler's sending HSSPF Friedrich Jeckeln to destroy the Jews of Riga. In some cases there was interaction between Berlin and local authorities, such as with the preparation of the first death camps at Belzec and Chelmno.

But in many cases, Berlin seemed to play little role, as various local authorities reached consensus to deal with their local problems by murdering their local Jews. In their recent studies on Galicia, Dieter Pohl and Thomas Sandkühler have shown that the fall massacres there were not yet part of an overall plan but the response of local and regional authorities to a housing shortage and a ghettoization edict. Starting in Stanislawow on the notorious "bloody Sunday" of October 12 and continuing into December in Lwow, the Germans carried out large-scale massacres to reduce the Jewish population in many towns in conjunction with ghettoization.[40] In Lithuania and Byelorussia, according to the recent research of Christoph Dieckmann and Christian Gerlach, food shortages played a crucial role for reaching consensus among the SS, military, and civil administration that the killing of Jews was not only ideologically desirable but economically necessary.[41]

[40] Dieter Pohl, *Nationalsozialistische Judenverfolgung in Ostgalizien 1941–44*, pp. 139–151; Thomas Sandkühler, *"Endlösung" in Galizien*, pp. 148–165.

[41] Christoph Dieckmann, "Der Krieg und die Ermordung der litauischen Juden," and Christian Gerlach, "Deutsche Wirstschaftsinteressen, Besatzungspolitik und der Mord an den Juden in Weissrussland, 1941–1943," both in *Nationalsozialistische Vernichtungspolitik*, (Frankfurt/M., 1998) ed. by Ulrich Herbert, pp. 292–329 and pp. 263–91 respectively.

In Serbia and Byelorussia, the Wehrmacht carried out extensive executions of Jews within the framework of antipartisan measures. In Serbia, these killings served to meet the horrendous 100 : 1 reprisal quotas that were increasingly counterproductive to fill by the indiscriminate shooting of Serbs. Again there was a consensus on this policy among the SS, military, and Foreign Office, even if the local head of the military administration, Harald Turner, at least in a private letter though not in official documents, admitted that the already-incarcerated Jews were obviously not the source of partisan resistance.[42] In Byelorussia the military commandant, Major General Gustav Freiherr von Bectholsheim, repeated his shrill exhortations so incessantly in the fall of 1941 to kill Jews as a precondition for pacification that one can only conclude that the connection between Jews and partisans was for him no formulaic pretext or defensive rationalization but an article of ideological true faith.[43] The SS credited the Wehrmacht units under Bechtolsheim with killing 19,000 people, more than half of them Jews, by December 1941.[44] With good reason Jürgen Förster has characterized the cases of Serbia and White Russia as the two "peaks" (*Gipfeln*) of Wehrmacht initiative and complicity in the murder of Jews.[45]

All of these factors – an overcrowded ghetto, a severe food shortage, and partisan activity – were also present in Brest. But in Brest none of these factors was embraced by local authorities to carry out mass killings of Jews, either in the fall of 1941 or for that matter even through most of 1942. If in some areas local authorities could initiate mass murder in the early months of the Final Solution, then in other areas they could also drag their feet even into the year of its most systematic implementation. Who were the local authorities in Brest and

[42] Christopher R. Browning, *Fateful Months: Essays on the Emergence of the Final Solution* (New York, 1985), pp. 39–56; and Walter Manoschek, *"Serbien ist judenfrei." Militärische Besatzungspolitik und Judenvernichtung in Serbien* 1941/42 (Munich, 1994).

[43] For the Bechtolsheim documents: Central State Archives Minsk, 378/1/698: Bechtolsheim reports of 2.10.41, 10.10.41; 16.10.41, 20.10.41, Order Nr. 21, of 10.11.41, Order Nr. 22 of 13.11.41, Order Nr. 24, 24.11.41 and 665/1/1, situation report, 19.10.41, Bundesarchiv-Militärarchiv Freiburg, RH 26-707/2, situation report, 10.11.41, and appendix 4.

[44] Latvian State Historical Archive, 1026-1-3, pp. 251-61, Abt. II, Burchardt memorandum, undated.

[45] Unpublished papers, American Historical Association, Seattle, Washington, January 1997; and German Studies Association, Salt Lake City, Utah, October 1998.

what did they do during this 13 and one-half month period of relative quiescence?

With the transfer of Brest from military to civilian administration, a 38-year-old SA-Standartenführer, Curt Rolle, became the *Gebietskommissar* for the Brest region.[46] The city itself came under the newly-appointed *Stadtkommissar,* Franz Burat, a very heavyset 42-year-old small-town mayor from East Prussia and party member since 1931.[47] In November 1941 a third key figure, 48-year old Friedrich Wilhelm Rohde, arrived. A veteran of World War I, he had joined the party and the SA "brown shirts" in the mid-twenties, made a career in the urban police (Schutzpolizei) in the 1930s, and been taken into the SS in 1939. He was now appointed by Himmler to be the SS and *Polizeistandortführer* in Brest, a somewhat ill-defined position whose occupant was in charge of coordinating joint actions of various SS and police units on the very local level – in effect a miniature HSSPF.[48] In February 1942 a branch office or *Aussenstelle* of the Security Police and Security Service (Sipo-SD) was established under 37-year-old Ernst Berger, a policeman since 1928 and Gestapo official since 1933 but SS and party member only in 1936 and 1937, respectively.[49]

When Burat arrived in Brest, the *Reichskommissar* for the Ukraine, Erich Koch, had just issued an order for ghettoization (along with the establishment of Jewish councils and ghetto police) in the district (*Generalberzirk*) of Volhynia and Podolia in which Brest was located.[50] Initially, Burat moved harshly against the Jewish population. He imposed a 2 million–ruble contribution, cut their rations below that of the non-Jewish population, and ordered that ghettoization be completed by mid-December. He pronounced the Jews to be "an extraordinary burden, especially in terms of food policy" ("*eine ausserordentliche Belastung, hauptsächlich ernährungs-politischer Art*").[51]

[46] Unfortunately, the Berlin Document Center (hereafter cited as BDC) files at the NA contain no material on Curt Rolle. The Germans did not investigate him, as he was transferred from Brest just before the liquidation of the ghetto.

[47] NA, BDC, Zentralkartei. ZStL, II AR 1040/72, p. 8 (testimony of Franz Burat).

[48] NA, BDC, SS officer file and RuSHA file. ZStL, AR-Z 334/59, pp. 1015-16, 1418-19 (Rohde interrogations).

[49] NA, BDC, SS officer file, ZStL, AR-Z 334/59, pp. 95–6 (Berger interrogation, after which he committed suicide in 1960).

[50] Zhitomir Archive, 1151-1-22, RK Ukraine, 5.9.41, to all *Gebietskommissaren* in Podolia and Volhynia.

[51] Bundesarchiv Berlin (hereafter BAB), R 94/6, Stadtkommissar Brest to Generalkommissar, 21.11.41, signed Burat.

More drastic in Brest than the food shortage,[52] however, was the economic standstill. Only two factories in the entire city were functioning, unemployment was high, and there was considerable discontent even among those who had jobs because German regulations had fixed wages so low.[53] Two other problems emerged in Brest in December 1941 that elsewhere were almost invariably – by ideological reflex – identified with the Jews, namely the appearance of both partisans and epidemic. But in Brest the diagnosis of *Gebietskommissar* Curt Rolle was quite different. The appearance of armed "bandits" was due to large numbers of escaped prisoners of war from the camps in the General Government who could now cross the frozen Bug River, he explained. And they brought with them not only weapons but also typhus.[54]

In the first months of 1942, the economic situation in Brest gradually improved. By late January 5 factories were operating; by late March this number had risen to 11.[55] Two trends concerning the ghettoized Jews of Brest became increasingly apparent during this phase of economic recovery. On the one hand, the Jews were fed less and less; on the other, their labor become more and more crucial to the economy.

On February 24, 1942, *Gebietskommissar* Curt Rolle wrote emphatically – in the context of criticizing the counterproductive policy before he arrived of stripping the peasants of all they had – that food shortages were becoming severe and "the Jews, for example, had not received one piece of bread for the last three months."[56] This was only a slight exaggeration. Until November 1, 1941, the Jews at least officially had received the same rations as others. Thereafter, the

[52] The head of the Schutzpolizei, Reserve Lieutenant Preissinger, pronounced on November 26, 1941: "In general the feeding of the population is satisfactory," as the population was still living off potatoes, cabbage, and vegetables they had stored. BAB, R 94/6, Lagebericht, Polizeidienststelle Brest–Litowsk, 26.11.41, signed Preissinger. One month later, Burat concluded: "For the moment, a special discontent due to the lowering of rations can not yet be ascertained." BAB, R 94/6, Der Stadtkommissar Brest–Litowsk, 23.12.41, to Generalkommissar of Volhynia and Podolia, signed Burat. In mid-January 1942 Preissinger still considered the food situation for most of the population to be satisfactory. BAB, R 94/6, Polizeidienststelle Brest, Lagebericht, 12.1.42, signed Preissinger.

[53] BAB, R 94/6, Polizeidienststelle Brest, Lagebericht, 12.1.42, signed Preissinger.

[54] BAB, R 94/7, Lagebericht, Gebietskommissar Brest, Abt. I, 24.12.41, to Generalkommissar.

[55] BAB: R 94/7, Monatsbericht, Gebietskommissar Brest, Abt. I, 24.1.42; R 94/6, Der Stadtkommissar Brest–Litowsk, Abt. I, to GK for Volhynia and Podolia, 25.3.42.

[56] BAB, R 94/7, Monatsbericht, Gebietskommissar Brest, Abt. I, to GK, 24.2.42.

rations of both Jews and non-Jews had been cut, but the former much more severely than the latter. However scant the food supply and terrible the hunger, mass starvation as in Warsaw and Lodz did not set in. The Jewish population in the ghetto, estimated at 17,500 in November 1941, was estimated at 18,000 at the end of February 1942.[57]

If Jewish rations declined, use of Jewish labor increased. Even before ghettoization virtually all the construction projects of the Wehrmacht and civil administration for housing and offices were also using Jewish labor, both skilled and unskilled.[58] In the course of ghettoization, Burat had established city workshops employing skilled Jewish artisans, both to produce consumer goods at a controlled price and to facilitate the training of young artisans from the "Aryan population." Moreover, ghettoization did not end Jewish employment outside the ghetto, as special identification cards were issued to permit travel to work.[59] By early February 1942, over 4,000 such cards had been issued for travel to work at virtually every German agency in Brest.[60]

Even more than Burat, *Gebietskommissar* Rolle emphasized the necessity of using Jewish labor.[61] Because wages were fixed so low by German regulation, there was considerable lack of desire among the rest of the population to work for less than subsistence. As the SS and *Polizeistandortführer* Friedrich Wilhelm Rohde complained, even the women would not clean and wash unless paid in food rather than cash, since there were no consumer goods to buy in any case.[62] Indeed, the demand for Jewish labor was such that by late January it could be met in some cases only by employing women and children.

57 The non-Jewish population was supposed to receive 200 grams of bread per day (down from 250) and 100 grams of meat per week, plus a special allotment of 15 kilos of potatoes per person for the winter. In fact, 82 percent of the potato allotment was provided. In contrast, over the next 3 months, the Jews received no meat or potatoes, and only 180 grams of flour per day per person for bread. BAB, R 94/6, Ernährungsamt Brest–Litowsk, Statistischer Bericht, 28.2.42. In April 1842 the daily ration was reduced to 1,050 grams per week or 150 grams per day of bread per person. United States Holocaust Memorial Museum (hereafter cited as USHMM), 1996.A.169, reel 22 (Brest Archive, M-41/653), Das Stadtkommissariat, Ernährungsamt, Statistischer Bericht, 23.4.42.

58 BAB, R 94/6, Polizeidienststelle Brest–Litowsk, 26.11.41, signed Preissinger.

59 BAB, R 94/6, Der Stadtkommissar Brest–Litowsk to GK, 23.12.41, signed Burat.

60 USHMM, RG 1996.A.169, reel 18 (Brest Archive, M 41/630), contains copies of all of them.

61 BAB, R 94/7: Gebietskommissar, Abt. I, Monatsbericht, 24.1.42.

62 BAB, R 94/6, Der SS und Polizeistandortführer Brest, 15.3.42, signed Rohde.

With the pending Sauckel action for recruiting and conscripting large numbers of foreigners to work in the Reich, of which the authorities in Brest learned in late March 1942,[63] the rush for Jewish labor only intensified. Burat announced that he and SS and *Polizeistandortführer* Rohde, with whom he had developed a very close working relationship,[64] were going to create "a large workshop complex for the employment of Jewish skilled workers on the model of the Lublin workshops"[65] – that is, Odilo Globocnik's growing enterprises based on Jewish labor in the General Government. Construction began almost immediately, with the expectation that the first shops would be producing by mid-June. Rohde would be in charge of construction; Burat would supervise day-to-day operations thereafter.[66]

With the construction of their workshop complex in full swing and the first Sauckel transports of labor to Germany underway in April and May 1942, Rohde and Burat found themselves in competition with other German employers who did not want to give up their indispensable Jews. They solidified their control by withdrawing Jewish labor from small enterprises and ordering that henceforth Jews working outside the ghetto could not travel freely to work but could only leave the ghetto in closed formations guarded by the Jewish ghetto police.[67]

At this time Rohde and Burat also faced another development that would affect the use of Jewish labor, namely the systematic mass murder of the Jews that began across the Bug River in the Lublin district of the General Government in mid-March 1942. Both Rohde and Burat noted that as before the Jews were very reserved. But now there was "a certain nervousness" ("*eine gewisse Scheu*") because they had learned of the expulsion of Jews from the city of Lublin. They were worried about their "fate in the future" ("*Schicksal in der Zukunft*), as they reckoned with a similar expulsion from Brest.[68] One result of this growing fear among the Jews was considered quite positive by Rohde

[63] BAB, R 94/7, Gebietskommissar Brest–Litowsk, Monatsbericht, 24.3.42.
[64] BAB, R 94/6, Der SS und Polizeistandortführer Brest, Lagebericht, 15.3.42.
[65] BAB, R 94/6, Der Stadtkommissar Brest–Litowsk, Abt. I, to GK, 25.3.42.
[66] BAB, R 94/6, Der SS und Polizeiführer [*sic*] in Brest–Litowsk, Lagebericht, 15.4.42.
[67] BAB, R 94/6: Der SS und Polizeiführer [*sic*] in Brest–Litowsk, Lagebericht, 15.4.42; Der Stadtkommissar Brest–Litowsk, Abt. I, Monatlicher Bericht, to GK, 25.4.41; Der SS und Polizeistandortführer Brest, 15.5.42, Lagebericht; Der Stadtkommissar Brest–Litowsk, Abt. I, Lagebericht, 22.5.42.
[68] BAB, R 94/6: Der SS und Polizeiführer [*sic*] in Brest–Litowsk, 15.4.42; Der Stadtkommissar Brest–Litowsk, Abt. I, Monatlicher Lagebericht, 25.4.42.

and Burat. The Jews sought desperately to obey every German order and fulfill every Germany request more than 100 percent. There was not a whisper of a resistance movement, they reported.[69]

Burat, who considered nonworking Jews "an extraordinary burden" ("*eine ausserordentliche Belastung*") to feed, learned in late May 1942 that Security Police commander Ernst Berger "hoped . . . in the next weeks to be able to withdraw a large portion of the Jews from Brest–Litovsk"[70] ("*hofft er, in den nächsten Wochen einen grossen Teil des Judentums aus Brest–Litowsk herausziehen zu können*"). In fact, the murder of nonworking Jews occurred in several towns in Volhynia–Podolia in the last week in May, and then in nearby Kovel in the first week of June, followed by the total liquidation of the surviving Jews of Rovno on June 14–15.[71] However, despite Burat's proclaiming the nonworking Jews a burden, neither Burat nor Rohde took any initiative, and Brest remained as yet untouched by the mass murder program getting underway in the district of Volhynia–Podolia.

In the summer of 1942, in fact, the various German authorities in Brest had much else on their minds. They were facing multiple crises, which Rohde diagnosed with critical precision and considerable anger. By June food shortages had become so acute that ration cards often could not be honored, and every day, police razzias attempted to round up workers to be sent to Germany. "Totally inadequate" food supplies and the "ruthless" seizure of labor, combined with low wages, exorbitant prices, arbitrary confiscations, and the invalidation of ruble notes that reduced many to total poverty, had created "unbelievable circumstances" ("*unglaubliche Zustände*") that inevitably drove people into the hands of the partisans. The partisans could be combatted only by removing the "soil" of "discontent." But instead of increasing food supplies, the Germans pursued antipartisan measures that were universally rejected because they struck "too many innocents."[72] If Rohde diagnosed the

[69] BAB, R 94/6: Der SS und Polizeistandortführer Brest, Lagebericht, 15.5.42; Der Stadtkommissar Brest–Litowsk, Abt. II, Lagebericht, 20.5.42. In a recent, as yet unpublished study, Yehuda Bauer has established that a small resistance movement did exist in the Brest ghetto that was quite unknown to the unsuspecting Germans. The sudden liquidation caught the inexperienced resistance by surprise, and no concerted fighting occurred.

[70] BAB, R 94/6, Der Stadtkommissar Brest–Litowsk, Abt. I, Lagebericht, 22.5.42, initialed by Burat.

[71] Shmuel Spector, *The Holocaust of Volhynian Jews, 1941–1944* (Jerusalem, 1990), pp. 123, 184–5.

[72] BAB, R 94/6, Der SS und Polizeistandortführer Brest, Lageberichten, 12.6. and 15.7.42.

causes of the crisis facing the German occupiers, the *Gebietskommissar* Curt Rolle carefully diagnosed the composition of the swelling and now heavily armed partisan movement that resulted. At the core were Polish activists and escaped Bolshevik prisoners of war, but now Rolle noted that "we are driving into the hands of the partisans even the men who are still working well for us."[73]

In spite of the growing partisan threat, not one official in Brest even hinted at the ideologically axiomatic connection among Jews, Bolsheviks, and partisans. Perhaps because they all too well understood the mentality of those to whom they were reporting, they in fact emphasized just the opposite. Although non-Jewish workers slipped away from low-paying jobs and worthless ration cards to seek food or contact with the partisans in the countryside, over 8,000 Jews were constantly employed in Brest and more than 1,000 Jews from the provincial ghettos were now in camps working on road construction.[74] "Terribly alarmed" by the news of "the recent measures" in Kovel, "the Jews were making extraordinary efforts to achieve recognition of their right to exist through intensified labor and the taking up of work at home."[75]

By late August the interrelated crises of food shortages, flight from work, and partisan resistance had worsened yet further, and the desperate reports of Rohde, Rolle, and Burat became ever more shrill. As feeding the population was the alpha and omega for both pacification and incentive to work, the Germans in Brest pleaded that an adequate portion of the harvest be left in the district.[76] However, the local crisis in Brest reflected a wider food crisis throughout the German empire, to which the Nazi regime was planning to respond in quite a different manner. As Christian Gerlach has shown, the Nazi leadership lived under the specter of the blockade, hunger, and internal collapse at the end of the World War I and was resolved that German domestic consumption in the current war would be upheld at any cost. In early August 1942, it resolved to do this by yet further intensifying the extraction of food from the occupied territories of eastern Europe,

[73] BAB, R 94/7, Gebietskommissar Brest–Litowsk, Monatsbericht, 20.7.42.

[74] BAB, R 94/6, Der Gebietskommissar/Arbeitsamt, Brest–Litowsk, Monatsbericht, 6.7.42.

[75] BAB, R 94/6, Der Stadtkommissar Brest–Litovsk, Lagebericht, 12.7.42.

[76] BAB, R 94/6, Der SS und Polizeiführer Brest, Lagebericht, 15.8.42; R 94/7, Gebietskommissar Brest–Litowsk, Abt. I, 22.8.42; R 94/6, Der Stadtkommissar Brest–Litowsk, IIa, Lagebericht Entwurf, 27.8.42.

whose populations would in turn be reduced by further intensifying the murder of the Jews, including now even Jewish labor.[77] Between August 25 and 28, 1942, the *Reickskommissar* of the Ukraine, Erich Koch, met with Himmler and then Hitler, presumably to plead against the increased extraction of agricultural products just ordered. Instead Koch returned and announced that he had come "directly from the Führer headquarters" and that the food crisis in Germany was "serious" ("*ernst*"). The deficit would be made up from the Ukraine, for in this situation provisioning the population of the Ukraine was "entirely of no consequence"[78] ("*gänzlich gleichgültig*").

[77] Christian Gerlach, *Krieg, Ernährung, Völkermord* (Hamburg, 1998), pp. 214–26.

[78] Gerlach, *Krieg, Ernährung, Völkermord,* pp. 240–1, quoting from *Trials of the War Criminals before the International Military Tribunal* (hereafter cited as IMT), v. 25, p. 318 (Vermerk on Rowno Tagung, 26.–28.8.42). My interpretation of the course of Nazi Jewish policy in Volhynia–Podolia differs from Gerlach's on two points. He portrays the end of the killing of Jews there in the fall of 1941 as based on the successful intervention of the civil administration on behalf of the indispensability of Jewish skilled labor prevailing over the SS desire for total extermination. He concludes that where the civil administration saw no necessity to murder the Jews, the SS and police could not prevail (Gerlach, pp. 238, 249). Yet there is evidence from several Einsatzgruppen reports that even within the SS there was a strong appreciation of the need to exploit Jewish labor. Gerlach cites Ereignismeldung Nr. 133 of 14.11.41, urging total extermination of the Jews, who were characterized as insignificant as a labor force but very dangerous as the carriers of the bacillus of Communism. He does not mention Ereignismeldung Nr. 86 of 17.9.41, that noted that disregard of the Jewish labor force in the western and central Ukraine would make economic reconstruction impossible and urged "extensive utilization of Jewish labor" leading to a "gradual liquidation" of the Jews. Ereignismeldung Nr. 191 of 10.4.42 likewise characterized the Jews as the most peaceful and industrious portion of the population and vital as craftsmen. In short, as between Rohde and Burat in Brest–Litovsk, there was agreement on the use of Jewish labor between at least some elements in the SS and civil administration in Volhynia–Podolia. Moreover, the destruction of the Jews of Brest–Litovsk would occur despite the pleas of the civil administration and SS there. Their objections could not stop the killing; their support was not essential to carrying out the killing.

Second, Gerlach concludes that Koch's support for a 100 percent liquidation of the Jews in Volhynia–Podolia resulted from his visit to Hitler and his learning of the seriousness of the food crisis in late August. Yet other documents indicate that the beginning of 100 percent liquidation in Volhynia–Podolia, with no exemption of skilled labor, dates from early August and reflected a policy already in effect in other parts of the Ukraine. For example, the SS in neighboring Galicia, eager to add workers to the D-4 camps, complained that without its intervention, all the Jews, including those capable of work, in southern Volhynia–Podolia would have been killed. They thus requested the right to select work Jews in the regions bordering the D-4 camps before total extermination. Glowna Komisja Badnia Zbrondi Prezeciwko Narodowi Polskiemu, SS i policji, Sygnatura 77: SS-Hauptsturmführer Hilliges, KdS im Generalbezirks Wohynien u. Podolien, 18.8.42, to Aussenstelle der Sipo-SD, z. Hd. Hauptscharführer Fermer, Kamenez–Podolsk.

Meanwhile, the mass murder of the Jews in the district had paused again after the late May and early June killings but then resumed in late July and hit a full, uninterrupted stride in early August.[79] This now also included the liquidation of all working Jews, with the exception of some in the south who were taken off to the infamous D-4 road construction camps in Galicia. Sometime before August 22, the killing reached the Brest district for the first time, when the approximately 1,000 Jews in the nearby town of Maloryta were "evacuated."[80] Moreover, jurisdiction over the Jews of Brest – until now under Rohde and Burat – was transferred to Ernst Berger's Security Police.[81]

Just after Koch's return from his meetings with Himmler and Hitler but already weeks after the killing campaign was in full swing, the *Generalkommissar* for Volhynia and Podolia, Heinrich Schoene, summoned his *Gebietskommissaren* and police chiefs to a meeting in Luzk on August 29–31, 1942, that included a report by the district Security Police commander (KdS), Karl Pütz, on the "general resettlement of the Jews."[82] Pütz informed his branch offices more explicitly concerning "Jewish actions":

> The actions are to be accelerated, so that they are completed in your area within five weeks. At the meeting of the Gebietskommissaren in Luzk from August 29–31, 1942, it was explained in general that in principle a 100% solution is to be carried out. . . . This 100% cleansing is also the emphatic personal wish of the Reichskommissar.[83]

In rare cases of exceptional importance to the economy, small numbers of essential workers could be kept for a transition period of 2 months, but the so-called 100 percent solution was recommended for the sake of simplicity.

[79] Shmuel Spector, *The Holocaust of Volhymian Jews,* pp. 184–5. For copies of miscellaneous German reports, including a report of August 15 on the *Sonderbehandlung* of 13,802 Jews in Kremianez, Wischnowitz, Potschajef, Katrinburg, Schumsk, and Danowce, and a report of August 17 on the *Sonderbehandlung* of 3,399 Jews in Kamen–Kaschirsk, see: Glowna Komisja Badnia Zbrodni Przeciwko Narodowi Polskiemu, SS i policji, Sygnatura 77.

[80] BAB, R 94/6, Gebietskommisar Brest–Litowsk, Monatsbericht, 22.8.42.

[81] BAB, R 94/6, Der Stadtkommissar Brest–Litowsk, IIa, Lagebericht, 27.8.42.

[82] BAB, R 6/243, Der Stadtkommissar Brest–Litowsk, Abt. I, 4.9.42.

[83] Glowna Komisja Badnia Zbrodni Przeciwko Narodowi Polskiemu, SS i policji, Sygnatura 77: Sturmbannführer Pütz to Aussenstellen der Sipo-SD in Brest, Pinsk, Starokonstantinow, Kamenez–Podolsk, 31.8.42.

For the triple task of repressing partisan resistance, protecting the harvest, and murdering Jews, Police Battalion 310 (now designated as III. Battalion of Police Regiment 15) was dispatched to the Brest region on September 6, 1942.[84] Over the next 2 months it carried out a reign of terror and repression in the territories east of Brest. But the destruction of the remaining provincial Jewish communities in the immediate surroundings of Brest was left to the local Security Police, Gendarmerie, and Schutzmannschaften. On September 19 and 20, these units shot 2,900 Jews in Domachevo and Tomachovka. With this action, all Jews outside Brest excepting 300 Jewish workers in two small camps had been "completely exterminated" ("*völlig ausgerottet*").[85]

Rohde sought to ward off the impending fate of the Brest Jews, arguing:

> The shortage of labor makes itself felt more and more. . . . Insofar as the Jewish question is one day solved in Brest, I foresee terrible economic damage resulting from a shortage of labor. When it is alleged that after the cleaning up of the Jewish question in Kovel orderly conditions ensued and economic life began to operate as before, this allegation is contradicted by the fact that in Kovel at the moment everything is at a standstill and the most valuable goods were left to perish, because no artisans and workers were available. The same consequences, probably in even more drastic form, would occur in Brest after settling the Jewish question, *even if a portion of the Jews remained* [italics mine] ("*selbst auch dann, wenn ein Teil der Juden zurückbleibt*"). I will not fail to draw attention to this time and again.[86]

Rohde went on to describe the continuing construction in and expansion of his Jewish workshop complex, where production of furniture would begin in early October with completion of the joiners' workshop. As if to counter the argument that the murder of the Jews would save scarce food, Rohde concluded that the Jews were utterly willing

84 For Police Battalion 310, see: Edward B. Westermann, "'Ordinary Men' or 'Ideological Soldiers'? Police Battalion 310 in Russia," *German Studies Review* 21/1 (1998), pp. 41–68; and Central State Archives, 7021-148-2, for the war diary and various reports from the fall of 1942.

85 BAB, R 94/7, Gendarmerie-Gebietsführer Brest–Litowsk to KdG Luzk, 6.10.42.

86 BAB, R 94/6, Der SS und Polizeiführer Brest, Lagebericht, 15.9.42.

workers "despite the downright miserable provisions" ("*trotz der geradezu miserablen Verpflegung*") they received.[87] In short, killing the Brest Jews would certainly aggravate the labor crisis but not contribute to solving the food crisis.

Burat noted that the "sudden liquidation" of the Jews of Domachevo and Tomachovka had caused "profound distress" among the Jews of Brest who strove desperately "to prove their indispensability" through a "model organization of Jewish workshops." Unlike Rohde, who had argued for keeping the entire Jewish community, Burat, as in May, argued only for the working Jews. "Although a complete resettlement of the Jews . . . is desirable from the political standpoint," he wrote, "from the standpoint of use of labor, I must unconditionally plead for the retention of the most needed artisans and manpower"[88] ("*Obwohl vom politischen Standpunkt aus die restlose Aussiedlung der Juden aus dem Kreisgebiet erwünscht ist, muss ich vom Standpunkt des Arbeitseinsatzes aus mich unbedingt für die Belassung der notwendigsten Handwerker und Arbeitskräfte einsetzen*").

The economically grounded arguments of local authorities were totally in vain as the wave of systematic mass murder in the Ukraine, which had been approaching inexorably from the south and east, reached Brest–Litovsk in mid-October. The ad hoc force of ghetto liquidators was composed of the bulk of Police Battalion 310,[89] a so-called Nürnberg police company (made up primarily of middle-aged reservists), the 48th motorized police company, and the district Gendarmerie and Schutzmannschaften,[90] as well as the Schutzpolizei and Security Police of Brest – altogether a force of certainly less than 1,000 men.[91] On October 15 and 16, 1942, the ghetto was surrounded

[87] By the summer of 1942, Jewish rations had been cut to one half that of utterly inadequate non-Jewish rations. USHMM, RG 1996.A.169, reel 22 (Brest Archive, M-41/995), Leiter des Ernährungsamtes of Stadtverwaltung to Gebietslandwirt in Brest–Litowsk, 9.7.42.

[88] BA, R 94/7, Der Gebietskommissar in Brest-Litowsk, Abt. IIa, Lagebericht, 9.10.42.

[89] The war diary states succinctly for October 15: "The battalion was employed in Brest for the clearing of the ghetto" ("*Das Battalion wird in Brest zur Räumung des Ghettos eingesetzt*"). CSA Moscow, 7021-148-2, Kriegstagebuch, entry of 15.10.42.

[90] This was composed of 9 career police, 14 reservists, and 304 Schutzmänner. BAB, R 94/7, Der Gendarmerie-Gebietsführer Brest–Litowsk, Lagebericht, 8.11.42.

[91] The liquidation of the Brest ghetto was the subject of an investigation by the Zentralstelle im Lande Nordrhein-Westfalen attached to the Oberstaatsanwalt in Dortmund. It could identify the participating units but it could not procure sufficient evidence to indict any single individual or even identify the unit(s) that carried out the actual shooting after clearing the ghetto. ZStL 204 AR-Z 334/59, pp. 1134–1216: Verfügung, 45 Js 8/61 Dortmund, 8.12.65.

and the Jews of Brest, including the workers, were rounded up. Those who were deemed too frail to march were taken out of the columns and shot on the spot. The rest were driven to the train station, packed into cattle cars, and taken eastward on the Brest–Minsk rail line. The trains halted some 100 kilometers from Brest on a side track at Brona–Gora. Here there was a well-prepared shooting site; barbed-wire fences funneled the unloaded Jews some 400 meters to the pits, where they were all shot.[92]

The Brest ghetto was then combed repeatedly over the next several weeks, with 70–80 Jews uncovered daily.[93] A relentless "Jew hunt" for the bunkers of those Jews who had escaped the city at the last moment followed.[94] The Germans in Brest rounded off their body count to roughly 20,000.[95] Of these, 9,000 had been employed, 2,000 of them as irreplaceable, highly skilled workers in Rohde and Burat's workshops.[96] After Brest, the killing wave continued to sweep to the north and west. It engulfed Pinsk, the last remaining ghetto in the Reichskommissariat Ukraine, on October 30–November 2, and then the Bialystok district immediately thereafter. There, however, in contrast to the Ukraine, the work Jews in the ghettos of Grodno and Bialystok were spared until the following summer.

In conclusion, let us return to the initial theme concerning the scope and importance of local initiative. In Brest there was both consensus between the civil administration and SS – Burat and Rolle on the one hand and Rohde on the other – on the importance of using Jewish labor as well as considerable initiative, especially in the construction of a workshop complex, to exploit Jewish labor most effectively. Not only did they defend the use of Jewish labor to the end but this trio of local officials was also quite confident and assertive in its criticism of a whole range of occupation policies. In Brest there was strong local initiative, but it ran counter to both implementation of the Final Solution as well as other central aspects of Nazi occupation policy.

92 The killing site at Brona–Gora is known almost only through the report of the postwar Soviet commission. ZStL 204 AR-Z 334/59, pp. 1646–50.

93 BAB, R 94/7, Abt. II, Beitrag zum Monatsbericht for October 1942.

94 BAB, R 94/7, Gendarmerie-Gebietsführer Brest–Litowsk, Lageberichten: 8.11.42; 5.12.52; and 4.2.43; CSA Moscow, 70211-148-2, Police Battalion 310 war diary, entries of late October and early November 1942.

95 BAB, R 94/7, Gendarmerie-Gebietsführer Brest–Litowsk, Lagebericht, 8.11.42; Der Gebietskommissar in Brest–Litowsk, Abt. IIa, Lagebericht, 31.12.42.

96 BAB, R 94/7, Der Gebietskommissar/Arbeitsamt, Monatsbericht, 27.10.42.

Such independence and assertiveness did not harm the careers of any of the local German authorities in Brest. Curt Rolle, the most biting critic of German occupation policies, was shifted as *Gebietskommissar* from Brest to Staro–Konstantinow in September 1942 and highly recommended by his boss, *Generalkommissar* Heinrich Schoene, for special recognition.[97] The position of *Stadtkommissar* was then merged with the now vacant position of *Gebietskommissar* in Brest, and in September 1942 Burat was promoted to fill it. In short, Burat stepped into Rolle's position while keeping his previous one.[98] In January 1943 Rohde left Brest, joined the antipartisan campaign of the so-called battle group (*Kampfgruppe*) von Gottberg, and won numerous decorations.[99]

Despite their sharp criticisms of occupation policy and open advocacy for the use and retention of Jewish labor, these men were clearly and correctly perceived as fundamentally loyal to the Nazi regime. Indeed, their advocacy of Jewish labor did not stem from humanitarian scruples or aversion to racism. Prior to the liquidation of the ghetto, according to one witness who had frequent contact with him, Rohde "had always made a peaceful, benevolent impression" ("*immer einen ruhigen, wohlwollenden Eindruck gemacht hatte*") on the Jews with whom he dealt personally. He had gained a reputation in the ghetto as "a kind of protector or possibly even savior of the Jews"[100] ("*eine Art Beschützer oder möglicherweise sogar Retter der Juden*"). But during the liquidation of the ghetto, he revealed a different face. Though witness identification was not certain enough to bring him to trial, Rohde was accused by German witnesses of directly and brutally conducting the selections, whereby those Jews judged too frail to march to the train station were shot in a courtyard outside the ghetto.[101] His decoration-winning performance in the

97 BAB, R 6/47, Schoene to Koch, 16.8.43.

98 ZStL, II 204 AR 1040/72, p. 8 (Burat testimony).

99 NA, BDC, SS officer file.

100 ZStL, 204 AR-Z 334/59, pp. 1326–7, 1336 (Berta B.). This witness was among the Jews who regularly delivered requisitioned goods and gifts to Rohde's office and thus observed him personally. She testified that he gave the appearance of being "friendly and ready to help" ("*freundlich und hilfsbereit*"). Yehuda Bauer has identified 19 survivors from Brest. In his as yet unpublished study, he notes that virtually all survivors other than Berta B. held utterly negative views of Rohde as corrupt and devious.

101 ZStL, 204 AR-Z 334/59, pp. 962 and 980 (Dr. Oswald C.) and 1005 (Dr. Walter G.).

murderous antipartisan activities of battle group von Gottberg are likewise revealing.

And Franz Burat, while defending the use of Jewish labor, railed against some 1,000 "Gypsies" who had been expelled from the Bialystok district to Brest and whom he considered an economic liability. In June 1943, he wrote in murderous exasperation: "Begging and stealing are the main occupation of this scourge. I consider it urgently necessary that these professional thieves be treated as the Jews are and request the appropriate authorization."[102] ("*Betteln und Stehlen ist die Hauptbeschäftigung dieser Landplage. Ich halte es für dringend notwendig, dass diese Tagediebe wie die Juden behandelt werden und bitte um entsprechende Vollmacht*"). For whatever reason, Burat's murderous request for authorization to murder the "Gypsies" remained unfulfilled, and he did not take the initiative to murder them on his own, for the "Gypsies" were still in Brest in the spring of 1944.[103]

When the local initiatives and pleas of Rohde, Rolle, and Burat for the use of Jewish labor conflicted with the policies of Berlin and the explicit orders of *Reichskommissar* Koch for a 100 percent solution to the Jewish Question, they were simply brushed aside, but with no detriment to the careers of the initiators. Clearly the "machinery of destruction" was not dependent upon the initiative and enthusiastic support of such local authorities, as long as orders, once given, were in fact obeyed. And in Brest–Litovsk, the destruction orders were indeed obeyed and carried out with terrible and total compliance.

There was a line, however, that could not be crossed, as can be seen in the fate of Brest's neighboring *Gebietskommissar* in Kovel, Arwed Kempf from Worms. Kempf did not carry out the ghettoization of the Jews of Kovel, as ordered by Koch in September 1941. When he departed Kovel for home leave in April 1942, he was apparently denounced. His apartment was searched, incriminating Jewish property was allegedly found, and he was arrested, brought to trial, convicted, and shot. Others stationed in Kovel merely heard that it was a simple case of corruption, and that he had enriched himself with

[102] BAB, R 94/8, Der Gebietskommissar in Brest–Litowsk to GK für Wolhynien und Podolien (persönlich!), 24.6.43.

[103] BAB, R 94/8, Der Gebietskommissar in Brest–Litowsk, Lagebericht, 21.3.44

Jewish property.[104] But the sentence of the court indicated that there was something much more serious at stake than corruption, which was utterly pervasive throughout the German occupation in the east and seldom investigated much less punished. The judgment did cite that Kempf was convicted in part for the minor offense of "passive corruption" ("*passiver Bestechung*") – that is, receiving though not actively extorting gifts; it also alleged "suborning perjury." But much more serious, the crux of the judgment was conviction on the charge of "grave disloyalty" ("*schwere Untreue*"), and for this Kempf was executed.[105] Although we know of no individual German who was harshly punished for refusing to shoot unarmed civilians, clearly the same cannot be said for those who were entrusted with positions of authority and then deemed to have sabotaged Reich policy as a matter of principle.

In summary, therefore, local initiatives that suited the purposes and policies of the regime – such as the early killings by Police Battalion 309 and the Tilsit commando – were seized upon and institutionalized with alacrity. Local initiatives – such as the use of Jewish labor in Brest – that clashed with the long-term goals and policies of the regime were temporarily tolerated but brushed aside when the time came. But local initiatives that challenged the regime's policies in principle – such as Arwed Kempf's failure to ghettoize the Jews of Kovel – were crushed with draconic severity.

104 ZStL, 206 AR-Z 26/61, Investigation of Erich Kassner: pp. 17 (Josef F.), 65 (Egon S.), 71 (Johann W.), and 111 (Karl S.).

105 ZStL, 206 AR-Z 26/61, p. 331 (Abschlussbericht); Anklage StA Oldenburg 2 Js 52/63, pp. 40–1; Urteil LG Oldenburg 2 Ks 1/64, p. 12

6

GERMAN KILLERS

Behavior and Motivation in the Light of New Evidence

One of the most elusive tasks facing historians of any event is to uncover the attitudes and mindset of the "ordinary" people who "make history" but leave behind no files of official documents and precious few diaries and letters. When "ordinary" people behave in ways completely at odds with the previous patterns of their everyday life and become the perpetrators of "extraordinary" crimes, this task becomes both more difficult and more essential to undertake. But how to undertake this task is a difficult question in its own right. In the case of Nazi Germany, one approach has been to shift the focus of study from the prominent and high-ranking perpetrators of the SS to the many individuals of the bureaucracy and business community, the medical and legal professions, the German railways, and even the German churches who contributed to the implementation of Nazi Jewish policy in one way or another. Among the new subjects of study, attention has been drawn in recent years above all to the German Order Police.

It is no longer seriously in question that members of the German Order Police, both career professionals and reservists, in both battalion formation and precinct service or *Einzeldienst,* were at the center of the Holocaust, providing a major manpower source for carrying out numerous deportations, ghetto-clearing operations, and massacres.[1]

[1] Christopher R. Browning, *Ordinary Men: Reserve Police Battalion 101 and the Final Solution in Poland* (New York, 1992); Daniel Jonah Goldhagen, *Hitler's Willing Executioners: Ordinary Germans and the Holocaust* (New York, 1996); Heiner Lichtenstein, *Himmlers grüne Helfer. Die Schutz und Ordnungspolizei im "Dritten Reich"* (Köln, 1990); Raul Hilberg, "The Bureaucracy of Annihilation," *Unanswered Questions: Nazi Germany and the Genocide of the Jews,* ed. by François Furet (New York, 1989), esp. pp. 124–6, and *Perpetrators, Victims, Bystanders* (New York, 1992), pp. 87–102;

(footnote continues)

The professional or career Order Police, who were merged with the SS in 1936, differed in age, career aspirations, institutional identification, training and indoctrination, and percentage of party and SS membership from the reservists. It is especially the reservists, not the career professionals, of the Order Police who could be said to be representative of "ordinary Germans." Conscripted virtually at random from the population of those middle-aged men who enjoyed no exemption for providing skilled labor essential to the war economy, they represented an age cohort that was socialized and educated in the pre-Nazi period and was fully aware of the moral norms of a pre-Nazi political culture.

What was the motivation and mind-set of the Order Police reservists who became Holocaust perpetrators? Did they come to their task possessed by virulent anti-Semitism and eager to kill Jews, or were they transformed by the situation in which they found themselves in eastern Europe? Did their attitude toward killing Jews differ from that toward killing other victims? Did they act with uniform enthusiasm, or did they display a spectrum of response – including evasion and nonparticipation by a significant minority – when killing?

Several scholars have answered these questions in sharply contrasting ways owing to very different readings of the admittedly problematic postwar judicial testimony given by the Order Police themselves.

(footnote continued)

1 Konrad Kwiet, "From the Diary of a Killing Unit," *Why Germany? National Socialist Anti-Semitism and the European Context,* ed. by John Milfull (Oxford, 1993), pp. 75–90; Andrej Angrick/Martina Voigt/Silke Ammerschubert/Peter Klein, "'Da hätte man schon ein Tagebuch führen müssen.' Das Polizeibataillon 322 und die Judenmorde im Bereich der Heeresgruppe Mitte während des Sommers und Herbstes 1941," *Die Normalität des Verbrechens. Bilanz und Perspektiven der Forschung zu den nationalsozialistischen Gewaltvebrechen,* ed. by Helge Grabitz, Klaus Bästlein, and Johannes Tuchel (Berlin, 1994), pp. 325–85; Jürgen Matthäus, "What About the 'Ordinary Men'?: The German Order Police and the Holocaust in the Occupied Soviet Union," *Holocaust and Genocide Studies* 10/2 (fall 1996), pp. 134–50, and "'Reibungslos und planmässig.' Die zweite Welle der Judenvernichtung im Generalkommissariat Weissruthenien (1942–1944)," *Jahrbuch für Antisemitismusforschung* 4 (1995), pp. 254–74; Martin Dean, "The German *Gendarmerie,* the Ukrainian *Schutzmannschaft* and the 'Second Wave' of Jewish Killings in Occupied Ukraine: German Policing at the Local Level in the Zhitomir Region, 1941–1944," *German History,* 14/2 (1996), pp. 169–92; Paul Kohl, *Der Krieg der deutschen Wehrmacht und der Polizei 1941–1944: Sowjetische Überlebende berichten* (Frankfurt/M., 1995); Klaus-Michael Mallmann, "Vom Fussvolk der 'Endlösung.' Ordnungspolizei, Ostkrieg, und Judenmord," *Jahrbuch für Geschichte,* 21 (1997), pp. 355–91; Edward B. Westermann, "'Ordinary Men' or 'Ideological Soldiers'? Police Battalion 310 in Russia, 1942," *German Studies Review,* 21/1 (February 1998), pp. 41–68.

The task of the historian now is to locate and analyze rare contemporary sources that can shed additional light on these issues. For that purpose I would like to consider two other kinds of sources: first, the eyewitness accounts by Jewish survivors who possessed a unique vantage point from which to observe the internal dynamics and individual behavior of German Order Police reservists, and second, three collections of unusual documents: (1) the records of the Schutzpolizei station of Czeladz, an industrial suburb of Sosnowiec, in East Upper Silesia[2]; (2) the letters of a member of Reserve Police Battalion 105 in the Baltic[3]; and (3) the records of a German wartime investigation of an unplanned massacre of the Jews of Marcinkance in the Bialystok district in November 1942, in which both career and reserve police participated.[4]

Let us look first at East Upper Silesia. After the publication of my book *Ordinary Men,* I received the following letter:

Your book deeply affected me, because I personally experienced the German Schutzpolizei, the good and the bad. As a 15 year old Jewish boy, I was sent by the Judenrat as a punishment to my father to do maintenance work in the headquarters of the German police. The town then called Auschwitz had no running water. I carried water and polished their boots until March 1941 when the whole Jewish population had to leave. The whole police company came from the town of Waldenburg in Silesia. I came across men that in my opinion could not hurt a fly. Walter Stark, Max Maetzig, Walter Kraus, Joseph Grund, Polizeimeister Sebranke, his deputy Orlet, and so on. Two of them were willing to make out false papers and send me as a Pole to work in Germany, apparently knowing what was coming. . . . As I mentioned before this whole company came from the town of Waldenburg. As faith [*sic*] wants it, in October 1944 I was taken to the KZ Waldenburg. In January 1945 we were taken to dig so-called Panzergraben [anti-tank ditches] on the outskirts of town in the direction of Breslau. One evening going back to the camp a child was playing on the sidewalk. I recognized him as Horst Maetzig, who[m] I met with his parents in Auschwitz. His father Max Maetzig was one of the

[2] United States Holocaust Memorial Museum (hereafter cited as USHMM), Record Group 15.033m, 8 reels (from Glowna Komisja Badnia Zbrodni Przeciwko Narodowi Polskienu Instytut Pamieci Narodowej, Archival Nr. 171), especially files 17, 31, and 32.

[3] Ludwig Eiber, ed., ". . . ein bisschen die Wahrheit": Briefe eines Bremer Kaufmanns von seinem Einsatz beim Reserve-Polizeibataillon 105 in der Sowjetunion 1941," *1999: Zeitschrift für Sozialgeschichte des 20. und 21. Jahrhunderte,* I/91, pp. 58–83.

[4] USHMM, Record Group 53.004m, reel 1 (from Grodno Oblast Archive, fond 1, opis 1), folder 59.

policemen. Of course, you know we were guarded by SS. I could not help it as we lined up with the boy, I exclaimed Horst. He took a look and ran away. The next day he was standing there with his mother Elisabeth, and [she] just nodded with her head. I appreciated that now very much. For the next two months, she and her boy stood there, it was a tremendous boost for my morale. I will never forget it. I wonder what happened to this police company, if they wound up to do what you describe in our book. Maybe you can find out for me, I would be grateful.[5]

I do not in fact know what this company of middle-aged policemen from Silesia did subsequently. But the newly accessible files of the Schutzpolizei police precinct in Czeladz indicate that the behavior of the policemen in Silesia was indeed atypical in comparison to elsewhere on occupied Polish and Soviet territory in ways that are very suggestive.

When East Upper Silesia was annexed to the Third Reich in October 1939, a network of German Schutzpolizei precinct stations was quickly established in the urban areas, including Sosnowiec and its industrial suburb of Czeladz. The Sosnowiec Schutzpolizei operated on the assumption that fully 70 percent of these men would be married and need family housing.[6] A roster from August 1942 reveals that fully one half of the men in the Czeladz police station had family names of Polish origin.[7] And the police commander in Sosnowiec had to make explicit that it was forbidden for his men to speak Polish in public while in uniform because this was damaging to the image of the police.[8] Thus it is likely that, as in the case of the Kattowitz Schutzpolizei, the Czeladz police were reservists from Silesia. They lived with their families in a milieu with which they were relatively familiar. They were not an isolated group of men living alone far from family and home in an alien environment. Their situation was far closer to that of reservists serving in precinct service near home in Germany than of those serving on occupied Polish and Soviet territory.

From the surviving documents of the Czeladz police station, we see that the commander of the Schutzpolizei in Sosnowiec was a stickler for

[5] Personal letter of J. H. to the author, 21.11.95.

[6] USHMM, RG 15.033m, reel 1, folder 4, p. 18 (KdSchupo in house, 16.1.41).

[7] USHMM, RG 15.033m, reel 6, folder 208, p. 61 (roster of 4. Polizeirevier, Czeladz, 31.7.42).

[8] USHMM, RG 15.033m, reel 4, folder 175, p. 42 (Abschnitts-Kommando-Befehl Nr. 31, 6.6.40).

ideological training and indoctrination. In this regard, he was extremely disturbed by the attitude of these men. For instance, he complained about the "previous indifference" ("*bisherige Gleichgültigkeit*") of the men toward meetings and written materials devoted to ideological indoctrination.[9] He also voiced his obvious disappointment in related matters as well. When the singing of the SS-Treuelied had to be abandoned because the men did not know the words, he ordered special hours of singing practice until the words were mastered. "In the future at all official and social occasions as well as at the conclusion of the monthly ideological training sessions, the SS-Treuelied must be sung. Because of our close organizational ties with the SS, this song is also the basic hymn of the police," he ordered.[10]

Concerning the attitude of these reservists toward Jews, it should be noted that the experience of the 90,000–100,000 Polish Jews of East Upper Silesia was significantly different from that of their fellow Jews in the Warthegau and the General Government. Many were moved into certain towns and Jewish residence areas within East Upper Silesia,[11] but only a few were expelled into the General Government.[12] Though their freedom of movement was curtailed by curfews as well as prohibitions against use of public transportation and entering certain streets and buildings in 1941,[13] the Jewish quarters of East Upper Silesia were not transformed into sealed ghettos until the spring of 1943.[14] Unlike the rest of Poland but instead as in pre-1939 Germany,

[9] USHMM, RG 15.033m, reel 1, folder 17, pp. 79–80 (KdSchupo Sonderbefehl Nr. 1, Sosnowiec, 20.7.42).

[10] USHMM, RG 15.033m, reel 1, folder 17, Sonderbefehl Nr. 2, 10.11.42.

[11] The Jews were concentrated in the eastern strip of East Upper Silesia that had not been German territory even before 1919. USHMM, RG 15.033m, reel 1, file 32: p. 4, KdSchupo Kattowitz, 16.4.40, Umsiedlung der Juden aus dem altschlesischen Raum, and p. 41, KdSchupo Sosnowitz, 25.11.41, betr.: Umsiedlung der Juden.

[12] Two Jewish transports left Kattowitz for Nisko on October 20 and 28, 1939, before that operation was halted. Alfred Konieczny, "Die Zwangsarbeit der Juden im Schlesien im Rahmen der 'Organisation Schmelt,'" *Beiträge zur nationalsozialistischen Gesundheits- und Sozialpolitik,* V (1987), p. 94.

[13] USHMM, RG 53.004m, reel 1: on the public transportation ban, file 31, p. 1: Polizeipräsident Sosnowiec, 19.3.41, betr: Ausschaltung der Juden aus den öffentlichen Verkehr, and p. 15, KdSchupo, Sosnowiec, 30.4.41, to 44. Polizeirevier Czeladz, betr: Benutzung der Züge durch Juden; on the curfew, file 32, p. 22, Schupo-Abschnittskommando I, Sosnowiec, 13.6.41, to all agencies; on banning Jews from certain streets and conducting business with German officials outside early morning hours, file 32, pp. 8–9, Polizeipräsident Sosnowiec, 18.1.41, to all authorities.

[14] For the ghetto in Czeladz: USHMM, RG 15.033m, reel 1, file 31, p. 12, Polizeipräsident Sosnowiec, 14.4.43, an die Zentrale der jüd. Altestenräte in Oberschlesien.

the Jews here were not marked until September 1941.[15] By the spring of 1942 some 6,500 Silesian Jews had been rounded up and interned in the Jewish labor camps of *Organisation* Schmelt, but prior to the deportations the majority continued to work in privately owned shops.[16] The strongest single indicator of the stark contrast between Lodz and Warsaw on the one hand and East Upper Silesia on the other is that despite the discrimination, expropriation, and forced labor roundups, in the first 2 years of the German occupation of East Upper Silesia there was no significant rise in the natural death rate among the Jewish population.[17]

In short, the reserve police in the "incorporated territory" of East Upper Silesia were more like German police serving at home than on occupied territory. And the Jews they encountered were treated more like German than Polish or Soviet Jews. How did the German Schupo of East Upper Silesia react toward a Jewish population that was not stigmatized by marking, isolated by ghettoization, emaciated by starvation rations, and decimated by epidemic? Scattered references in the surviving documents hint at a very different atmosphere and rank-and-file police behavior than in the rest of German-occupied Poland. In November 1939 the commander of the Schutzpolizei in East Upper Silesia warned all of his men that "the greeting of a Jew is not to be acknowledged at all," and that any police engaged in contact with Jews outside official business could be expected to be sent to a concentration camp.[18] This was not simply a one-time setting of policy, for the following spring, the commander of the Schutzpolizei felt compelled

[15] USHMM, RG 15.033m, reel 1, file 31, p. 2, Schutzpolizei-Abschnittskommando I, Sosnowiec, 17.9.41, Polizeiverordnung über die Kennzeichnung der Juden vom 1. Sept. 1941.

[16] Nuremberg Document NO-1386: Schmauser to Himmler, 20.4.42; Konieczny, "Die Zwangsarbeit der Juden im Schlesien," pp. 97–100. Though Jewish businesses were taken over by German trustees, at least initially they often continued to employ the former Jewish owners and workers. As the young survivor Abe Kimmelman remembered in 1946 about German-Jewish business relations in the early months of the occupation: ". . . during the first winter, the cruelty of the Germans was not yet recognized. . . . They were not so much Germans on the *inside* as on the *outside.* And when they were together with the Jews they could get along." USHMM, David Boder Collection, vol. I, pp. 9–10 (interview of Abe Kimmelman).

[17] Avihu Ronen, English abstract of "The Jews of Zaglembie during the Holocaust," Ph.D. thesis (Hebrew), Tel Aviv University, 1989, p. 7.

[18] USHMM, RG 15.033m, reel 3, file 144, pp. 1–3, circular KdSchupo Scheer, Kattowitz, 20.11.39.

once again to warn his men. He had repeatedly witnessed how Jews did not promptly and sufficiently make way for Germans on the sidewalks, which he deemed to be intentionally provocative. The police were told to demand respect from the Jews and Poles, not chat with them. "An even more regretful case has come to my attention," he continued, "that a police official has extended his hand to greet a Jew." The police were to watch for and report any such "abuses."[19] There were also complaints that the curfew and ban on use of public transportation were not being enforced.[20]

On the eve of the May 1942 deportations, the Schutzpolizei commander felt the need to exhort his men to be tough: "You must proceed ruthlessly in the Jewish actions. . . . Racial struggle is harsh – sentimentalism is out of place."[21] In July 1942, however, even after the first deportation action of May–June 1942 and on the eve of the second deportation action of August, the unthinkable had happened once again – "A German police official was said to have greeted a Jew. . . . Jews should not be greeted on the open street at all." Thus, all the men and noncommissioned officers were to be reminded once again about the exact fulfillment of duties. "In case of lapses, especially in dealings with Jews and Poles, they can reckon with no consideration."[22]

Although the Schupo commander continued to see disturbing signs of insufficient harshness and disdain toward the Jews on the part of his men, between the first and second deportation actions (May–June and

[19] USHMM, RG 15.033m, reel 4, file 175, p. 15, Major Nowack, Schutzpolizei-Abschnittskommando V, Sosnowiec, 10.4.41, Abschnitts-Kommandobefehl Nr. 10.

[20] USHMM, RG 15.033m, reel 1, file 32: p. 15, Major Nowack, KdSchupo, Sosnowiec, 30.4.41, betr. Benutzung der Züge durch Juden; p. 22, Schutzpolizei-Abschnittskommando I, Sosnowiec, 13.6.41, an alle Dienststellen. Even more disturbing for the police commanders were instances of police dereliction making use of Jews. In February 1941 a policeman entered a fabric store accompanied by a Jew. The latter – acting as an expert adviser and allegedly behaving "very impudently" – found fault with goods on the shelves and asked for those kept in the back of the store. The store owner refused to show him these goods, and the policeman "very rudely" left store. Despite an investigation, his identity was not discovered. USHMM, RG 15.033m, reel 3, file 144, p. 24, Schutzpolizei-Abschnittskommando I, Sosnowiec, 13.2.41 (sehr frech . . . sehr unhöflich). In May 1942, a Schupo accompanied by a Jew entered the apartment of a Polish woman. He confiscated her food supply without receipt, which the Jew then carried off for him. This case too remained unsolved. USHMM, RG 15.033m, reel 1, file 52, pp. 7–11, KdSchupo Gerichtsoffizier, Sosnowiec, 8.5.42.

[21] USHMM, RG 15.033m, reel 6, file 209, Diesntstellenleiter-Besprechung, 14.5.42.

[22] USHMM, RG 15.033m, reel 6, file 209, Dienststellenleiter-Besprechungen, 16.7. and 30.10.42.

August 1942) in East Upper Silesia, for the first time he had also to give his attention to another phenomenon – namely, the curbing of unseemly and public police violence. In July 1942 – after some 17,000 Jews had been sent to their deaths in nearby Auschwitz–Birkenau – he advised his men that beating Poles or Jews in public was "in no way permissible." "This is freebooter behavior that has no place in the German police."[23] ("*Dies sind Landsknechtnamieren, die nicht in die Deutsche Polizei gehören*").

These are admittedly quite fragmentary references, but they are suggestive. In East Upper Silesia, where the police were still living as at home rather than as occupiers in a foreign land and the dehumanization of the Jews through marking, ghettoization, and starvation proceeded well behind the pace set in the Warthegau and General Government, the brutalization of the police seems also to have been a much slower process. This would suggest that imposing racial imperialism was corrupting. Acting as a "master race" on occupied territory changed attitudes and behavior, and each step in degrading and mistreating victims made the next step easier. For the policemen stationed in East Upper Silesia this process went relatively slowly, in sharp contrast to those involved in Operation Barbarossa. Let us turn to the letters from Reserve Police Battalion 105 in the Baltic.

A 40-year-old Bremen salesman who had previously served as a reservist in Norway wrote his wife about the battalion's orientation on the eve of the invasion: "The major said that every suspect is to be shot immediately. Well, I'm in suspense," he noted sarcastically. ("*Der Major sagt, jeder Verdächtige ist sofort zu erschiessen. Na, ich bin gespannt.*") Not hiding his antipathy toward his officers, he suggested that they might shoot as they had in the comfort of the officers' casino in Oslo, where they had been previously stationed. "The gentlemen fancy themselves as very important and martial," he concluded.[24] ("*Die Herren kommen sich sehr wichtig und kriegerisch vor.*")

Two days later, after the first execution of seven civilians, his tone changed abruptly. "In comparison to our present action," he admitted,

[23] USHMM, RG 15.033m, reel 6, file 109, Dienststellenleiter-Besprechung, 2.7.42.

[24] "'. . . ein bisschen die Wahrheit.' Briefe eines Bremer Kaufmanns von seinem Einsatz beim Reserve-Polizeibataillon 105 in der Sowjetunion 1941," ed. by Ludwig Eiber, 1999. *Zeitschrift für Sozialgeschichte des 20. und 21. Jahrhunderte*, I/91, p. 67 (letter of 24.6.41).

"Norway was nothing at all."[25] He assured his wife that he would tell her "a little bit of the truth"; otherwise, she would perhaps get "a false picture" from others. However, he warned: "Only you must give it no thought, there's no point to it."[26]

Initially he made detailed references to the Jews he encountered. Sent to a village to arrest all communists, the police rounded up 19 men and 6 Jewish girls. He fully expected to be part of a firing squad. However, after interrogation, the 6 Jewish girls and 11 men were released. The 8 remaining men – none of them Jews, he noted specifically – were taken away amidst the "terrible wailing and howling" ("*fürchterliches Gejammer und Gejaule*") of their mothers, wives, and children.[27] Clearly Reserve Police Battalion 105 did not enter Soviet territory with prior instructions to kill all Jews but had received the *Kommissarbefehl* concerning the liquidation of communist functionaries.

In early July his company was lodged in commandeered Jewish houses, where every morning the "chosen people" ("*auserwählte Volk*") had to appear and work. He himself had two young Jews, a 15-year-old boy and 19-year-old girl, as his servants, but they had to be provided with identification cards or otherwise someone else would grab them. "The Jews are free game. Anybody can seize one on the streets for himself. I would not like to be in a Jew's skin." ("*Die Juden sind Freiwild. Jeder kann sich auf der Strasse einen greifen, um ihn für sich in Anspruch zu nehmen. Ich möchte in keiner Judenhaut stecken.*") The Jews had no food, he noted. "How they actually live, I don't know. We give our bread and more. I cannot be so tough," he confessed. ("*Von was die eigentlich leben, weiss ich nicht. Wir geben unser Brot und auch sonst was ab. Ich kann nicht so hart sein.*") In addition to food, he noted: "One can only give the Jews some well-intended advice: bring no more children into the world. They have no future"[28] ("*Mann kann den Juden nur noch einen gut gemeinten Rat geben: Keine Kinder mehr in die Welt zu setzen. Sie haben keine Zukunft mehr.*")

Two weeks later, when the company moved to Mitau, the reserve policeman noted that there were "no more Jews" in town to act as

[25] Ibid., 68 (letter of 26.6.41).
[26] Ibid., p. 70 (letter of 4 or 5.7.41).
[27] Ibid.
[28] Ibid., pp. 70–1 (letter of 7.7.41).

servants. "They must be working, I suppose, in the countryside," he wrote once again with a possible tone of sarcasm.[29]

In early August he wrote first on a theme that dominates much of the correspondence – namely, the most recent packages of food that he had sent home to his wife and mother, in this case butter and cheese, which he hoped "will taste good to you." He then added cryptically: "Here all Jews are being shot. Everywhere such actions are underway. Yesterday night 150 Jews from this place were shot, men, women, children, all killed. The Jews are being totally exterminated" ("*Hier werden sämtliche Juden erschossen. Überall sind solche Aktionen in Gange. Gestern nacht sind aus diesem Ort 150 Juden erschossen, Männer, Frauen und Kinder, alles umgelegt. Die Juden werden gänzlich ausgerottet*"). He advised his wife once again not to think about it – "it must be" – and at least for the moment to "say nothing about it" to their eldest child.[30] ("*Liebe H., mache Dir keine Gedanken darüber, es muss sein. Und dem R. nichts davon erzählen, später mal!*")

In short, in the first month of Operation Barbarossa the Bremen reserve policeman wrote about Jews in two distinct ways. When referring to Jews in general, his tone was sarcastic and unsympathetic: "the chosen people" had had their houses commandeered, and they were presumably "working in the countryside." But when he wrote of the Jews that he actually encountered, the tone was quite different. The first Jews arrested by his company were released, and he was relieved not to be part of a firing squad. The Jewish youths working as his servants were portrayed as victims facing a pitiless future, and he confessed himself not tough enough to deny them a few handouts. One month later, when systematic killing of all Jews was clearly underway, he shifted to yet another voice – what I would call the "anonymous passive" that is so prevalent in postwar testimony as well. He openly wrote that all Jews were being shot, but without mentioning in any way his own or even his unit's participation. He expressed no feelings of his own except acceptance of the inevitable – "it must be." He urged willed indifference on his wife and silence before his eldest child. There was no celebration or boasting and even a hint of shame.

[29] Ibid., p. 72 (letter of 20.7.41)
[30] Ibid., p. 73 (letter of 7.8.41).

The reserve policeman wrote of Russians, especially partisans, quite differently. The partisans were "beasts" (*Biester*),[31] "dogs" (*Hunde*),[32] and "trash" (*Lumpen*) who had to disappear.[33] He provided vivid descriptions of executions that were "the order of the day." For example, "The arrested communists and snipers are made to lie facedown in graves that they have dug themselves and then shot in the neck from behind."[34] The sight of partisans whose bodies were left hanging for "deterrence" was so common it no longer affected the men, he admitted.[35] Concerning one execution that he missed following a "partisan hunt," he wrote explicitly: "It was said to have been fun"[36] ("*Es soll toll gewesen sein*").

It is clear from the letters that the civilian population at large was not spared. His company had burned down every house and barn within 25 kilometers to deny lodging to the partisans. "We were 'arsons' in the true sense of the word," he confided.[37] Russians were forced to march in front of patrols to set off possible mines.[38] Any Russian found in the forest was shot out of hand.[39] When his unit suffered casualties, he and his comrades become angry; they "would like best of all to shoot down all Russians"[40] ("*möchte am liebsten alle Russen über den Haufen schiessen*").

He complained that the retreating Russians had burned everything in their flight, leaving nothing to be plundered. "For that their own prisoners must go hungry, yes, that is quite clear," he wrote. And he left no doubt as to what that meant. "When one sees a prisoner camp, one can see miserable scenes. The people would be better off dead"[41] ("*Hungern müssen die eigenen Gefangenen dafür, das ist ja ganz klar. Wenn man mal Gefangenlager sieht, kann man trostlose Bilder sehen. Die Leute wären besser tot*").

31 Ibid., p. 68 (letter of 3.7.41).
32 Ibid., p. 77 (letter of 28.9.41).
33 Ibid., p. 82 (letter of 25.10.41).
34 Ibid., p. 74 (letter of 22.8.41). Other executions are described on pp. 81–3 (letters of 25.10 and 18.11.41) as well.
35 Ibid., p. 79 (letter of 8.10.41).
36 Ibid., p. 81 (letter of 8.10.41).
37 Ibid., p. 77 (letter of 28.9.41).
38 Ibid., p. 78 (letter of 3.10.41).
39 Ibid., p. 76 (letter of 7.9.41).
40 Ibid., p. 81 (letter of 8.10.41).
41 Ibid., p. 75 (letter of 7.9.41).

Now there is no "anonymous passive" voice and certainly no hint of shame. On the contrary, he was "proud of" what he had gone through and experienced. He openly regretted that he missed filming an execution, in which the company's so-called revolver hero (*Revolverheld*) had shot three people "before the eyes of the company"[42] ("*vor den Augen der Kompanie*"). Subsequently, however, he was able to film at least one execution. "In the future my film will be a document and of great interest for our children,"[43] he assured his wife. ("*Mein Film wird später nochmal ein Dokument sein und für unsere Kinder hochinteressant.*")

If the Bremen reservist fully identified with the regime's antipartisan policies and passively accepted the mass murder of the Jews, he maintained a critical stance in regard to the behavior of his officers. Although the company posted placards announcing that "whoever plunders will be shot," his captain filled his suitcase with whatever he could lay his hands on in the houses of the villagers, despite the tearful pleas of distraught mothers at least to leave their children's winter clothing. "Well, that's what we go through along the way, and it reflects on our officers. I can't bring myself to take anything from the poor people. But the career policemen don't even question it."[44]

In comparison to the very gradual and belated brutalization of the reserve police in the less violent environment of East Upper Silesia, this Bremen reservist initially mocked the murderous exhortations of his officers but then adapted himself to the viciousness of the "war of destruction" on Soviet territory with breathtaking speed. Though he referred briefly and in passive voice to the mass murder of the Jews, he proudly and enthusiastically detailed and filmed his unit's antipartisan activities. Where does he fit into the spectrum of reaction among the German police? Indeed, was there even a spectrum? Let us turn to two cases in which we can identify with some precision both the entire range of behavior and the proportional distribution of the individual perpetrators along this spectrum: the village of Mir in Byelorussia (what the Germans called Generalkommissariat Weissruthenien) and the village of Marcinkance in the district of Bialystok near the Lithuanian border.

42 Ibid., p. 74 (letter of 22.8.41).

43 Ibid., pp. 75 and 83 (letters off 7.9. and 18.11.41).

44 Ibid., p. 80 (letter of 8.10.41).

For the village of Mir there is the testimony of a survivor, Oswald Rufeisen.[45] The special quality of his testimony derives from two factors. First, he had a unique vantage point. Born and educated in Silesia, Rufeisen spoke Polish and German without a detectable accent. Following his escape from Vilna, he was passing as a person of mixed Polish-ethnic German parentage when in November 1941 he was ordered to serve as the interpreter for the chief of the regional auxiliary police living in the village of Mir. Two months later, he was commandeered to serve as translator at the German Gendarmerie station in Mir under the command of Sergeant Reinhold Hein. For the next 7 months, until August 1942, Rufeisen slept in the house of the Byelorussian police commander at night. By day he worked at the German police station across the street and took his meals seated next to Sergeant Hein.

Second, Rufeisen's formidable memory has been tested and proved in an unusual way. He had given a detailed account of his escape from the Mir police station on several occasions. When the archives in Brest–Litovsk were finally made accessible to the west, a contemporary report by Sergeant Hein on Rufeisen's escape was found.[46] The coincidence between Rufeisen's postwar recollections and the written report is remarkable to say the least.

The German Gendarmerie unit in Mir was composed of 2 career policemen – Sergeant Hein and his second in command, Corporal Karl Schultz[47] – and 11 reservists from the north German region of Pommern. Hein was the only Catholic. Virtually all the men were in their forties. Relations among them were formal. They addressed one another by their last name. Mealtime conversation was dull and humorless. There was no political conversation either, and Rufeisen had no idea who was or was not a party member. Hitler's name was mentioned only on the Führer's birthday. The only anti-Semitic expression Rufeisen

[45] This account of Oswald Rufeisen is based on three sources: his interviews with Nechama Tec, recorded in her book, *In the Lion's Den* (Oxford, 1992); his pretrial testimony in the case of *Crown v. Semion Serefinowicz*; and my own interview with him on June 17, 1998, just 6 weeks before he died on August 1.

[46] USHMM, RG 19996.A.169, reel 22 (Brest Archive, M-41/1021): Hein to Gend.-Gebietsführer in Baranowitsche, 20.8.42.

[47] In his account to Nechama Tec, Rufeisen identified Schultz as a baker by trade. In his interview with me, he corrected Tec's account and stated that Schultz was an *Aktiv,* or career policeman.

could remember was when one of the Protestants once referred to Mary, mother of Jesus, as an "old Jewess" – a remark that was as anti-Catholic as it was anti-Semitic.

Among the 13 German Gendarmes, Hein's deputy Karl Schultz was a notorious sadist and drunkard, whom Rufeisen described as "a beast in the form of a man." He kept a notebook listing all those he had killed, a tally that reached more than 80 before Rufeisen escaped. His closest companions were Rothe and Schmelzer, whom Rufeisen did not characterize as sadists. But they also killed "without remorse or conscience." A fourth policeman, Steinbach, was also placed by Rufeisen in this group of those he considered the "worst" policemen.

In contrast, identified as the "best" policemen were the *Volksdeutscher* from the Netherlands, Roth, and a man named Proksch. In his interview with me, though not in other accounts, Rufeisen also added to the list of the "best" policemen the man in charge of the kitchen, whom he remembered only by the first name of Adolf. These men did not take part in the killing of Jews, and their absence on these occasions was accepted without incident or repercussion. As Nechama Tec summarized Rufeisen's account: "No one seemed to bother them. No one talked about their absences. It was as if they had the right to abstain."[48]

The remaining policemen were characterized by Rufeisen as "passive executors of orders," who killed without hate or ideological motivation. Concerning the spectrum of attitudes, Rufeisen noted:

> It was clear that there were differences in their outlooks. I think that the whole business of anti-Jewish moves, the business of Jewish extermination they considered unclean. The operations against the partisans were not in the same category. For them a confrontation with partisans was a battle, a military move. But a move against the Jews was something they might have experienced as "dirty."[49]

Sergeant Hein was the most enigmatic figure among the 13 Germans. He, too, did not take part in the anti-Jewish expeditions

[48] Tec, *In The Lion's Den*, p. 102.
[49] Tec, *In the Lion's Den*, p. 104.

and flatly told his young interpreter that he would never shoot a Jew. However, he added: "But someone must do it. Orders are orders." Thus he meticulously organized the killing expeditions that he left to Schultz to carry out. According to Rufeisen, Hein was always "very gentle" and even "reverent" toward the *Judenrat* members, whose community he would eventually liquidate. When delegates of the *Judenrat* attempted to bribe Hein to spare the ghetto, he refused their gifts on the grounds that he could promise them nothing in return. When one of the Jewish leaders then asked him to see that they at least would "die a humanitarian death," Hein replied affirmatively: "I can promise you this," and showed them respectfully to the door.[50]

Let us turn to the second example of Marcinkance, a small village and customs station in the district of Bialystok just west of the Lithuanian border. The Einsatzgruppen and police battalions that passed through the district of Bialystok in the first month of Operation Barbarossa carried out numerous killings of Jews, but thereafter an eerie calm settled over the district. During the same months in which the bulk of Soviet and Polish Jewry were being destroyed, the Jews of the Bialystok district were being ghettoized and put to work. Finally, on November 2 and 3, 1942, all the Jews in the district except those in the two major ghettos of Grodno and the city of Bialystok itself were simultaneously rounded up and placed in transit camps, from which they were subsequently deported to Treblinka and Auschwitz–Birkenau.

This simultaneous roundup throughout the district stretched German manpower to the limit. In the case of Marcinkance, two career policemen from the Gendarmerie station in Sobakince – 47-year-old Sergeant (Hauptwachtmeister) Albert Wietzke and 35-year-old Corporal (Oberwachtmeister) Paul Olschewski – were sent to Marcinkance, where they joined two reserve policemen stationed there – 44-year-old Wilhelm Pohl and 43-year-old Fritz Thomsch. By order of the local *Amtskommissar,* Czapon, virtually every German official in town had to report for duty, in order to form a squad of 17 men, who were assigned the task of clearing a ghetto of some 200 Jews. Unlike further east, in the district of Bialystok large numbers of native auxiliary police or *Schutzmänner* had not been recruited to help the

50 Tec, *In the Lion's Den,* p. 134.

Germans in such activities, and thus the ghetto-clearing squad in Marcinkance was composed of Reich Germans.

Included were eight officials from the customs office, two officials of the forestry office, the local agricultural officer, and a railway employee. At least two were so-called old fighters, or *Alte Kämpfer* – Corporal Olschewski and the 41-year-old chief forester Hans Lehmann – who had both joined the party in March 1932. The secretary of the customs office, 40-year-old Emil Marquardt, was a 1937 joiner. The railway man, Otto Fahsing, also claimed party membership. The most recent membership of 1940 belonged to the overall commander, Sergeant Wietzke.[51]

In short, of the 17 Germans assigned to the ghetto-clearing commando, 2 were career policemen and 2 were reserve police. The remaining 13 were drawn from five sectors of the civil administration: the *Amtskommissar,* customs office, railway, forestry office, and agricultural office. Of the 7 known by full name, 5 were party members, including 2 "old fighters." The average age of these 7 was 40 years. These men were not a cross-section of German society in either age or party affiliation, but they were probably not untypical of Gendarmerie and civil administration personnel serving far behind the lines in the occupied eastern territories.

In fact, the ghetto-clearing squad was ultimately composed of only 15 men. After the Germans had assembled early on the morning of November 2, the *Amtskommissar* and the police sergeant ordered the Jewish council to assemble all Jews at the ghetto entrance by 8 A.M. to be transported for "labor." The *Amtskommissar* then left to check on transportation but was unable to return "because he was summoned to a suicide of a customs official."[52] In the entire file this suicide is referred to only once, without elaboration. Given the fact that this customs official took his life at the very moment when all customs officials were to report for the ghetto-clearing operation strongly suggests, however, that the suicide was not purely coincidental or unrelated to the task at hand.

[51] For party membership, see: National Archives, Berlin Document Center microfilms, Ortsgruppenkartei and Zentralkartei. I could find no card for Otto Fahsing, but in the investigation, he proudly claimed party membership.

[52] USHMM, RG 53.004m, reel 1 (Grodno Oblast Archives, fond 1, opis 1, folder 59, p. 3: Hauptwachmeister Wietzke to Gendarmeriekreis in Grodno, 6.11.42) (*da er zu einem Selbstmord eines Zollbeamten gerufen wurde*).

What actually happened at Marcinkance on the morning of November 2, 1942, was the subject of a German investigation triggered not by the suicide, however, but rather by a complaining letter of the chief forester Hans Lehmann, written that very day to the *Kreiskommissar* of Grodno. According to Lehmann, when the 15 Germans took up their positions around the ghetto of Marcinkance at 5 A.M., the Jews were totally unsuspecting. With the break of dawn, individual Jews who attempted to leave were easily turned back without resort to weapons. After the *Judenrat* had been informed that the ghetto was to be cleared, the Jews assembled quietly at the ghetto entrance. Then, according to Lehmann:

> Without any visible reason (*Ohne jeden ersichtlichen Grund*) the two Gendarmes suddenly opened fire on the densely packed mass of people. All broke into wild flight, leaving the dead and wounded behind. In panicked fright the Jews then naturally tried to break through the ghetto fence. Here they came under fire from the guards outside the fence, and there were many dead and wounded. Nevertheless given the general confusion and very thin cordon a very considerable number of Jews managed to flee into the nearby forest. . . . I am convinced that the entire shoot-out, in which above all we Germans were also greatly endangered, was completely senseless and without any reasonable cause (*vollkommen sinnlos und ohne jeden vernünftigen Grund*).

Lehmann further noted that his deputy, Gemmer, had been injured in a hand-to-hand scuffle with a fleeing Jew. Once things had quieted down, Lehmann had taken him for medical treatment. Lehmann then returned to his forestry work, "all the more because it cannot be my task as head of the forestry office here in the east to shoot Jews dead"[53] ("*zumal da es hier im Osten nicht meine Aufgabe als Forstamtsvorstand sein kann, Juden tot zu schiessen*").

An investigation of Lehmann's complaint was launched immediately. Wietzke was asked to submit a written report, and a two-man commission composed of a local official of the civil administration and a lieutenant of the Gendarmerie interviewed five other participants on November 6. In his written report, Wietzke noted that before the action he had been warned that the ghetto was near the forest and

[53] Ibid, p. 1: Forstmeister Lehmann to Kreiskommissar Grodno, 2.11.42.

poorly fenced, and he was explicitly instructed to counter any attempt at flight with use of weapons. *Amtskommissar* Czapon and he had ordered the Jewish council to assemble all Jews at the ghetto entrance for "labor" ("*Arbeitseinsatz*"), but only some 80 Jews initially appeared as ordered. Therefore, Wietzke continued, after Czapon departed to check on the train, he entered the ghetto again with Corporal Olschewski and the railway man Fahsing. They ordered the Jews they encountered to go to the assembly point, where the total number of Jews increased to some 150. When Olschewski ordered them to form up in rows of 6, the Jews "with one accord" ("*wie auf ein Kommando*") scattered in all directions, some trying to escape to the woods and others fleeing again to the houses. "Before this not a single shot had been fired," Wietzke claimed, but now he, Olschewski, and Fahsing opened fire with automatic weapons to prevent the attempted escape.

After the shoot-out, the same three men, joined by the customs head Marquardt, went on a house-to-house search through the ghetto, uncovering bunkers under five houses with disguised entrances sawed in the floorboards. This was proof, Wietzke wrote, that the Jews had prepared their hiding places long before. As not a single Jew could be induced to leave the bunkers either through coaxing or threat, "only the use of weapons remained to carry out the measures that had been ordered." In the end a total of 132 Jews were "shot trying to escape" ("*beim Flucht erschossen*").

When *Amtskommissar* Czapon finally returned, Wietzke continued, Lehmann left his post without orders, openly accused him of shooting "peaceful Jews" ("*friedliche Juden*"), and then went home even though 2 hours of obligatory service remained. Lehmann had admitted that many Jews had escaped through the fence near him, but Wietzke had never heard a shot fired in this area. Thus Lehmann, who in any case had not brought a rifle but only a small pistol with him, had not obeyed orders to use his weapon to prevent escape. Moreover, Wietzke charged, Lehmann's position was 800 meters from the ghetto entrance, so he could not possibly have seen what had actually happened. Everyone else except Lehmann had kept their nerve and done their best to prevent "the scum of humanity, the Jews" ("*der Abschaum der Menschheit, die Juden*") from fleeing. In conclusion, Wietzke again asserted, all his actions were in accordance with orders and no "unauthorized actions" had occurred.[54]

The visiting commission interviewed only five men: the two reserve policeman – Pohl and Thomsch – who had been in the cordon and who were subordinate in rank to Wietzke, the two men – Olschewski and Fahsing – who had been inside the ghetto with Wietzke and taken part in the very actions for which Wietzke was being investigated, as well as the customs man Marquardt, who had joined the hunt for hidden Jews. In short, the commission did not interview anyone likely to contradict Wietzke's account and confirm Lehmann's. The strong suspicion must exist that this investigation was not an evenhanded search for the truth but from the beginning was aimed at collecting the testimony necessary to dismiss a bothersome complaint.

Reserve policeman Pohl had been in charge of the cordon on the north side of the ghetto. Around 8 A.M., he said, two or three shots rang out, and the Jews attempted to break through the dilapidated ghetto fence. As ordered, he opened fire to prevent escape and shot four Jews. "Subsequently," there was a burst of fire from automatic weapons, but he could not see who was shooting from his vantage point.[55] Reserve policeman Thomsch was still in the police station in Marcinkance when he heard gunfire from the ghetto. He rushed to the unguarded west side of the ghetto where Jews were streaming through the fence. As previously instructed, he opened fire to prevent escape and shot eight Jews.[56] Each volunteered that he had undertaken another task after the breakout had ended; Pohl had supervised the burial of bodies and Thomsch had returned to man the police station in town. Neither had joined the killing in the house-to-house search, and neither expressed any anti-Semitic sentiment to the investigators.

Fahsing and Olschewski – the two men in addition to Wietzke who had been equipped with automatic weapons and were inside the ghetto – gave such similar accounts in near identical language that it is difficult to avoid the conclusion that their testimony was coordinated

[54] Ibid., p. 2–5: HWM Wietzke, Gend.posten Sobakince, to Lt. Porzig, Gendarmeriekreis Grodno, 6.11.42.

[55] Ibid., p. 12: Statement of WM Wilhelm Pohl, 6.11.42.

[56] Ibid., p. 13: Statement of WM Fritz Thomsch, 6.11.42.

beforehand. Each emphasized that no shots had been fired until "with one accord" the Jews scattered. By Olschewski's estimate, 50–60 Jews were shot at the assembly point by the three Germans within the ghetto. He gave no estimate for how many had been shot at the fence by those forming the cordon. During the subsequent search of the ghetto, the Jews had stubbornly refused to come out of their hiding places and bunkers despite "soothing assurances," so that "the customs man" ("*der Zoll*" – i.e., Marquardt) had had to throw in hand grenades. The well-prepared hiding places were proof, they noted, of long-held Jewish intentions to escape the roundup. Each emphasized that Wietzke's behavior had been "composed" ("*ruhig*") and "sober" ("*besonnen*"). And each emphasized that from Lehmann's assigned post, the chief forester could not possibly had seen the ghetto entrance. If he had not left his post, he could not have seen what happened; if he had seen what happened, then he had against orders left his post and thereby helped Jews to escape.[57]

The two men also made no attempt to hide their anti-Semitic credentials. Fahsing testified that while guarding the fence before entering the ghetto, he had warned one Jew who approached the fence to turn back or he would fire. The Jew had, as he put it, "impudently" ("*frech*") answered that "it was no great feat to shoot at defenseless human beings" ("*es wäre kein Kunststück auf wehrlose Menschen zu schiessen*"). Concerning Lehmann's accusation that they had shot upon "peaceful" Jews, he noted: "I am a party member, and was dumbfounded by the behavior of Lehmann regarding the Jews." Lehmann's accusation of Wietzke was not only "fully unjustified" and "uncomradely" but "proved Lehmann's comical attitude to the Jewish question." In the same vein, Olschewski testified, "Personally I cannot rid myself of the impression that Lehmann sympathized with the Jews and even protected them. Apparently Lehmann does not yet understand the racial question . . ." ("*dass Lehmann die Juden bedauerte order sogar in Schutz nahm. Scheinbar ist Lehmann über die Rassenfrage noch nicht im Bilde . . .*"). In contrast, as an old party member, Olschewski proudly claimed to be "fully aware" of it.

[57] Ibid., pp. 9–11, 14–16: Statements of Otto Fahsing and Paul Olschewski, 6.11.42. Although Wietzke and Olschewski spoke only of Marquardt or the customs man in the house-to-house search, Fahsing did speak of "customs men" in the plural.

Emil Marquardt testified that from his post in the cordon he saw the Jews milling around and pressing toward the fence when, like Pohl, he heard two shots. A burst of automatic gunfire then erupted, and many Jews broke through the fence. As ordered beforehand, he opened fire on the fleeing Jews. Twenty-four Jews were killed along the fence line where he was stationed. He, too, testified that the breakout appeared to have been "planned and organized." Marquardt then joined the search of the ghetto, where any Jews found hiding were shot. As not a single Jew would leave the bunkers, hand grenades were thrown in. In short, all Jews were killed and not a single prisoner was taken. Unlike Fahsing and Olschewski, Marquardt did not identify himself as the one who threw the hand grenades, though he did state: "I don't see myself being made to look ridiculous by Jews, but rather take the standpoint that any order of any German official, if resisted even only passively, must be carried out energetically."[58]

Wietzke was fully backed by the investigating police officer, Lieutenant Porzig, who added his own report to the file. Porzig alluded to previous unspecified quarrels between Wietzke and Lehmann, implying that the latter was habitually quarrelsome and had acted out of personal spite. Furthermore, he questioned Lehmann's "scruples" ("*Hemmungen*"). How could Lehmann speak of "peaceful" Jews, Lieutenant Porzig queried. "As a National Socialist he [Lehmann] must know that there is no such thing as peaceful Jews, otherwise we would have been spared the present war." In contrast, Porzig noted, Wietzke was "no novice" in the Jewish Question.[59]

On the following day, the investigative commission, joined now by yet another police officer, Lieutenant Müller, confronted Lehmann, who initially reiterated his charge that the Gendarmes had fired on peaceful Jews for no visible reason. When pressed, Lehmann admitted that he was 300–350 meters away, too far to see what had caused the Gendarmes to open fire. Lehmann maintained that "he had worked very well together with the Jews for 9 months and without complaint, and he did not want to make himself responsible for the shooting." To Lieutenant Müller's accusation that Lehmann should view the matter

[58] Ibid., pp. 6–8: Statement of Emil Marquardt, 6.11.42.

[59] Ibid., pp. 117–18: Schlussbericht of Lt. Porzig, Gendarmerieabteilung Porzecze, 6.11.42.

from the "National Socialist standpoint," the forester allegedly replied that "if occasionally one were shot, that would not be so bad, but he could not do it. In that case he should be transferred; in that case he was not suited for this territory" ("*Man solle ihn dann versetzen; dann würde er sich für dieses Gebiet nicht eignen*"). Lieutenant Müller then concluded in his report that according to convincing testimony, the Jews had not assembled peacefully as claimed by Lehmann but instead had milled around trying to find openings in the fence. When several shots had been fired against individual attempts to break out, the Jews had scattered in mass. As ordered beforehand to prevent escapes, the Gendarmes had then opened fire. To Lehmann's allegation that the agricultural officer shared his view, Müller cited *Amtskommissar* Czapon to the contrary. There is, however, no written record of testimony by either. Müller ruled that his fellow Gendarmes had behaved properly, and he recommended action be taken against Lehmann for his "frivolous and totally unjustified false accusation and defamation" ("*leichtfertig und durch nichts gerechtfertigten falschen Anschuldigung und Beleidigung*") against them.[60]

Further up the hierarchy, *Landrat* Dr. von Ploetz added to the charges against Lehmann. Not only had he made a frivolous and false accusation, which if true was of sufficient gravity to have led to Wietzke's conviction in a SS court, but Lehmann had also not performed his duty properly: he had not brought a rifle with him, he had not fired on the escaping Jews, and he had left his post early. Furthermore, he had displayed an attitude toward the Jews that was "not worthy of a high official serving in the east." *Landrat* Dr. von Ploetz concluded that Lehmann, who already had a record of run-ins with other officials, had this time gone too far. He recommended that Lehmann be taken into custody.[61]

Lehmann was astonished, for the report of the two investigators, he said, "must have confirmed the full truth of my report." Indeed it was true that he had not been able to see who fired the first shot and for what reason, but he could see perfectly well that the Jews had offered no resistance until shooting by Gendarmes "*within* the ghetto fence" had caused panic and mass flight. He then elaborated on his previous

[60] Ibid., pp. 19–20: Müller report, Grodno, 10.11.42.
[61] Ibid., pp. 26–8: Ploetz to Dr. Brix, Ploetz to Forstmeister Lehmann, 12.11.42.

account to protect himself against the countercharges that had now been made. The charges against him, he concluded, were not only unjustified but an attack upon his honor as an official and party comrade.[62]

On December 15, 1942, Lehmann and the head of the Bialystok forestry administration met with Dr. von Ploetz and the head of Grodno Gendarmerie, Lieutenant Haag. In the interests of sparing time on further investigation and restoring cooperation between the forestry office, the Gendarmerie, and the *Amtskommissar,* all sides agreed to drop their various accusations.[63] Although quarrels between the German occupiers continued and von Ploetz was soon demanding the troublesome Lehmann's removal once again,[64] the Marcinkance massacre was no longer at issue.

For the historian, it is not unuseful that the investigation was conducted by outspoken anti-Semites who made no secret of their dismay over Lehmann's complaint. Only those likely to confirm the account of the accused sergeant were interviewed. And as was not the case in postwar judicial investigations, they had every incentive to boast of their anti-Semitic motivation, exaggerate their role in the killing, and provide evidence that Lehmann was an isolated troublemaker. Despite all of these biases in the investigation, what do we discover? Of the 17 Germans assigned to clear the ghetto at Marcinkance, 1 committed suicide and 1 protested openly. In addition to Lehmann, 2 other men on one side of the ghetto – the agricultural officer and one customs official

[62] Ibid., p. 22: Lehmann to Ploetz, 21.11.42. Lehmann's elaboration and defense was as follows: Two other witnesses – customs officer Kanis and agricultural officer Grafke – could confirm that Jews had not escaped through his sector of the cordon, which was not the point of any breakout attempt. He had not brought a rifle with him because he had received no instructions to that effect, but like several others – including *Amtskommissar* Czapon – he had been armed with a pistol. When the shooting and breakout occurred, he, along with the customs officer and the agricultural officer, had rushed to help two other customs officials at a point where the Jews where fleeing through the fence in mass. At this point they had been greatly endangered by the automatic fire coming from within the ghetto and had been forced to take cover. He had fired his pistol twice but then stopped because the distance was too great. When the shooting and breakout were over, he had approached *Amtskommissar* Czapon and asked if he was still needed. Receiving no answer, he had left the ghetto to take his deputy for medical attention.

[63] Ibid., n.p.: Niederschrift, Grodno, 15.12.42.

[64] USHMM, RG 53.004m, roll 3 (Grodno Archive, fond 1, opis 1, folder 271, pp. 2–4): Ploetz to Brix, 22.1.43.

– refrained from shooting at escaping Jews. And Lehmann's subordinate, the other forester, suffered a shoulder injury while trying to tackle an escaping Jew, which would indicate he, too, had been unwilling to shoot unarmed, fleeing Jews at point-blank range. Once the shooting was over, only 2 men – the senior customs official and the railway man but not the 2 reserve policemen – joined the 2 career policemen in the hunt for hidden Jews with the opportunity to continue killing. The 4 eager killers were indeed all Nazi Party members and avowed anti-Semites. It is hard to imagine that others could not have joined in the "Jew hunt" if they had wished. And it is hard to imagine that others would not have joined in the anti-Semitic denunciation of Lehmann if they, too, had found his views so alien and his behavior so objectionable.

From postwar testimony of Marcinkance survivors we learn additional relevant information. First, there is not a single reference to a planned and organized breakout, as alleged by the eager, ideological killers during the investigation. Those who survived spoke only of escape and hiding. Indeed, if there had been any such plan, the Jews would hardly have assembled at the gate first, presenting a compact target for the three Germans with automatic weapons, before making their breakout attempt. Second, 105 Jews were killed that day (Wietzke had claimed 132). Nearly 100 Jews escaped, out of whom 45 survived the war. And finally, in the winter of 1943 Jewish partisans derailed a German train in the forests of eastern Bialystok. Among those taken prisoner was Hans Lehmann. Identified by a Marcinkance escapee as having "actively" helped in the liquidation of the ghetto, Lehmann was promptly executed.[65]

This evidence that offers rare and unusually precise insight into the behavior and attitudes of individual participants of two groups of German perpetrators suggests several conclusions. First, in each group there was a significant core of eager and enthusiastic killers – 4 of 13 in Mir and 4 of 17 in Marcinkance – who required no process of gradual brutalization to accustom themselves to their murderous task. And certainly in Marcinkance, though less in Mir, the evidence for their strong anti-Semitic convictions is clear.

[65] Yad Vashem Archives, 0.33/2112: Collective eyewitness report of Shloyme Peretz, Kahne Garfing, Leyb Kobrowsky, and Khayem Kobowsksy, written down by Leyb Konykhosvky, Ulm, August 25, 1948.

In both cases there was a middle group that followed orders and complied with standard procedures but did not evince any eagerness to kill Jews. The evidence from Mir and Marcinkance does not indicate any transformation over time into eager killers, though certainly the evidence from the Czeladz Schutzpolizei and Reserve Police Battalion 105 suggests that such a process was at work among the German perpetrators elsewhere.

And finally in both Mir and Marcinkance there was a significant minority of men who did not participate in the shooting of Jews – 3 or 4 of 13 in Mir and at least 3 and perhaps as many as 5 of 17 in Marcinkance. Abstention from shooting by itself did not have disciplinary consequences for these men. Nor did the presence of this minority of nonshooters create significant tensions within the group. Their nonparticipation was both tolerated and brushed aside as inconsequential. The killing went on without them.

What did create tension and invoke disciplinary consequences was crossing the line from abstention to protest. What made the Marcinkance case so unusual was not that a number of the Germans did not fire their guns during the breakout but that one German committed suicide on the morning of the action and a second wrote a strong letter of protest. Passive abstention was one thing; an open and official challenge to the system was another. The eager killers and their supportive superiors banded together to discredit and crush their upstart accuser.

Emphasizing once again the fragmentary nature of the evidence that is therefore more suggestive than conclusive, what else can one nevertheless hazard to infer from these unusual and rare documents? In East Upper Silesia, where the pace of Jewish persecution was slower than elsewhere in eastern Europe, the hardening of police attitudes also took longer. In contrast, plunged into the murderous environment of Operation Barbarossa, the transformation of the men in Reserve Police Battalion 105 took place much more quickly. Both in this battalion and among the policeman stationed in Mir, the men were far more eager to kill those who could be classified as partisans than Jews. In Reserve Police Battalion 105 the Bremen reservist was proud of his unit's antipartisan actions, which he documented on film for his children. And at times he expressed a murderous bitterness toward the Russian prisoners of war and the Russian people as a whole. These attitudes stood in contrast to his willed indifference toward and muted acceptance of the mass murder of the Jews, about which he did not want his child to hear. Likewise in Mir, the men did not speak about the killing of Jews, which was viewed as a "dirty" task, but they spoke eagerly and proudly about their antipartisan actions.

What also emerges more starkly in these documents than in postwar testimony is the difference between career police and reservists.[66] From the documents we see that in East Upper Silesia the commander of the Schutzpolizei was disturbed by the insufficient hostility toward and enforcement of measures aimed at Jews and furious about occasional instances of public fraternization. In Reserve Police Battalion 105 the reservist from Bremen criticized both the pompousness and hypocrisy of his officers. In Marcinkance the reserve police found things to do other than join the "Jew hunt," and their testimony was both devoid of anti-Semitic comment and less than effusive in providing support on behalf of their sergeant.

Career policemen like Sergeant Hein in Mir or Major Wilhelm Trapp of Reserve Police Battalion 101 were the exception. They clearly had no great liking for their task of killing Jews and personally distanced themselves from these actions. But simultaneously they ensured that the men under their command carried out the policies of their government and the actions that had been ordered by their superiors.

At the opposite extreme of Hein and Trapp were career Order Police officers like Fritz Jacob, the commander of 25 Gendarmerie and 500 *Schutzmänner* in Kamenetz–Podolsk in the south Ukraine, who wrote a series of revealing letters to one of the very highest ranking Order Police officers, Generalleutnant Rudolf Querner.[67] Jacob's virulent hatred of Jews and commitment to the Final Solution were total. The Jews he characterized as "venereal, deformed, and feeble-minded" ("*Venerische, Krüppel, und Blöde*"). They were "not humans but

[66] For example, in Reserve Police Battalion 101 one noncommissioned officer (NCO) hinted at "certain tensions" between the older reservists and the younger NCOs who were career policemen – so-called *Aktiven.* Because he fraternized with and played cards with the reservists, he testified, he was disliked by his fellow NCOs for his unseemly behavior in this regard. Staatsanwaltschaft Hamburg, 141 Js 1957/62, testimony of August W., p. 3304.

[67] *"Schöne Zeiten." Judenmord aus der Sicht der Täter und Gaffer,* ed. by Ernst Klee, Willi Dressen, and Volker Riess (Frankfurt/M., 1988), pp. 148–51 (letters of Fritz Jacob to Generalleutnant Querner: 24.4.41, 29.10.41, and 21.6.42).

rather ape men" ("*keine Menschen, sondern Affenmenschen*") whom he killed "without the slightest prick of conscience" ("*ohne Gewissensbisse*"). But Jacob was not limited to Jews in his appetite for killing. "We do not sleep here," he wrote. "Weekly 3–4 actions. One time Gypsies and another time Jews, partisans, or other riffraff."

In addition to his ideological commitment to do "practical work" for his Führer, Jacob was also an ambitious careerist. He welcomed his assignment in the east because "hopefully" he would "finally" receive advancement, for in Saxony "the promotion path is really slow and scarcely conceivable without favor from above" ("*der Beförderungsgang wirklich schleppend und ohne Protektion kaum denkbar*"). The sycophantic and obsequious tone of his letters to Generalleutnant Querner were hardly indicative of someone unmindful of his future career. Even avowedly anti-Semitic killers could act from more than one motive.

Clearly the German Order Police was not monolithic, but in the end the diversity of attitudes and motives made little difference. Even if the "ordinary Germans" who were conscripted as reserve policemen did not go to the east exuding ideological commitment to National Socialism and eager for the opportunity to kill Jews, when the deportations and killing began, most did as they were told and many were changed by the actions they undertook. Both the men of the Reserve Police battalions – such as 101 in Lublin, 133 in Galicia, and 45 in the Ukraine, to name several of the most notorious – as well as the countless Gendarmerie and Schupo stations throughout the German empire in the east became efficient perpetrators of the Final Solution. A core of eager and committed officers and men, accompanied by an even larger block of men who complied with the policies of the regime more out of situational and organizational rather than ideological factors, was sufficient. Unfortunately, the presence of a minority of men who sought not to participate in the regime's racial killing had no measurable effect whatsoever.

POSTSCRIPT

In recent years the pace of Holocaust scholarship has so intensified that almost inevitably significant new works by other historians appear during the hiatus between the writing and the presentation of one's own work. In particular, I would note that Peter Longerich's recent comprehensive study of the Nazi persecution of the Jews[1] appeared just before these lectures were delivered and could not be taken adequately into account at that time. I value many aspects of Longerich's intrepretation, such as his emphasis on the continuities in Nazi Jewish policy that bridge or tie together the various "stages of escalation" ("*Eskalationsstufen*") on the one hand and his extension of the decision-making process into 1942 on the other. But in one regard at least, our portrayals of the decision-making process differ significantly. We both portray the decision-making process as incremental. However, within this prolonged and gradual decision-making process, Longerich delineates four stages of escalation (fall 1939, summer 1941, fall 1941, and spring 1942) and deems the first to be the most important "caesura."[2] In contrast, I have placed much greater emphasis on and attached more importance and scope to the decisions made in the summer and fall of 1941.

For Longerich, the fall of 1939 marks the beginning of *Vernichtungspolitik* ("policies of destrution"). In his perspective, the fall of 1941 is seen as important. For instance, Longerich writes that "in the fall of 1941 the murder of hundreds of thousands but not mil-

[1] Peter Longerich, *Politik der Vernichtung: Eine Gesamtdarstellung der nationalsozialistischen Judenverfolgung* (Munich and Zurich, 1998).
[2] Ibid., esp. pp. 577–86.

lions of human beings was being prepared" but that "the decision for the immediate mass murder of all European Jews had not been taken." In the same vein, he notes that as of the "end of 1941 there was still no general authorization for the murder of central European Jews." Nor was a "program or plan for systematic destruction" as opposed to a "climate for the development of such a program or plan" yet perceptible.[3] These cautious and carefully worded conclusions are not invalid. However, the focus on the technical questions of "preparations," "plans," "programs," and "authorizations" for "immediate" mass murder ought to inform but not obscure our search for the answer to a different and in my opinion more important question: When was it clear to Hitler, Himmler, and Heydrich that their ultimate goal was the imminent mass murder of every last Jew within the German grasp?

In my opinion the evidence points most plausibily and persuasively to early October 1941. Many questions remained open. How, when, where, at what rate, and with what temporary exceptions this task was to be accomplished remained issues subject to a series of decisions in the following months and years. It was also unclear to what extent the Final Solution was to be a wartime or postwar project. But the fact that the Germans were considering the construction of gassing facilities in at least six locations on Soviet and Polish territory in the last months of 1941 indicates that the potential of this second killing method in addition to shooting was going to be fully explored and expectations were high. The key watershed between expulsion and decimation on the one hand and comprehensive mass murder on the other had been crossed. In early September 1941 Rolf-Heinz Höppner was still asking for "total clarity" on the basic issue concerning the fate of "undesirable ethnic elements" deported to the east: "Is it the goal to insure them a certain level of life in the long run, or shall they be totally eradicated?" Concerning the fate of Jewish deportees, I continue to argue that Hitler, Himmler, and Heydrich achieved clarity in early October on the goal of total eradication.

In trying to articulate the dynamics of how Nazi Jewish policy developed, Longerich correctly rejects the simple, linear, "top-down" model of decision-order-implementation in favor of a triangular model of

[3] Ibid., pp. 448, 457, 465.

vaguely worded orders requiring intuitive comprehension according to political climate, personal initiative of local authorities who possessed considerable latitude, and subsequent formulation into uniform policy by higher echelons. The result was a dialectical interaction between central and local authorities that produced mutual radicalization.[4] To Longerich's sophisticated and nuanced model, I would only reiterate the conclusions drawn from the example of events in Brest–Litovsk. When local intuition and intiative did not produce the desired result, central authorities imposed uniform policies. Loyalty and obedience invariably succeeded when local intuition and initiative did not.

Within this complex process, Longerich places particular emphasis on the crucial role of Heinrich Himmler as peripatetic intermediary. The emphasis on Himmler is fully justified, in my opinion.[5] Indeed, I would argue that in addition to the dialectical interaction between central and local authorities, there is a similar and utterly crucial dialectical interaction between Hitler and Himmler. Himmler become the second most powerful man in the Third Reich during this period precisely because he shared Hitler's vision of a racial empire in the east, intuitively understood Hitler's vague exhortations, and took the initiative to formulate proposals and policies that would transform Hitler's nightmarish visions into reality. He understood what was expected of him without needing explicit orders.

Thus, I would suggest further that if one wants to know what Hitler was thinking about racial policy during this period, one should look first of all at what the reliable and perceptive Himmler was doing. In 1939–41, Himmler was pushing massive schemes of ethnic cleansing to remake the demographic map of Germany's new *Lebensraum,* including a sequence of increasingly radical and destructive plans for the expulsion of the Jews. Before Operation Barbarossa he was laying the groundwork for a war of destruction in the Soviet Union, entailing the death of millions by hunger, execution, and starvation. In July and August 1941, he was visiting and reinforcing his killing units in the field and fomenting the accelerated and expanded execution of Soviet Jews, especially women and children. In the fall of 1941, he was reversing the

4 Ibid., pp. 416–17, 464–5.

5 See also: Richard Breitman, *The Architect of Genocide: Himmler and the Final Solution* (New York, 1991).

previous German policy of expulsion and blocking the exit of Jews from the German sphere who would thereby "be too much out of the reach of measures for a basic solution to the Jewish question. . . ." He was also meeting with key people, such as Odilo Globocnik on October 13, who shortly thereafter began construction of the death camp at Belzec; Friedrich Jeckeln in early November, who was dispatched to liquidate the Riga ghetto[6]; and Alfred Rosenberg on November 15, who promptly announced that a solution to the Jewish Question required "the biological eradication of the entire Jewry of Europe."

In the spring of 1942, Himmler and his deputy Heydrich visited Lodz and Minsk, respectively, shortly before the systematic killing of Reich Jews began at those two sites. On July 17–18, 1942, Himmler visited Auschwitz, shortly after which plans for Birkenau crematorium construction suddenly leaped from one to four.[7] One day later he issued issued explicit orders that all but a remnant of interned Jewish workers in Poland were to be "resettled" before the end of the year.[8] And on July 28, 1942, he affirmed that "the occupied eastern territories will be cleared of Jews. The implementation of this very hard order has been placed on my shoulders by the Führer. No one can release me from this responsibility in any case. So I forbid interference."[9] Until late 1943, he worked ceaselessly for the systematic and total liquidation of Jewish work camps instead of a gradual process of "destruction through labor." Whatever the varying impact of local authorities on Himmler, it was clearly not proportionate or symmetrical to his impact on them. The relationship between Himmler and local authorities might have been interactive, but it was most certainly not equal and reciprocal.

In addition to the publication of new scholarship, new documents also continue to come to light. One set of documents that has come to my attention since these lectures were given are particularly relevant to

[6] Helmut Krausnick and Hans-Heinrich Wilhelm, *Die Truppe des Weltanschauungskrieges: Die Einsatzgruppen der Sicherheitspolizei und des SD 1938–1942* (Stuttgart, 1981), pp. 566–7, 570. Jeckeln dated this meeting to November 10, 11, or 12, 1941.

[7] Jean-Claude Pressac with Robert Jan van Pelt, "The Machinery of Mass Murder at Auschwitz," *Anatomy of the Auschwitz Death Camp,* ed. by Yisrael Gutman and Michael Berenbaum (Bloomington, 1994), pp. 216–19, and Francizsek Piper, "The Gas Chambers and Crematoria," *Anatomy,* p. 165. Danuta Czech, *Auschwitz Chronicle* (London, 1990), pp. 198–99. Deborah Dwork and Robert Jan van Pelt, *Aschwitz: 1270 to the Present* (New Haven, 1996), pp. 317–21.

[8] Nürnberg Document NO-5574: Himmler to Krüger, 19.7.42.

[9] Nürnberg Document NO-626: Himmler to Berger, 28.7.42.

my argument concerning the importance of the key decision for the Final Solution in the fall of 1941. They are four reports of an ardently pro-Nazi and anti-Semitic Dutch collaborator and informer to the SS in the Netherlands.[10] On November 20, 1941, the collaborator noted that "the dragging off of all German Jews to Poland" *("Die Verschleppung aller deutschen Juden Nach Polen")* had been ordered, and he vehemently urged that Dutch Jews also be deported as soon as possible, "best of all likewise to Poland" *("am liebsten ebenfalls nach Polen").* On December 4, that is before Pearl Harbor and Hitler's alleged *Grundsatzentscheidung* of December 11, he was aware that the deportation of all Geman Jews, "which means a partial extermination of Jewry" *("was eine teilweise Ausrottung des Judentums bedeute"),* would be followed by the deportation of all Dutch Jews in the spring, "also to East Poland" *("ebenfalls nach Ost-Polen").* He thus urged the immediate introduction of preparatory measures such as marking, restrictions on movement, and the "starvation of the Jews in the Netherlands" *("Aushungerung der Juden in den Niederland").* By December 18, 1941, the informant proclaimed that "Extermination, destruction, and dragging off of the Jews shall make a revival of the Jews impossible for all time." *("Ausrottung, Vernichtung, und Verschleppung des Judentums sollte für alle Zeiten eine Wiederaufstehung des Judentums unmöglich machen.")*

I would suggest that these documents are reflections of information circulating within the SS in the Netherlands to which a well-connected Dutch collaborator was privy. Eichmann had, after all, summoned the various SS Jewish experts stationed in both Germany and abroad to orientation meetings in Berlin in the fall of 1941. If it was known already in late November and early December 1941 to SS circles and their close collaborators in the Netherlands that the deportation of German Jews was underway, that the deportation of Dutch Jews would follow the next spring, that both were destined for east Poland (the site of the Operation Reinhard camps), and that deportation in fact meant extermination with the avowed goal of making a revival of the Jews impossible for all time, then the key decision concerning the fate of

[10] Rijksinstituut voor Oorlogsdocumentatie, HSSPF 25 A–B: reports of Denis H., 20.11. and 4., 11., and 18.12.41. I am very grateful to Thomas Sandkühler for drawing my attention to these documents and to Peter Romijn for sending copies to me.

German and west European Jews must have been taken in Berlin somewhat earlier.

In the course of the lectures, one question was raised more frequently than any other: How had my subsequent research into new sources about low-level perpetrators altered the conclusions I had reached in *Ordinary Men* on the basis of my study of the problematic postwar testimonies of the men in Reserve Police Battalion 101? There I had concluded that a significant minority of the men became eager killers as they were transformed by what they were doing. I also concluded that a small minority – more than 10 percent but less than 20 percent – sought ways to evade participating in the killing itself, even though almost all of them continued to perform other duties – such as cordon duty and searches – that aided the killing process.

I think that the new evidence clearly confirms my latter conclusion about the presence of a minority exceeding 10 percent (indeed, in Mir and Marcinkance even exceeding 20 percent!) that evaded taking direct part in the killing itself but with very rare exceptions did not hinder or protest against the killing process. Evasion was easily tolerated but protest and obstruction most emphatically were not.

The evidence also necessitates a partial revision of my first conclusion about the eager killers. They were indeed a significant minority, not a majority, and some were transformed by the situation in which they found themselves. But many were ideologically motivated men ready to kill Jews and other so-called enemies of the Reich from the start. Situational/organization/institutional factors played no key role in shaping their behavior. On the local level, they formed a crucial nucleus for the killing process in the same way as eager and ambitious initiators at the middle echelons and Hitler, Himmler, and Heydrich at the top. Their influence was far out of proportion to their numbers in German society.

INDEX